Artists of the Possible

Studies In Postwar American Political Development

Steven Teles, *Series Editor*

Series Board Members

Paul Frymer
Jennifer Hochschild
Desmond King
Sanford Levinson
Taeku Lee
Shep Melnick
Paul Pierson
John Skrentny
Adam Sheingate
Reva Siegel
Thomas Sugrue

Series Titles

The Delegated Welfare State: Medicare, Markets, and the Governance of Social Policy
Kimberly J. Morgan and Andrea Louise Campbell

Rule and Ruin: The Downfall of Moderation and the Destruction of the Republican Party, from Eisenhower to the Tea Party
Geoffrey Kabaservice

Engines of Change: Party Factions in American Politics, 1868–2010
Daniel DiSalvo

Follow the Money: How Foundation Dollars Change Public School Politics
Sarah Reckhow

The Allure of Order: High Hopes, Dashed Expectations, and the Troubled Quest to Remake American Schooling
Jal Mehta

Rich People's Movements: Grassroots Campaigns to Untax the One Percent
Isaac William Martin

The Outrage Industry: Political Opinion Media and the New Incivility
Jeffrey M. Berry and Sarah Sobieraj

Artists of the Possible: Governing Networks and American Policy Change since 1945
Matt Grossmann

Artists of the Possible

Governing Networks and American
Policy Change since 1945

MATT GROSSMANN

OXFORD
UNIVERSITY PRESS

OXFORD
UNIVERSITY PRESS

Oxford University Press is a department of the University of Oxford.
It furthers the University's objective of excellence in research, scholarship,
and education by publishing worldwide.

Oxford   New York
Auckland   Cape Town   Dar es Salaam   Hong Kong   Karachi
Kuala Lumpur   Madrid   Melbourne   Mexico City   Nairobi
New Delhi   Shanghai   Taipei   Toronto

With offices in
Argentina   Austria   Brazil   Chile   Czech Republic   France   Greece
Guatemala   Hungary   Italy   Japan   Poland   Portugal   Singapore
South Korea   Switzerland   Thailand   Turkey   Ukraine   Vietnam

Oxford is a registered trademark of Oxford University Press
in the UK and certain other countries.

Published in the United States of America by
Oxford University Press
198 Madison Avenue, New York, NY 10016

© Oxford University Press 2014

Cataloging-in-Publication data is on file with the Library of Congress

ISBN 978-0-19-996784-1
ISBN 978-0-19-996783-4

9 8 7 6 5 4 3 2 1
Printed in the United States of America
on acid-free paper

To Sarah and Norah

CONTENTS

ACKNOWLEDGMENTS

This book is the product of countless consultations with colleagues and friends. The research depended on hundreds of hours of reading and content analysis by dozens of research assistants. Without tremendous aid, I would never have completed it. Exceptionally helpful students and research assistants included Martina Egerer, Janee Prince, Michael Thom, Kurt Pyle, Lydia Hawthorne, Liz Petoskey, Emily Kieliszewski, Ernscie Augustin, Milton Gilder, Erik Jonasson, Matt Phelan, Haogen Yao, Erica Weiss, Heta Mehta, Lindsay Vogelsberg, and Chris Heffner. The inspiration for the project developed from discussions with Todd LaPorte, Chris Ansell, Laura Stoker, Eric Shickler, and Neil Fligstein. Paul Pierson and Nelson W. Polsby stimulated my interest in policy history since 1945 and provided copious models of large-scale policy history research. I sought to emulate their approaches to political science.

For helpful feedback on the project, I sincerely thank many Michigan State University faculty: Steve Kautz, Dan Lee, Ani Sarkissian, Cory Smidt, Jeff Conroy-Krutz, Eric Juenke, Ryan Black, Cristina Bodea, Paul Abramson, Chuck Ostrom, Eric Chang, Mike Colaresi, Valentina Bali, Laura Reese, Ric Hula, Bill Jacoby, Brian Silver, Melinda Gann Hall, Barry Stein, Ben Appel, Jakana Thomas, Sandy Schneider, and Zak Neal. I want to single out Josh Sapotichne, who provided feedback at every stage of the project, and Tom Hammond, who offered detailed and comprehensive feedback on the entire book. At other institutions, I received useful input from Adam Sheingate, Brendon Swedlow, McGee Young, Kristin Goss, Jennifer Hochschild, Neal Caren, Holly Brasher, Hans Noel, Frank Baumgartner, Michael Heaney, Bird Loomis, John Sides, Ray La Raja, Jennifer Victor, Paul Culhane, Deirdre Mulligan, Margaret Weir, Dara Strolovitch, Amanda Hollis, and Jonathan Adler. Bryan Jones helped me formulate the project and aided in its evolution. David Mayhew was the most important commenter on early materials and provided the most critical suggestions for revising the book. I also thank David Hopkins, Brendan Doherty, Lee Drutman, Angelo

Gonzales, Jill Greenlee, Rachel VanSickle-Ward, Jen Bussell, and Thad Dunning for their support. I appreciate early interest in the book from David McBride and Steven Teles and their advice during the publication process.

The book is dedicated to my wife Sarah and my daughter Norah. Sarah is a helpful collaborator in all of my projects, a constant sounding board for good and bad ideas, and the best life partner anyone could ask for. Norah was the motivation for making faster progress on a project that took six years to complete; she is a constant source of joy in my life. I am also blessed to have a great mother, father, and sister, who always provide encouragement.

M. G.

Introduction

In the summer of 2011, the United States approached a possible credit default. House Speaker John Boehner and President Barack Obama spent weeks negotiating spending cuts and tax increases, but the duo failed to reach an agreement just as the country approached its legislated debt ceiling. The task of cobbling together a minimal compromise instead fell to Vice President Joe Biden and Senate Minority Leader Mitch McConnell. Biden and McConnell had worked together in the US Senate for two decades. They found a way through the impasse, just as they had 18 months earlier when other leaders failed to find common ground before a series of tax cuts were set to expire. As 2013 approached, the country faced another legislated deadline dubbed the "fiscal cliff." Obama and Boehner traded a series of proposals and stretched negotiations to the last possible moment, but again fell short. Once more, Biden and McConnell came to the rescue, negotiating their third compromise economic proposal that became law.

Their first negotiations began following the overwhelming Republican victories in the 2010 congressional elections; their third followed Obama's historic re-election in 2012; these electoral shifts coincided with dramatic moves in public opinion. The relevant issues ranged from taxes to education to health care to employment policy, but historians will credit the same pair of actors—working in tandem despite their ideological and partisan division—with all three significant policy changes. Other administrative and congressional officials, and perhaps some interest groups, helped make the changes possible, as did the built-in deadlines of previous policy decisions. Yet Biden and McConnell will receive their due credit from most observers; they were the artists of the possible who got the deals done.

Political science theories of policy change attempt to generalize away from the specific actors and negotiations involved in policymaking to broader patterns of partisan and ideological change. These efforts to attribute policy changes to broad macro-political patterns are incomplete. Leadership by two policymakers may not be a sufficient explanation for these three significant policy decisions, but neither is any model that excludes their role.

This book presents a new view of American policymaking, focusing on networks of actors responsible for policymaking. Policy change is not easily predictable from election results or public opinion because compromise and coalitions among individual actors make a difference in all three branches of government. The amount of government action, the issue content of policy changes, and the ideological direction of policy all depend on the joint actions of executive officials, legislators, and interest group leaders. The patterns of cooperation among policymakers and activists make each issue area and time period different from the others and undermine attempts to build an unchanging unified model of American policymaking.

To investigate the actors and circumstances responsible for policy change, this book uses secondary sources of policy history: reviews by policy area specialists of extensive case evidence on the political process surrounding policymaking. These authors, who I call "policy historians," catalog the important output of government and explain how, when, and why public policy changes. They identify important policy enactments in all branches of government and produce in-depth narrative accounts of policy development. I use this historical record to assess when and where policymaking takes place and which circumstances and actors were responsible.

To introduce the book, I begin with the four theories of American policy change that I seek to challenge. I then sketch my own argument and the evidence I bring to bear. Next, I describe the role of theories of policymaking in our evaluations of democratic government. Finally, I preview the arguments and analyses in each of the book's chapters.

Limitations of Current Views of Policymaking

The most actively studied policymaking system in political science is the US federal government, especially its activities since World War II. Scholars studying the nation's recent history are collectively conducting a long and in-depth case study about how political institutions and behavior produce public policy. The many moving parts of the policymaking system and the complexity of their interactions have led most scholars to partition their investigations, making the simplifying, if untrue, assumption that they can analyze one or two pieces in isolation. A few scholars, however, have produced wide-ranging accounts designed to holistically understand the policymaking system.

This book considers and critiques four different families of theory that explain significant policy change. First, *agenda setting* theories emphasize how policymakers prioritize problems.[1] They point to factors outside of government that drive attention to particular issues, such as public opinion, media coverage, and focusing events. The common assumption among these theories is that policy change occurs when an issue makes it onto the agenda, usually via an increase in attention to a problem. I argue that policy change occurs occasionally in many issues areas, including those off the public and government agenda, and it rarely follows directly from agenda setting. Policymaking is driven by the relationships among institutional actors, rather than their collective prioritization of problems or the signals they take from the public or media.

I also challenge *macro politics* models that explain change over time in the level and ideological content of policy output. Researchers find that public opinion and party control of legislative chambers and the presidency determine the ideological direction of policy change.[2] More Democrats and more liberal public opinion lead to more liberal policy and vice versa. Other *macro politics* research investigates the causes of changes in productivity—the number of important laws passed—using analogous determinants such as unified partisan control of government and ideological polarization.[3] I argue that, after accounting for a single long period of active liberal policymaking from 1961 to 1976, neither policy productivity nor its ideological direction can be predicted from the ebb and flow of public opinion, institutional partisanship, or ideology. Furthermore, changes in productivity and the ideological direction of policy go hand-in-hand because most policy changes expand the scope of government responsibility.[4]

The third family of theories I assess uses *issue typologies* to explain variation across issue areas.[5] These typologies share the assumption that, once scholars know a few pieces of information about who benefits and who loses from policy change, they can categorize the likely circumstances and actors that contribute to policymaking in each area. I argue that the policy process varies idiosyncratically across issue areas, but not in a way that any policy typology can predict. Instead, the composition of issue networks, the structure of the relationships among actors, and the circumstances driving policy change all vary independently. Differences are best conceptualized as a series of issue-specific exceptions to the general policy process.

Finally, I consider a class of scholarship I call *actor success* models in which scholars focus on one set of actors and assess their influence. The most common of these focus on the proposals and actions of the president or congressional leaders. Others consider only the influence of scientists, interest groups, or the public. No scholar claims that only their chosen actor matters but they start from the premise that their actor's goals are achievable and analyze deviations between their preferences and policy outcomes. I argue that each category of actors sometimes influences the policy process, but no single actor's agenda drives policymaking. Most actors matter only in definable and narrow circumstances.

Analyzing Policymaking

The American policymaking system is decentralized, complex, and open. All three branches of government are potential policymaking institutions. Congress, the key policymaking branch, is divided by party and chamber and split into many committees with overlapping jurisdictions. The operations of the administration and the courts are also diffuse. The national government is connected to state, local, and international institutions. Interest groups, the media, and the public can target and potentially influence all parts of government. The agenda of government concerns is broad, encompassing a wide array of social and economic problems. The potential policy tools are numerous and can be recombined in new ways. Arguments of diverse origin make their way into policy debates. Policymaking, at any given time, is constrained and animated by the institutions and results of past policy debates and decisions.

This book attempts a new holistic analysis of American policy history that attends to all of these factors. It covers American federal domestic policymaking since 1945, including a broad range of issues across all three branches of government.[6] I aggregate the findings of policy historians, who have accumulated a substantial trove of data about American policymaking, identifying long-term trends and painstakingly recording the steps and people involved in the policy process around a large range of concerns. Covering more than 60 years ensures that the view of policymaking developed here is not dependent on trends in any one historical era or participation by any one key participant. The domain is much more expansive than most studies of policymaking but has clear boundaries; readers cannot assume that the findings extend beyond the time period, to other levels of government, or to foreign policy.

I assess the factors relevant to policy changes, identifying and analyzing significant policy enactments by Congress, the president, administrative agencies, and courts. In addition to the passage of new laws, important policy changes often happen from executive branch actions and court decisions. I focus on enactments, rather than policy results. This enables a search for the factors relevant to particular decisions made in national political institutions, rather than an accounting of trends in practice or changes in the goals of policy.[7] I analyze the actors involved in all significant domestic policy enactments and the political circumstances that enabled change.

The structure of the analysis matches previous theories with my alternative views. Chapters 1 and 2 explain my theory and data. Chapter 3 assesses *agenda setting* theories and analyzes the most important contributors to policy enactments. Chapter 4 reviews *macro politics* theories and assesses how and why policy productivity and direction change over time. Chapter 5 assesses *issue typologies* and variations in the policy process across issue areas. Chapter 6 reviews *actor success* models and compares explanations for policy change across observers. In assessing each theory, the book contributes a new view of the factors driving policy change.

The Argument

The most important system-level characteristic of American policymaking is pervasive status quo bias. That is, in most times and issue areas, little policy change should be expected. There are many veto points and checks and balances that, in a decentralized system, have the effect of disadvantaging proponents of change.[8] There are numerous institutional mechanisms that force actors to revisit the same questions and make similar decisions, such as the legislative appropriations process, the administrative preparation of budgets, and precedent in the federal courts. Due to the many obstacles, when change does occur, it usually reflects broad consensus or willingness to compromise across institutions, parties, and primary issue interests. The need for supermajorities, tacit approval, and consensus-building means that the interactions among institutional actors that make policy change possible are unlikely to be predictable based only on changes in elected actors or political circumstances.

Yet status quo bias is ideologically asymmetric. The scope of government responsibility tends to grow over time; proposals to contract government face a steeper uphill battle than those designed to expand it. Existing policies have built-in constituencies and compel policymakers to adjust their expectations regarding the proper concerns of government. Most policy changes expand existing government programs, establish new endeavors, or exchange new responsibilities for old ones. Status quo bias is more severe in spoiling attempts to contract the scope of government, eliminating public programs or responsibilities. This means that the ideological direction of government is a product of the system-level capacity for policymaking: when government enacts more policies, it is usually moving policy to the left. This puts liberals and conservatives in different positions in their efforts to advance policy change and implies that policy output will not respond equivalently to leftward and rightward political movement.

Policy enactments are made possible by agreements among institutional actors. Understanding policymaking requires a consideration of who allied with whom in specific times and places. Policy change is made more likely by myriad other factors, but the role of each is circumscribed. What does not change is that institutional actors must cooperate with one another to develop and pass policy changes.[9] The governing arrangements among institutional actors are not produced by a single mechanism; shared experience, social relationships, shared goals and ideology, electoral incentives, and negotiating strategies all sometimes play a role in coalitions and compromises. Scholars must look beyond political circumstances to the alliances that directly enact policies.

The previous literature that takes endogenous policy change most seriously is historical institutionalism, especially with its interest in policy entrepreneurs.[10] Individual agents make policy, in this view, by acting in concert with the opportunities available in their time and place. Some agents are better than others at recognizing the character of their political environments and mobilizing others to support their views. Yet policy entrepreneurs cannot act in isolation. The character of their political environments is mostly a product of their relationships with other political actors. Policy entrepreneurs are embedded in what I call "governing networks," arrangements of ties among political actors to pursue policy change.[11]

Not all actors are equally equipped to serve central roles in governing networks. Presidents, long-serving members of Congress, and prominent interest groups, the actors that I call "institutionalized entrepreneurs," most often jointly produce policy enactments. Each of these actors has influence on many others inside and outside of government. Presidents influence legislation and administrative agency decisions, interact most directly with the public and media, and possess some unilateral power. Congressional leaders oversee the bureaucracy and the courts, are the key point of contact for outsiders, and control the branch of government where most new policy is developed. Prominent interest groups can be central for a different set of reasons: they help organize proponents of policy options and seek change over an extended period, simultaneously working in all branches of government.

None of these actors is automatically a successful policy entrepreneur. Presidents are the most likely to help achieve policy change, but they vary dramatically in their ties to legislators and activists and their productivity. Most members of Congress, in any given session, play little role in producing policy change—but a few workhorses make a lasting mark. Of the thousands of interest groups that mobilize to influence policy, similarly few make inroads. Yet the largest, broadest, and oldest of these groups are sometimes involved in several policy changes across many decades. Although each actor is equipped to help produce policy change, they can only achieve it in cooperation with one another.

The capacity of each of these actors to change policy is a product of their role in governing networks. That is, each actor is dependent on the relationships among all of the others. Most presidents, legislators, and interest groups are active in time periods where the structure of relationships is not conducive to much policy change. To enable extensive policymaking, participants with many different issue concerns and institutional affiliations must ally or compromise in pursuit of the same program. Since 1945, the most successful period of policymaking involved a stable cross-issue coalition of diverse but powerful actors.

During an era that I call "The Long Great Society" from 1961 to 1976, a similar cast of central participants dominated policymaking in many issue areas in the legislative, executive, and judicial branches. Advocacy, coalition, and compromise among these institutionalized entrepreneurs mobilized the entire political system to achieve substantial results.

The distinct governing networks that develop in each time period and issue area are not artifacts of political conditions. Actors are not simply pursuing pre-existing preferences in strategic games with other actors. They are developing political relationships, learning about policy and political feasibility, paying attention to others' reactions, and adjusting preferences along the way. That is why variables like public opinion and election results are unable to explain policymaker action. The patterns of cooperation emerge instead from the behavior of the entrepreneurs themselves. Observers cannot know in advance whether actors will be able to join forces on the basis of their partisanship, ideology, issue concerns, or branches of government. The institutional actors themselves have to decide to work with one another to achieve policy change across a range of issues. In any given issue area, time period, and governing institution, there are many other factors beyond network composition and structure that contribute to policy change; everything matters, a little bit, sometimes. Yet the actors in the governing network consistently and jointly produce policy change.

In explaining policy change as a product of endogenous patterns of cooperation in governing networks, I am necessarily acknowledging that many outcomes are possible given the same political circumstances. To move beyond idiographic explanations involving the specific individuals and political contexts involved in each policy change, I seek generalized empirical patterns. The analysis pursued here focuses between the macro-level patterns sought by political scientists and the micro-level explanations offered by policy historians. Governing networks are the context within which the micro-level explanations develop but they are not mere reflections of the macro-level political environment.[12] They are instantiations of the patterns of coalition and compromise among institutionalized actors that are necessary for policy change.

In three famous maxims, German statesmen Otto von Bismarck captured the difficulty of predicting policy output with political inputs. "Politics is not an exact science," he reminded us. Later, he went further: "Politics is not a science, as the professors are apt to suppose. It is an art." Finally, he defined politics as "the art of the possible."[13] This book pursues the science of politics, but does so with a bit of Bismarck's skepticism. Political inputs like public opinion, partisanship, and election results will not fully explain changes in the amount and character of policymaking. Neither differences in the types of political conflict across issue domains nor the relative public concern over different problems will explain the issues that are addressed by policymakers. No one set of predictive variables will explain when policymaking diverges from the normal pattern of limited action. Policy changes are achieved when policymakers and activists, the artists of the possible, make them happen.

The Evidence

To assess theories of American policymaking, this book uses a comprehensive content analysis of policy area histories. My data originates from 268 sources of policy history, mostly books. The sources all cover at least 10 years of policymaking since 1945 in one of 14 domestic policy issue areas: agriculture, civil rights and liberties, criminal justice, education, energy, the environment, finance and commerce, health, housing and development, labor and immigration, macroeconomics, science and technology, social welfare, and transportation. This excludes defense, trade, and foreign affairs, but covers nearly the entire domestic policy spectrum.[14] My content analysis follows David Mayhew's coding of landmark laws using the retrospective judgments of policy historians but expands his source list by more than 300%.[15]

The policy histories I analyze collectively uncover 790 notable policy enactments in these issue areas since 1945.[16] Using this population, the content analysis enables new measures of policymaking productivity and its ideological direction but expands the analysis to all branches of government and incorporates a wider variety of assessments. With some limitations, coding of these historical sources can produce reliable data that matches previous trends (as chapter 2 assesses).

The content analysis of policy histories also provides data on the circumstances that each author judged significant in each policy enactment. To capture their explanations, I included more than 60 questions about each author's explanation of each enactment. I rely on the judgments of experts in each policy area, who have already searched the most relevant available evidence, rather than impose one standard of evidence across all cases and independently conduct a new investigation that is less sensitive to the context of each policy debate. This analysis provides a database of which factors each author judged important for each policy enactment. In chapter 6, I review several minor effects of differences in author explanations based on their background and the methods that they use.

I also record every individual and organization that historians credit with policy change. I catalogue all proponents of policy change that were seen as partially responsible for each enactment.[17] Combined, the policy histories identify 1,306 actors that they credit with at least one policy enactment (usually in coalitions, rather than in isolation). This book uses social network analysis to connect the actors, assessing the structure of relationships in each issue area and time period.[18] I categorize the actors based on which of the three branches of government they came from, if any, and their ideological orientation. The network analysis enables discovery of the patterns of cooperation that helped produce policy change.

To compare and compliment the data from policy history, I incorporate the best available existing data. I use information on the topics of congressional hearings, public laws, executive orders, Supreme Court cases, and news articles from the Policy Agendas Project.[19] I also rely on previous indicators of the number of landmark laws per year, the ideological orientation of laws, the ideological mood of the country, and polarization.[20] Integration of past data demonstrates more robust findings and facilitates an assessment of the degree to which traditional political inputs presage changes in policy output.

I combine these data in several analyses: I predict time series data on policy productivity and its ideological direction, analyze separate datasets linked to policymaking in each issue area, and construct a cross-sectional time-series model of policy enactments by topic. I assess differences in explanations for the same enactments based on the claims of each policy historian. I create and analyze networks associated with each time period and issue area. Collectively, this enables a thorough quantitative review of evidence originally collected from qualitative sources.

Policymaking and Democracy

The book challenges Americans' views of democratic government. Despite Abraham Lincoln's vision that our government is "of the people, by the people [and] for the people," there is little evidence that the most important outcomes of the policy process follow uniformly from the opinions of the American public or their expression in elections.[21] Instead, these inputs matter for policymaking only alongside factors like research and interest group lobbying, each under a limited set of circumstances. Policymakers can and do collectively ignore public opinion and the direction of election results, sometimes by enacting contrary policy but most often by making no change at all. The results of the policy process are determined by the interactions among policymakers themselves, and the public appears to have quite limited impact.

Political accountability is difficult in a decentralized policymaking system. The success of entrepreneurs in changing public policy in any issue area at any given time is dependent on institutional capacity. The American government has a cross-issue system-level capacity for policy change that varies over time, rather than any inherent and constant constraint on its agenda. Its capacity for action is more influential than the relative attention that policymakers pay to each social problem and is associated with the cumulative ideological direction of policy. During many time periods, government is capable of accomplishing very little. Judging each elected official on the basis of his or her accomplishments is quite difficult in a governing system in which all the parts have to fit together for much of importance to happen.

The context-dependent story of policymaking told here makes for thorny judgments of democratic government. The many different pictures of policymaking in different historical eras and issue domains mean that governance cannot be reduced to variations on a few ideal types. Whatever normative visions we construct of ideal democratic procedures, whether they are premised on the consent of the governed or simply good governance, our aspirations are likely to diverge from the true process in any time and place. Our vision of democracy and its execution in the policy process are quite far apart.

The Structure of the Book

The book begins with an outline of theory and evidence, proceeds to consider broad patterns and differences across time and issue areas, and concludes with an evaluation of contemporary policymaking. Chapters 1 and 2 introduce the theoretical and methodological tools of the investigation. Chapters 3-6 assess theories based on *agenda setting, macro politics, issue typologies,* and *actor success* in turn, presenting my alternative perspectives. Throughout, I emphasize how institutionalized entrepreneurs operating in governing networks make policy change possible. I articulate a view of national policymaking as insular and policy change as irregular, a process of government expansion through clustered significant enactments.

In chapter 1, I outline the difficulty of achieving policy change and critique four families of theory designed to explain significant enactments. I explain the many premises that I borrow and adapt from previous theories based on separation of powers, historical institutionalism, and issue networks. I develop a view of policymaking based on the ideological asymmetry of significant enactments, the role of institutionalized entrepreneurs, and the characteristics of governing networks (especially the unique policymaking formula of the Long Great Society). Because the perspective places little emphasis on the power of the American public, I also address the implications for our normative view of democratic government.

In chapter 2, I explain the use of policy histories, scholarly accounts of the political activities surrounding American national policymaking in each issue area, for understanding policy change. I describe the rationale and procedures for aggregating information from my 268 sources and detail the steps to create comprehensive data from narratives of policy development. I also review the limitations of the method and address common objections. I illustrate the method with data from one policy area: civil rights and liberties. I review the times and places of civil rights policy change, the relevant political circumstances, and the actors credited with policy enactments. I build networks of actors credited with policy change and demonstrate their use. The results show that many political circumstances and actors occasionally influence policy change. But even in civil rights—the issue area most associated with social movements and public mobilization—the internal machinations of government institutions and bargaining among traditional interest groups are the most commonly influential factors in policy change.

Chapter 3 argues that the agenda setting focus of previous research is misplaced. *Agenda setting* theories are limited by the notion that government prioritizes problems before deciding which policies to consider. I demonstrate that objective measures of the public and government agenda are a poor guide to when and where policy change will occur in any branch of government. To explain why, I detail how often each political actor and circumstance reportedly influences policy change and analyze the most commonly influential actors across all issue areas. The most frequently mentioned actors are presidents, members of Congress, and prominent interest groups. The most frequently credited circumstances involve negotiations in the administrative and legislative branches and interest group advocacy. The results are inconsistent with the focus of previous research, which expects public opinion, focusing events, and election results to direct policymakers to particular problems.

Chapter 4 reviews policy development over time, arguing that the unique features of a single period of policymaking better explain policy history than *macro politics* models relating political inputs to policy outputs. From 1961 to 1976, the US federal government enacted hundreds of significant new public policies that dramatically expanded its scope and responsibility. The period effect associated with the Long Great Society is the most important determinant of changes in the productivity and policy direction of all branches of government since 1945. Changes in public opinion, partisanship, and ideology predict neither this era's success nor the aggregate patterns of policy change outside of the period. A large and diverse cross-issue governing network—held together by a core of interest groups, long-serving legislators, and four successive presidents—enabled extensive liberal policymaking. Rather than a policymaking system responsive to public opinion or party control, what emerges is a single unique era driven by system-level changes in the governing network.

Chapter 5 argues that the long-standing effort to use *policy typologies* to categorize issue areas based on their types of politics is unhelpful. The most important factors in the policy process are broadly consistent across issue areas, but each area is somewhat distinct in the venues where policies are enacted, the frequency and type of policy development, the relative importance of different circumstantial factors in policy change, the composition of participants in policymaking, and the structure of governing networks. The differences are not reducible to a few dimensions or categories. The politics of each issue area stand out in a few important but unrelated aspects: issue area differences are best viewed as exceptions to general patterns.

Chapter 6 analyzes explanations for policy change from different authors. I review five types of *actor success* models that focus on one category of policymaking actor, arguing that all are myopic. Scholarship on presidential and congressional success begins with the proposals that each makes, assuming influence if their agendas match results. Three other literatures also match preferences and policy output, but start from the agendas of the public, the scientific community, or interest groups. Instead of analyzing deviations between any particular actor's preferences and outcomes, I assess when and where each author includes each type of factor in their explanations for policy change. I find few consistent differences in explanations across types of authors and research methods. Most factors influence policy in some circumstances but are not universally recognized as regular contributors. The exception is internal processes of advocacy, coalition, and compromise within government institutions.

The conclusion reviews the limitations of each theory of American policymaking, forwarding a new set of consistent findings that enable a credible evaluation of democratic government. The policymaking system is built with a status quo bias, but significant government expansion is more likely than contraction. The Madisonian system succeeds in limiting policymaking, making it likely only when many institutional actors pursue cooperation across many issue areas—empowering the president, long-serving legislators, and interest groups. American policymaking is rarely responsive to the public; the role of opinion and elections is limited and inconsistent. National institutions have not created an effective match between our expectations for democratic accountability and their execution in American government.

The book offers a revised perspective on old questions, aggregating information collected by policy historians to enable a reevaluation of previous research on American policymaking and a new view of the perennial questions of democratic governance. Scholars must learn from the close analysis of policy history as well as an assessment of the connections between political trends and policy outcomes in multiple issue areas. The broad patterns of influential factors in the policy process are discernible and important foundations of American government.

The patterns do not comport with the textbook view of political institutions, macro-level theories, or the hopeful image of government "by the people." They do incorporate the story of how Biden and McConnell jointly negotiated three consecutive landmark policy changes into our systematic understanding of policymaking. The aggregation of policy history encourages a context-rich view of the policy process in which a few important actors have real agency to affect policy independent of their political circumstances, but only if they collectively pursue a shared program. Policy change is not simply the product of political inputs. It emerges instead from governing networks among institutionalized actors—the artists of the possible.

CHAPTER 1

The Insularity of American Policymaking

Following the Republican takeover in 2010, the House of Representatives voted to repeal the Affordable Care Act, better known as Obamacare, more than 35 times. All of the votes were largely along party lines, with Republicans voting for repeal and all but a few Democrats voting against. These votes are consistent with the party-line votes that originally passed the health care law, but they will not result in any revisions because no new bill was signed into law.

The partisan and ideological alignments that lead to policy change do not always fit the pattern of ideological division. Bill Clinton's health care bill faced the same partisan division but never came to fruition. In between, Republican George W. Bush sought a Medicare prescription drug benefit program, a major expansion of government responsibility. That 2003 act passed via a bipartisan majority in the Senate and a party-line vote in the House (but with Republicans voting for government expansion). The development of the law was credited to a bipartisan coalition including Edward M. Kennedy, Tom DeLay, the AARP, and the pharmaceutical and health insurance industries.

Both polarized voting patterns and bipartisan coalitions of legislators and interest groups are important components of the policymaking process in Washington. The former has received much more attention, but the latter is more important. Polarized voting has not produced alternating one-party coalitions to enact policy changes. Instead, significant policy changes tend to pass with overwhelming and bipartisan support.[1] There are some final votes like the Affordable Care Act, where the parties split down the middle and the majority party determines the ideological direction. There are others like the prescription drug bill, with Republican votes in support of government expansion. Still other important laws pass by near-universal consensus with votes that are foregone conclusions. Other policy change occurs in the executive or judicial branches and not simply as a product of partisan appointments by elected officials.

Understanding what determines public policy change is among the most important questions in political science. Policy output is the chief product of government, and public policy choices are the main decisions of politicians. Traditionally, political scientists assume that policy decisions are made based on the preferences of elected officials or the public. Institutions aggregate individual preferences, which stem from pre-existing ideologies or a desire to respond to public opinion. In the health care example, the Democrats want national health insurance and the Republicans oppose it. Whether the nation enacts and repeals health reform depends on which party wins elections and how the public responds.

I argue that current theories fail to explain American policy history since 1945. Rather than responding to public concerns, national policymaking is insular. Policy change occurs primarily as a result of coalition and compromise within the political class. Election results, ideological preferences, and public opinion explain neither the amount nor direction of policy change. There is no type of political debate that proceeds primarily due to forces external to government, although the most important factors driving policy change differ slightly across issue areas. The structure of policymaker relationships is not simply a product of who stands to gain and lose from policy action in each area. Although many political circumstances sometimes affect the likelihood of policy change or the form it takes, the relationships among institutionalized entrepreneurs, the active and central policymakers, are the one constant force in American governance. No individual actor's agenda drives the policy process; together, the artists of the possible shape policy development.

This chapter outlines my perspective on American policymaking. It begins by reviewing the central feature of American governance: status quo bias and the associated norm of incremental change. It then critiques four families of theory designed to explain rare but significant policy change: theories based on *agenda setting, macro politics, issue typologies,* and *actor success.* Each represents a reasonable starting point for investigating policymaking and makes claims that can be assessed empirically, but each comes up short. To build a new view of policymaking, the chapter builds on premises borrowed from several other theories. The building blocks include separation of powers models, historical institutionalism, and theories of entrepreneurship. The chapter then outlines the important outcomes the book seeks to explain and details a new theoretical approach based on cooperation among institutionalized entrepreneurs in governing networks. Finally, it points to the problems that the new view raises for democratic accountability.

Status Quo Bias and Incremental Change

Theories of American policymaking generally agree that policy change is difficult, with institutions set up to block change. The constitutional system was designed to limit aggressive action. Power is divided by branch and chamber and each branch has checks on the powers of the others, limiting action without broad consensus.[2]

Political scientists detail the operations of American institutions and model their effects. Thomas Hammond and Gary Miller, for example, argue that the stability-inducing mechanisms of bicameralism and the executive veto combine to make the status quo a common equilibrium, narrow the range of possible outcomes, and put the proponents of policy change at a major disadvantage.[3] Keith Krehbiel argues that current policy often falls within a "gridlock range"; no change is possible, even with majority support, because bicameralism and supermajoritarian institutions require agreement among many ideologically opposed actors.[4] This logic of veto players has been extended to many political institutions; each additional actor whose acquiescence is necessary for policy change leads to fewer enacted proposals.[5]

Scholars have uncovered other reasons why it is difficult to get anything done—even given relatively wide agreement across the political system. The two-party system produces few stable majorities with overwhelming partisan control of government. Entrenched interest groups often oppose reforms. A potentially active court system can limit lawmaking. The federalist division of responsibility can frustrate national action.

Status quo bias is a consistent finding in studies of institutions across all political systems, but that does not mean no policy change occurs. Incremental policy changes that build on previous policies are typical. Institutional development often has an innate logic due to the increasing returns of maintaining current arrangements.[6] Policies can build on themselves because they create constituencies to support them and raise the costs of switching to alternatives.[7] The few leaders paying attention at early stages in a policy process may create institutions that determine the future course of policymaking.[8] Yet path-dependent policymaking need not entail preordination or planning by institutional designers.[9]

The notion of incrementalism draws from a venerable tradition of theory on public administration. Herbert Simon argues that individuals are boundedly rational; instead of seeking out and evaluating all possible alternatives, they "satisfice" with an easily available option.[10] Charles Lindblom contributes the complementary notion that policy change is rarely revolutionary.[11] Policy evolves through a pattern of "partisan mutual adjustment" where independent actors analyze policies through their partial viewpoints but react to one another, eventually reaching an available compromise that slightly modifies current policy.

Since early scholarship expected gradual evolution, it left open a large void: explaining significant policy change. Contemporary policy scholars view this as their primary challenge. *Theories of the Policy Process*, Paul Sabatier's influential compendium, covers theories that attempt to explain the sources of major policy change.[12] Each of the theoretical traditions within the field sees incremental policy adjustment as the norm, but seeks to explain how policy development is occasionally abrupt. Frank Baumgartner and Brian Jones recognized this as the central problem of policy theory: explaining significant policy change given the strong incentives for incremental adjustment and the strong status quo bias of American political institutions.[13]

Alternative Theories of Significant Policy Change

This book challenges four families of theory that seek to explain significant changes in American national policy. I outline the focus of each theory in table 1.1, along with my primary critiques. *Agenda Setting* theories focus on the attention that policymakers give to different problem areas on the national issue agenda, emphasizing how events, public priorities, and media coverage influence how government prioritizes problems. *Macro Politics* theories use changes in political inputs like election results, the ideological positions of policymakers, and public opinion to predict changes in policy productivity and the aggregate ideological direction of policy choices. *Issue Typologies* categorize issue areas into ideal types, usually based on how policies distribute benefits and costs, and expect different types of policies to produce unique political conflicts. *Actor Success* theories focus on how well policy outcomes match the preferences of a particular actor such as the president, congressional leaders, or the American public.

Table 1.1 includes examples of seminal texts in each theoretical family. My intellectual categorization is not meant to fully convey the claims of these authors, but to supply the essence of their views as compared to others. *Agenda Setting* theories say significant policy change stems from a large change in attention to a problem, taking the issue area away from the incremental adjustment of policy specialists and bringing it to the center of political debate. *Macro Politics* theories argue that significant change is made possible by wide partisan and ideological agreement among policymakers and the public. *Issue Typologies* claim that, because the stakes of policy debates differ, policymaking in some issue areas will proceed without public involvement whereas others will generate wider mobilization. *Actor Success* models analyze what a particular actor wants to achieve, explaining when they fail to achieve their goals.

I find theoretical limitations with each previous view and empirical generalizations that are inconsistent with them. Each is associated with a chapter that assesses conflicting evidence: chapter 3 covers the relationship between issue agendas and policy change; chapter 4 covers whether policy change follows from trends in elections, ideology, and public opinion; chapter 5 covers the fit of issue

Table 1.1 **Alternative Theories of Policy Change**

	Agenda Setting	Macro Politics	Issue Typologies	Actor Success
Examples	Baumgartner and Jones, Agendas & Instability in American Politics; Kingdon, Agendas, Alternatives and Public Policies	Erikson, Mackuen, and Stimson, The Macro Polity; McCarty, Poole, and Rosenthal, Polarized America	Lowi, "American Business, Public Policy, Case-Studies, and Political Theory"; Wilson, "The Politics of Regulation."	Light, The President's Agenda; Binder, Stalemate; Gilens, Affluence and Influence
Essence or focus	Problem prioritization via issue attention	Time-series analysis of policy productivity and direction	Categorizing issue areas based on how policies distribute benefits	Success rates of key actors
Common explanations for policy change	Events, public priorities, media coverage	Election results, ideological change, public opinion	Public opinion or interest groups; differs by issue area	Agendas of president, Congress, the public, interest groups, or researchers
Theoretical limitation	Cooperation on proposal for policy change is critical, not a shared issue agenda	Consensus proposals usually required; entrepreneurial roles and eras of cooperation key	Politics does not conform to ideal types based on styles of policy conflict	No actor's agenda drives policymaking
Empirical evidence at odds with theory	Issue agendas not closely associated with policy change; internal factors often matter alone	Amount and ideological direction of policy change do not follow from party, ideology, and opinion	Issue areas vary on many dimensions, do not divide into clear types; each issue network is distinct	No one type of actor dominates; taking an actor's perspective assumes their influence
The alternative view in Artists of the Possible	Policy change occurs mostly through internal dynamics of cooperation among activists within institutions	Policy productivity and liberalism linked; patterns of leader cooperation created unique 1961-1976 policymaking era	Each issue area features a subtle variation on the generic policy process; network composition and structure vary	Many factors matter sometimes but central actor relationships matter most; actor agendas are secondary
Chapter assessed	Chapter 3	Chapter 4	Chapter 5	Chapter 6

Note: The table reports characteristics of four families of policymaking theories and this book's alternative views.

area differences with policy typologies; chapter 6 assesses when each actor plays a role in policymaking and how views differ based on where observers focus. This chapter lays out how my views are at odds with the essence of each theory.

AGENDA SETTING

Agenda setting, the process by which policymakers decide which issues to prioritize or which problems to address, is a major focus of research. It plays a central role in three of the most productive research traditions: the Punctuated Equilibrium theory associated with Jones and Baumgartner, the Independent Streams theory associated with John Kingdon, and the Advocacy Coalition Framework (ACF) associated with Paul Sabatier and Hank Jenkins-Smith.[14]

Punctuated Equilibrium theory makes the most direct case for a relationship between issue agendas and outcomes, repeatedly finding examples of policy changes that followed shifts in the government agenda associated with an upsurge in public concern. External forces like interest groups, media coverage, and real-world events disrupt the normal incremental adjustment of the policy process. The updated version of the theory focuses on disproportionate information processing.[15] During normal periods, policymakers fail to respond to many signals they receive about social problems or current policy. As these signals build without response, they enable an abrupt change in policy (a punctuation) coinciding with an increase in attention. Punctuated Equilibrium scholars assess their theory by analyzing distributions of policy changes and indicators of attention, arguing that both tend to be intermittent and skewed (with a few large changes and many small changes). The assumption is that these two series are causally related—that policy changes follow increased attention. Both the examples used as case studies and the data used to assess attention focus mainly on the impact of public opinion and media coverage.

Kingdon's Independent Streams theory argues that social problems, potential policy options, and political trends all develop independently.[16] Two of these three "streams" rely on agenda-setting inputs: the politics stream uses public opinion to determine what can be enacted; the problems stream uses focusing events, media coverage, and new information to help policymakers match their proposed solutions with agreed-upon problems. The key to policy change is "windows of opportunity" that emerge when the streams are joined during shifts in the public agenda.

The ACF also usually requires factors external to government to change the settled arrangements among policymaking participants in an issue area. Because these issue-specific coalitions are usually in agreement, it takes external pressure or disruptions in participation to produce significant policy change.[17] Final votes in Congress, administrative agencies, or courts may function merely as a ratification of a decision that has already been reached through a consensus of issue stakeholders.

The main theoretical limitation of *Agenda Setting* theories is that agreement on which problems or issues to address is not a necessary step in policymaking. It is far less critical to share a topic of debate than to coalesce or compromise around a specific proposal for policy change. Proposals that elicit wide support or minimal objection can move toward enactment without much attention. Critical compromises among policymakers or competing coalitions can produce changes, whether a policy area is constantly on the agenda or well out of public view. Since policy agendas can also expand and contract to incorporate policy options that develop wide support, problem prioritization is not always critical.

As a result, changes in the issues on the public or media agenda do not presage changes in policy. Focusing events, public opinion, campaign issue discussion, and media coverage can all occasionally help move the policy process along, changing policymaker expectations about the likelihood that something will be enacted. Yet issues that become new objects of policymaker attention do not necessarily lead to laws, executive actions, or court decisions.

Policymaking is more insular than *Agenda Setting* theories perceive, but not because it occurs largely in cloistered issue subsystems that design policy for later acquiescence. Instead, policymakers and advocates play critical roles in coalition and compromise across the issue spectrum. Some are veto players, whose assent is required. Other entrepreneurs are workhorse advocates who have developed reputations for productivity and compromise.

MACRO POLITICS

The second family of theories I assess uses traditional political inputs to predict policy change. Scholars start with a model of actor preferences, explaining how they aggregate through institutions. If there is a proposal that everyone agrees on, it should pass. Policy change results from general agreement among liberals or conservatives or complete control of government by one side or the other. Yet if the preferences are largely constant, widely acceptable proposals that have not already passed should be infrequent. Thus, *macro politics* models need to find a way around gridlock by changing actor preferences. The easiest way to change the preferences is to change the actors: have elections with different results. When new party majorities or political leaders with different ideologies are elected, new policy can pass. *Macro Politics* models also allow actor self-preservation instincts to rule: actors can exchange public preferences for their personal preferences in anticipation that they may lose the next election.

In *The Macro Polity*, Robert Erikson, Michael Mackuen, and James Stimson argue that internal ideological trends in Congress are associated with their antecedents: public opinion and elections.[18] The authors predict the ideological direction of policy based on liberal or conservative trends in public opinion and the results of presidential and congressional elections. This is one example in a class of models designed to predict change over time in policy output, but subsequent analyses have focused more on the total output of significant policy changes rather than their ideological direction. Nolan McCarty, Keith Poole, and Howard Rosenthal view the rise in ideological polarization as the main impediment to significant policy change.[19] Few policy changes are possible because actors' ideal points, especially those of the two political parties, are too far away from one another.

Most *macro politics* models focus on Congress, but there have been some attempts to predict the output and ideological direction of the administration and the courts as well.[20] Scholars argue that the courts and agencies all make policy in response to the preferences of their median actors or those of the public. Another literature tracks whether, and under what circumstances, the branches move in the same direction over time—with each responding to ideological or partisan changes in other branches.[21] Despite the diversity of *macro politics* models, they tend to rely on a similar set of input variables: election results, ideological trends, and public opinion.

The main theoretical difficulty is that the American system requires widespread consensus for significant policy change; elections rarely produce such clear-cut and sustained mandates regarding the overall direction of government. Fortunately, not all actors have immovable ideological preferences that extend to all policy issues and not all voting members of political institutions are involved in developing policies. Instead, a small subset of policymakers and advocates develop and build support for compromise policies to gain broader acquiescence.

Macro-political variables are but one component of the policy process. Emmette Redford usefully divided the determinants of policy into three levels of analysis: (1) the macro level, including the electoral and public opinion patterns referenced in *macro politics* models, (2) the subsystem level, including factors specific to particular issue areas or institutions, and (3) the micro level, the patterns of cooperation among specific policymakers.[22] Rather than emerging solely from the American public, I argue that even macro-level patterns can develop from the sustained patterns of cooperation among policymakers and advocates. A liberal or activist mood among elites may be able to sustain itself without much input from the public.

Public opinion is an unlikely fundamental source of policy change. The public lacks consistent and expressed opinions on many policy issues. Most citizens do not hold ideologically consistent opinions that correspond to those of elites.[23] Many survey respondents express different opinions if called twice and asked about the same issue or if a question is worded slightly differently on the same survey.[24] Most citizens also lack the information necessary to evaluate public policy choices or to understand the actions of government.[25] Many voters lack information on the policy positions of candidates.[26]

As *macro politics* models find, public support for policies does not translate into continued support for the politicians that enact them; as policy gets more liberal, public opinion grows more conservative.[27] Neither a conservative nor liberal ideological perspective is likely to maintain a majority of adherents. As a result, policymakers view public opinion as malleable and responsive to their framing choices.[28] They use public opinion to change their messages, but not their policies, because they believe that they can convince voters to support the policies they favor. These numerous disconnects mean that shifts in the public mood cannot account for the ideological direction of policy.

The historical record presents one major example of a self-sustaining policymaking era that is not explained by public opinion or policymaker partisanship and ideology: a liberal and productive era of policy change across all three branches of government from 1961 to 1976. I will argue that this unique era, The Long Great Society, corresponds to productive patterns of cooperation among central policymakers and advocates across all issue areas.

ISSUE TYPOLOGIES

A third family of theories seeks to explain variation across issue areas. The logic is that significant policy change occurs in each issue area but perhaps for different reasons. The policies in place and the options under review govern the type of associated politics. The categorizations are usually based on what is at stake in each debate and the likely proponents and opponents of policy change.[29]

Theodore Lowi proposes a three-part typology: redistributive, distributive, and regulatory.[30] Regulatory policies involve limits on choices to restrict behavior; distributive policies involve efforts to provide benefits to specified populations; redistributive policies involve taxing some people to provide benefits to others. The political process surrounding regulatory policy involves adjudication, but can feature swiftly implemented new restrictions. The process surrounding distributive policies involves satisfying client-like interest groups for each relevant agency. Redistributive policies involve intense partisan and ideological conflict.

Similarly, James Q. Wilson argues that policy issues can be divided into four types based on whether the costs and benefits of policy action in the area are concentrated or dispersed: interest group politics where both costs and benefits are narrow, entrepreneurial politics where only costs are concentrated, client politics where only benefits are concentrated, and majoritarian politics where both are broad.[31] The idea is that policy change in some areas will be achievable via interest group negotiation alone. In others, policy change will require a few populist proponents overtaking their opposition using public support. Client politics will instead involve alliances between interest groups and allied politicians, usually avoiding public scrutiny. Majoritarian politics should require public and elite ideological debate.

In other words, policy change has different causes depending on the likely winners and losers of policy change in a particular issue area. Although these authors differ in identifying the important categories dividing some policy debates from others, they all tend to focus on a few ideal types that will supposedly correspond to more than one issue area. They expect issue politics to differ based on broad distinctions on a few underlying dimensions.

The key theoretical problem with this style of analysis is that there is no reason to expect issue debates to correspond with any of these ideal types. There are considerable differences between health care and criminal justice policy but not on any one underlying dimension; their differences will not assist our understanding of the differences between any other two issue areas. It makes more sense to acknowledge that issue areas vary on many dimensions, without clustering into distinct types associated with different types of policymaking. Each issue area has several subtle variations from the policy process evident in most other issue areas.

The critical actors may not follow from the types of policies under consideration. There is little reason to expect that the policymakers responsible for change will result automatically from any quintessential feature of each issue area. Policymaking in all issue areas is likely to involve patterns of coalition and compromise between leading political figures and advocates, with only limited influence from the American public.

ACTOR SUCCESS

Another area of scholarship, which I label *Actor Success* models, considers the influence of one set of actors at a time. These studies begin with an agenda of potential policy changes, based on the attempts made by an actor to change policy, and assess how many of these attempts lead to policy change.

Paul Light finds substantial variation in success rates across presidents but a consistent honeymoon effect of success near the beginning of each term.[32] Light argues that the agendas of the presidents have contracted in recent years, along with the scope of their attempted policy initiatives. Others analyze similar trends but attribute success to the partisan and ideological composition of

Congress that a president inherits.[33] Others find that presidential influence is conditional on whether the majority of the public is closer to the presidential opinion than the median opinion in Congress.[34] This presumes that the president's role is central and restricts the scope of the investigation to items that the president attempts to influence.

Other scholars start with the agenda of important items on the congressional docket and assess the success rate of congressional leaders. In *Stalemate*, Sarah Binder argues that divided government and polarization can lead to lower levels of success for each party and more gridlock.[35] The reason is that agendas expand during divided government and many of the proposals from each party fail. The success of congressional leaders, however, may also depend on their mobilization of interest groups and public opinion.[36]

I also categorize studies of the match between public, interest group, and scientific opinion and policy output as *actor success* models. Like the presidential and congressional studies, they focus on the agenda of one set of actors. For example, studies analyze whether policymakers follow the majority opinion in public opinion polls on individual policy proposals.[37] In *Affluence and Influence*, Martin Gilens demonstrates that opinion among high-income earners is most predictive of policy results; this raises questions about whether public opinion has a strong role at all, as it is consistent with many other causal explanations.[38] This analysis also begins with a limited agenda of possible changes: questions asked in opinion polls.

Studies of the influence of scientists on policy tend to compare federal policy to an ideal type where technocrats utilize scientific research to decide optimal policy.[39] Scholars have found some evidence of research-driven policy, particularly early in the policy process.[40] Previous studies find evidence of influence by scientists, usually in concert with other political actors.[41] Researchers, journalists, and policymakers all use research tactically to advance proposals.[42]

Theories of interest group influence argue that policy should match interest group preferences. In the pluralist approach, some social groups begin with advantages in social status, generate cohesion and develop a political orientation, and face a receptive government.[43] Elitist accounts of interest groups are also born of the idea that government institutions are an arena for conflicts between groups—but one where the upper class always wins.[44] Contemporary studies assess which lobbyists get their way in Washington policy debates, assuming that possible policy choices will come from the agendas of the groups.[45] Analogous to literatures on public opinion and research, scholars only seek to explain policy based on the actions of other political actors and circumstances when interest groups do not seem to be driving policy. Political officials are still seen primarily as agents for, or organizers of, interest groups.

All of these *Actor Success* models can be viewed as "hedgehog" theories of policymaking.[46] They focus on one big thing influencing policy, rather than many small things. They look mainly at characteristics of one set of actors at a time: the behavior of the president, the cohesion of congressional parties, the character of research, the relative mobilization of groups, or the section of the public that shares an opinion. They consider all of the other circumstances that influence policy change only as potential mediating factors. This common myopia in research is associated with less accurate predictions of political outcomes than approaches that look for multiple categories of influence.[47]

The shared theoretical limitation of these approaches is that no one set of actors dominates policymaking and no one actor determines the agenda of possible policy goals. Taking an actor's perspective tends to assume their influence and is less likely to notice all of the other factors at play. When researchers select the point of view of a particular actor, they assume the items on the actor's agenda are more likely to be enacted and that a match between an actor's preferences and outcomes entails influence. Instead, a global perspective is superior; many actors can matter, but they tend to do so with vastly different frequencies.

Building Blocks for a New View of American Policymaking

This book assesses each family of alternative theories in its own chapter, presenting evidence for the views articulated here and describing empirical regularities that are inconsistent with each previous theory. Yet the book's goal is not merely critical. I hope to advance a new understanding of policymaking that is consistent with the findings from policy history. This view explicitly draws from the theories listed in table 1.2 and the associated authors. For each theory, the table includes the theoretical premises that I share and those where my view if somewhat different. Even though I do not wholly embrace their claims, each plays an important role in my view of policymaking and I want to credit prior scholarship. I detail each in turn below.

SEPARATION OF POWERS

Theories of separation of powers use rational actor models to assess likely policy changes based on the ideological positions of policymakers, including legislators and the executive. Given the difficulty of mobilizing the wide support necessary to achieve policy change, many status quo positions may be invulnerable to potential attempts to achieve change. Hammond and Miller argue that the bicameral legislature and the executive veto both induce stability, restricting potential new policies and circumventing large ideological swings in policy outcomes.[48] They also find a substantial role for the president. In a two-dimensional

Table 1.2 **Theoretical Building Blocks**

	Examples	*Borrowed Premises*	*Where Artists of the Possible Departs*
Separation of Powers	Krehbiel, *Pivotal Politics*; Hammond and Miller, "The Core of the Constitution"	Significant policy change is difficult and irregular, usually a product of supermajorities; status quo powerful	Policymaker preferences are adaptive and multidimensional; entrepreneurs critical, not pivotal voters
Historical Institutionalism	Pierson, *Politics in Time*; Carpenter, *The Forging of Bureaucratic Autonomy*	Even significant changes constrained by past decisions; government responsibility grows over time; leaders build reputations and coalitions	Path dependence not overwhelming force in policymaking; actor ties often independent of institutions
Activist Eras	Schlesinger, *The Cycles of American History*; Huntington, *American Politics*	Long periods can be more active and liberal; convergence of trends enables era of change	Eras not necessarily cyclical or built on public ideology
Policy Entrepreneurs	Kingdon, *Agendas, Alternatives, and Public Policies*; Mintrom, *Policy Entrepreneurs and School Choice*	Individuals with policy and political expertise drive policymaking; relationship building and mood reading creates options	Central political leaders most well positioned to serve; depend on overall structure of relationships
Issue Networks	Heclo, "Issue Networks and the Executive Establishment"; Hallacher, *Why Policy Issue Networks Matter*	Each issue area is associated with different actors who develop policy independent of the public	Policy productivity increases when same leaders active across issue areas; major actors still key

(*Continued*)

Table 1.2 **(Continued)**

	Examples	*Borrowed Premises*	*Where Artists of the Possible Departs*
Advocacy Coalitions	Sabatier and Weible, "Advocacy Coalition Framework"; Sabatier and Jenkins-Smith, *Policy Change and Learning*	Stable coalitions in policy debates include interest groups and government officials; insulated from public	Policymaking not usually in subsystems; research and ideas only of secondary importance
Presidential Leadership	Caro, *The Passage of Power*; Perlstein, *Nixonland*	Policy coalitions and compromises brought about by ambitious and cajoling presidents	Presidential leadership a product of ties among legislators and groups; public face less critical

Note: The table reports premises of seven policymaking theories and their relationship to this book's perspective.

policy space, the threat of the executive veto reduces the range of possible policies even without frequent use. The ideological location of widely acceptable policy changes is more responsive to changes in the president's preferences than those of legislators.[49]

Krehbiel's theory similarly envisions a large status quo advantage. He designs it to account for two basic facts about American policymaking: (1) gridlock is not constant but it is the norm and (2) winning coalitions are usually large and bipartisan. In a one-dimensional space, moderate current policies are usually impossible to change even if majorities prefer movement. The winning coalition is the final vote on major laws in Congress, which is usually far greater than required for passage. The average support level on final passage is 82% of legislators; only 12% of votes are near the majority threshold and more than 40% feature near unanimity.[50]

These empirical regularities represent a starting point for understanding policy change, as do the theoretical suppositions that illustrate the difficulty of achieving wide consensus on potential policy changes. Yet I do not endorse a rational actor model of policymaking. Krehbiel makes assumptions that are common in these models: issues are well defined on a single dimension of disagreement, the preferences of the actors are fixed and single-peaked on this dimension, the procedural rules leading to policy change are known to participants, and all actors are pursuing the action most likely to maximize their gain from policy.[51] With these assumptions, Krehbiel shows that some legislators will be pivotal decision-makers.

In my view, these assumptions do not reflect the American system. Policymaker preferences are multidimensional and fluid; both the dimensions and ideal points can change during policy debates and after interaction among policymakers and with activists. If and when preferences are fixed on a single dimension, it is usually too late for any policy change to occur. The preferences of many disinterested legislators are malleable as issues develop and proposals are articulated. Even the way that the status quo is understood can change. Policymakers also differ in how much they desire policy change for its own sake, even at the cost of an outcome not clearly preferred to the status quo. Presidents often strongly prefer action because they desire identifiable accomplishments. Liberals are also more likely to want government to act.

As a result, pivotal voters on final passage are less critical parts of the policy system than entrepreneurs willing and able to take leading roles in shaping policy debates and forging compromises. The critical steps toward policy change often take place well before a final vote comes forward and not necessarily in full anticipation of who is likely to be critical on the final vote. Because policymaking can also take place in the executive and judicial branches, it is incomplete to assign critical roles only to legislators and the president. Nevertheless, these theories point to the way that American institutions require widespread ascent for policy change.

HISTORICAL INSTITUTIONALISM

Historical institutional scholarship suggests that causal processes often take considerable time to develop. Alongside the historical inheritance of previous choices, many trends act in combination to influence current policymaking. Combinations of sequencing effects, slow-moving causal processes, and conjunctures (interaction effects between variables moving in a complementary direction over time) can create different potentials for policy change in different eras.[52] Paul Pierson argues that the significance of variables like public opinion on policy outcomes is "frequently distorted when they are ripped from their temporal context."[53] American state development is a long-term developmental process where government institutions typically grow over time.[54]

The historical institutional literature specifies the methods by which policy builds on itself and the determinants of the course that it takes, emphasizing path dependence and policy design.[55] Participants are hardly building policy from scratch in each moment; they are working within existing policies and revising. Adjustments may depend on aspects of the way the policy was initially designed and the skill of the entrepreneurs that support it. As Daniel Carpenter has described, individuals can develop networks of support, building on past achievements as they gain a reputation for influence.[56] The extent to which policy adapts over time is often dependent on its initial design, such as whether it mobilizes a constituency to support expansion and whether it aligns the interests of most actors.[57] Policy may have a trajectory of its own independent of contemporary political conditions and actor preferences.

My theoretical departure from historical institutionalism is one of degree: path dependence and sequencing play a role in policy change, but it may not be overwhelming. At any given time, contemporary political circumstances may play a greater role. Furthermore, the working relationships among policymakers need not be tied to a process of institutional development; actors may be pursuing policy change through coalition building and compromise in each issue area, forging agreement behind policy proposals not directly related to maintaining or enlarging the existing institutions within which they work.

ACTIVIST ERAS

Historical institutionalism also emphasizes the potential for system-level time period effects. All of the actors operating in the 1950s are subject to a similar set of opportunities, constraints, and norms that diverge from those of actors operating in the 1990s. In particular, some time periods may be much more conducive to large changes in political institutions or policy development. Especially when normally distinct realms of activity collide, the actors participating during the collision may have more opportunities for fundamental change.[58]

Some eras may benefit from lots of converging trends that promote change. Once a productive era of policy change begins, actors may change their expectations about what can be achieved and seek to expand on their success.[59] As a result, advocates, policymakers, and groups that move first to develop institutions and policies can sustain early advantages, consolidating support well past when their supportive political and social context dissolves.[60]

In postwar America, the most commonly referenced era of activism is the Long Great Society. Arthur Schlesinger, Jr. and Samuel Huntington both conceived of 1961–1976 as having a society-wide activist orientation. Schlesinger saw the era as part of a cycle, the next coming of the New Deal.[61] Huntington saw it as an era of "creedal passion," corresponding to the American Revolution, the Jacksonian period, and the Progressive era.[62] Huntington credited the rise in social protest and urban unrest; Schlesinger claimed broad changes in the public mood.

I endorse the view that long periods can be associated with active and liberal governance due to a convergence of institutional and social trends. Observers often notice that elites in one era have quite different norms of behavior and expectations about what is possible than those in another. I see no reason that these eras will follow a periodic cycle or necessarily result from changes in public opinion or social movement activity, but I do not doubt that both played a role in providing the environment that policymakers exploited in the 1960s and 1970s.

POLICY ENTREPRENEURS

Explanations for policymaking should incorporate policy entrepreneurs: individuals or organizations that promote a policy idea and create a practical path to enactment. Entrepreneurs help develop actionable proposals that are politically achievable, mobilize others to support their proposals, and find the most convincing arguments and information to support their view. As Kingdon argues, they are just as focused on political coalition building as policy content.[63] Entrepreneurs help develop proposals and shop them to decision-makers, finding workable solutions in an iterative process. Michael Mintrom elaborates the skills of policy entrepreneurs: they must be "creative and insightful," "socially perceptive," able to intermingle in various settings, and persuasive advocates.[64]

Mintrom also suggests that entrepreneurs are more effective at operating in networks and maintaining coalitions.[65] Entrepreneurs work with other advocates and decision-makers, molding and selling their ideas and learning from others.[66] He finds that greater involvement in policy networks increases their likelihood of success. Entrepreneurship requires lots of social activity; entrepreneurs must understand multiple audiences and the limits and opportunities of the time and place where they operate. Their knowledge, reputation, team-building skills, vision, and tenacity are all shown when they successfully operate within networks.[67]

Kingdon claims that entrepreneurs can be in or out of government—elected, appointed, or neither—as long as they are willing to invest long-term resources.[68] Mintrom agrees that entrepreneurs need not hold positions of power, pointing to roles played by concerned citizens, small group leaders, and backbench legislators. As a result, they need to cultivate relationships with key decision-makers and become a trustworthy source for them.[69]

The most prominent insiders characterized as policy entrepreneurs are bureaucrats.[70] Scholars appear to have an aversion to labeling presidents or congressional leaders as policy entrepreneurs. This is a mistake, considering that these are the people that play the largest role in final decisions. There is little reason to think that the entrepreneurial skill set or the ability to operate in networks is any less important for central policymakers. I depart from prior theory by arguing that few people are in a position to be a successful entrepreneur at any given time: their influence depends on their formal role and their connections to other decision-makers.

ISSUE NETWORKS

Political scientists regularly investigate networks of relationships between interest groups, policy specialists, and political officials. The work is commonly qualitative, using networks as a metaphor rather than network analysis as a technique.[71] In the classic formulation of "issue networks," Hugh Heclo argues that experts form relationships based on reputations for issue-specific knowledge.[72] Heclo emphasized that these networks emerge via contacts that cross institutional boundaries. Ideas and information can move throughout the network without regard to the organizational placement of the participants.

This view goes too far in de-emphasizing the composition of networks. Like policy entrepreneur scholarship, there is a bit too much faith that anyone can become a member of each network, regardless of institutional position. Heclo's emphasis on technocrats leaves out the critical role of elected officials. Brokered compromises and wide coalitions among these officials are usually a necessary component of policy change.

I also depart from the literature's focus on relationships within issue domains. Because major policy change still has to be enacted through government institutions, the key relationships may be between major political actors and advocates that bring together disparate issue concerns. Unlike Heclo, I see no evidence of a broad-based change in policy communities from iron triangles to issue networks.[73] Iron triangles relied on ties among congressional committees, administrative agencies, and client interest groups. The idea descends from a long tradition of understanding policymaking in subsystems, subsets of the political system associated with each issue area. Issue network research often finds that some type of issue-level structure is more likely to successfully lead to policy change.[74] I argue that network structure differs in more subtle ways over time and across issue areas, with substantial overlap in participation across issue areas. Networks also vary in the degree to which the relationships that define them are built on shared expertise, institutional location, or policy agreement.

ADVOCACY COALITIONS

Although I critique the emphasis on agenda setting in work on advocacy coalitions, I draw from it in other respects. The ACF starts from the realistic premise that there are relatively stable sides of a policy debate. The regular participants on each side include interest group advocates as well as government officials. Although not always in a formal coalition, the actors on each side are in communication and agree on a set of policy principles. The framework emphasizes discussions about the content of proposed policies and beliefs about their effects.

The ACF shares the problem that it tends to be less attentive to major institutional actors. It generally assumes that decentralized issue area experts determine policy in their areas of concern. ACF studies rarely mention actors like the
president and congressional party leaders.[75] Advocacy coalitions are made up
of people who share ideas about policy problems and solutions. ACF adherents
are not enamored with "coalitions of convenience," which they believe have less
impact on policy development.[76] In contrast, I view coalition building across the
political system, including compromises between typical political opponents,
as a critical aspect of successful campaigns for policy change. Policymaking in
national political institutions usually requires iterative modification, with communication across communities with different priorities and beliefs. Research
and shared policy ideas play only secondary roles in policy development.

PRESIDENTIAL LEADERSHIP

Rather than focus on policy subsystems, presidential historians emphasize the
abilities of the most central political actors and the quality and substance of their
relationships. They review personal ties and political rivalries, arguing that they
affect the capacity to find workable compromises. This approach should not be
confused with what has been termed the "great man theory of history," where
the abilities of famous people are exaggerated with little regard to their context.[77]
Rather than a singular focus on individual ability, presidential historians move
back and forth between discussions of personal relationships and ambitions, on
the one hand, and broad periodizations of social, demographic, technological,
and economic trends, on the other.

Robert Caro's *The Passage of Power*, the fourth installment in his long-running
series on "The Years of Lyndon Johnson," is typical of presidential biographies
in that it is centrally concerned with Johnson's personal skills and experience.[78]
It reveals Johnson's willingness to trade favors and engage in corrupt bargains for
personal and political gain, crediting him with most of the major policy initiatives during his presidency as well as the decade that preceded it. Caro describes
him as far more effective than Kennedy but puts great emphasis on contingen-
cies associated with public sympathy for liberal initiatives following Kennedy's
assassination.

Nixonland by Rick Perlstein picks up historically where Caro ends.[79] According
to Perlstein, Nixon draws from broad ideological trends in conservative public
opinion, learns from the example of Ronald Reagan in California, and successfully
bargains with southern leaders to reclaim the Republican nomination and become
president. Yet Perlstein reports a vast separation between Nixon's electoral project,
on the one hand, and his policy development, on the other. In office, Nixon works
on behalf of civil rights and relies on policy ideas from liberal friends.

Both Caro and Perlstein emphasize their president's abilities to cajole co-partisans and moderates from each party to reach deals that do not arouse public or interest group anger. I also view presidential action as central to national policymaking, but I place more emphasis on the president's role in a broader network of policymakers and activists. Although all presidents are well positioned to influence policy, those with stable connections to powerful interest groups and legislators are better able to build lasting legacies. Not all of this is under the control of the president; it depends on the relationships among all of the other active policymakers.

I depart from the historians' emphasis on the presidential role in mobilizing the public or molding public opinion. Although some political scientists argue that presidents can gain support for proposals by generating public support, most evidence shows little influence from their growing public activities.[80] I endorse the older political science view, associated with Richard Neustadt, that presidents influence policy through persuasion and bargaining with legislators, administrators, and interest groups.[81] Presidential power is constrained by the desires and incentives of all these other actors, but it is still more extensive than that of any other actor.

Understanding American Policy Change Since 1945

Since research on public policy is often bogged down by definitional and epistemological controversies, I want to specify where this book stands in relation to previous work. In a recent review of research on the determinants of policy change, Giliberto Capano and Michael Howlett characterize four major points of differentiation in studies of the policy process: (1) the extent to which policymaking is viewed as revolutionary or evolutionary, (2) the attempt to explain policy output or the process leading to it, (3) the focus on endogenous and exogenous sources of change, and (4) the role of institutional structure and individual agency.[82] The focus of studies is related to their findings; studies finding a high degree of agency tend to view the policy process as open to wide participation and more frequent change.[83]

This book considers sources of significant policy change since 1945. It is thus less concerned with incremental, evolutionary policy changes. Nevertheless, it seeks to identify instances where even major policy change builds on previous policies. By design, the research also seeks to explain policy output, rather than process. The point of the exercise, however, is to assess how different aspects of the process lead to policy outcomes. The theoretical orientation of the book is resolutely on the side of endogenous sources of policy change, with a more circumscribed role given to exogenous effects originating outside of the political class and national institutions. This is not a methodological choice: I consider both sources of policy change, but argue that the role of external factors has been overstated.

On the question of institutional structure and individual agency, I take an intermediary view. The actions of individuals and organizations are critical to policy change, but only in combination. Coalition and compromise among policymakers and advocates, reflected in their networks of regular cooperation, produce policy change. Yet institutional structure delineates the actors that can cooperate to achieve change: the president and congressional leaders gain a role because their acquiescence is usually necessary for policies to be adopted; prominent interest groups and backbench legislators play primary roles if they are consistently active on policy in multiple venues. This leaves quite a bit of room for agency, but only for a limited subset of policy actors.

This view of policymaking is reflected in the study's structure. Table 1.3 defines key concepts used throughout *Artists of the Possible* and reviews their role in the book. The study seeks to identify and analyze the most significant policy decisions made by the US Congress, the president, administrative agencies or departments, and federal courts. I seek to understand how policy productivity and ideological direction differ across time period and issue area. Productivity is the aggregate output of policy; ideological direction is the aggregate level of liberal versus conservative enactments. I assess explanations for both individual enactments and the overall level of policy productivity and its ideological direction.

The argument differs from the four previous families of theory described in table 1.1. Rather than prioritize problems in response to public concern, policymakers and activists operating inside institutions coalesce and compromise around particular proposals. Rather than respond to elections and public opinion, policymakers can pursue productive and sustained government expansion for long periods. These features of policymaking differ slightly across issue areas, but only in degree rather than in kind. Many different actors can influence policy change, but searching for influence based on the agenda of any one actor or group conceals more than it illuminates.

The argument nonetheless incorporates premises from the previous work described in table 1.2. To summarize, significant policy change is usually a product of supermajority agreement across branches. Government responsibility grows over time as institutions develop. Activist eras can come about via a convergence of social and institutional trends. Entrepreneurs, individuals with both policy expertise and political acuity, drive policy change. Issue areas are associated with networks of elites that debate policy outside of public view. Stable coalitions of interest groups and government officials produce and refine

Table 1.3 **Key Concepts**

	Definition	*Role in Artists of the Possible*
Significant Policy Enactment	Recognized change in US national policy in a domestic issue area due to an action taken by any of the three branches of government	Used to create aggregate measures of policymaking and track common explanations for enactments among historians
Policy Productivity	The aggregate number of significant policy enactments in the period	Used to assess *macro politics* theories as well as the relationship between issue agendas and policy change
Ideological Direction of Policy	The aggregate level of policy enactments that expand versus contract the responsibility of government in the period	Used to assess *macro politics* theories; rarity of conservative enactments makes policy process asymmetric
Institutionalized Entrepreneurs	Active policymakers with an institutional role in governance; presidents, long-serving legislators, and prominent interest groups	The key actors involved in policy change; their ongoing relationships enable policymaking
Governing Network	The patterns of cooperation among actors jointly responsible for policy enactments in an issue area or time period	Used to investigate the composition and structure of policymaking relationships; provides the mechanism for distinct policymaking in each era
The Long Great Society	The period from 1961 to 1976, associated with productive and liberal policymaking in all branches of government	Provides an alternative view of system-level changes in the policymaking process since 1945

Note: The table reports characteristics of six important concepts in the book.

policy proposals. Ambitious and cajoling presidents can lead the effort to build compromises for new policy.

In addition to my critiques of existing theory and the premises I borrow from the literature, my view incorporates three new points of emphasis. First, the ideological asymmetry of significant policy change (the tendency to expand government) affects the composition of actors regularly involved in policymaking and makes government less responsive to ideological change. Second, institutionalized actors with entrepreneurial skills are the primary agents in national policymaking, especially experienced presidents, long-serving legislators, and prominent interest groups. Third, these actors collectively create networks of cooperative relationships that differ by time period and issue area. To explain the Long Great Society, the most productive and liberal era of American policymaking since 1945, I focus on the regular patterns of coalition and compromise among institutionalized entrepreneurs across issue areas.

IDEOLOGICAL ASYMMETRY IN POLICYMAKING

In explaining policy productivity and its ideological direction, I emphasize that the two are closely related. As Simon and Lindblom observed, the slow growth of government is the most typical observed pattern in policymaking across issue areas. Governance usually has a built in direction: it expands toward new domains of administration and new tasks of responsibility. Policy change is usually in the direction of government expansion. This fundamental asymmetry between conservatism and liberalism deserves a central place in any assessment of policymaking. Because overturning existing programs and responsibilities of government is more difficult, most significant policy changes are expansionary.

Although my emphasis is distinct, the finding is hardly new. *Macro politics* models find that policy rarely contracts the scope of government (the common definition of conservative policy).[84] Few significant policy changes are strictly conservative; many expand government responsibility; others are not easily categorized as an expansion or a contraction because they have a mixture of both or no clear effect on how much government spends or regulates. Some proposals that are understood at the time as conservative still expand government (such as restrictions on abortion). Even including these rare instances of conservative expansion within the conservative category, Erikson, Mackuen, and Stimson code only 3.6% of landmark laws as conservative and 51.8% of landmark laws as liberal.[85] Conservative policy changes that produce major contractions of government do take place, but they are rare compared to liberal policy changes that expand government. Similarly, there are few time periods in which policy choices are mostly contracting government. When conservative policy changes are enacted, they tend to be enacted alongside other liberal policy changes. Although *macro politics* models notice that conservative policy changes are less common, they do not account for it theoretically; they just adjust the baseline, showing that conservatism is associated with less liberal policymaking.

Other studies treat the regular expansion of government responsibility as an important part of policymaking, but view it as an aspect of incrementalism. Agency responsibilities slowly expand over time as they successfully expand their mission. Budgets are built on baselines that assume an increase in spending each year. Policies tend to create supportive constituencies promoting expansion. In my view, these trends are just as important in major policy change. Across the world, government expands as an economy expands, with richer societies taking on more responsibility to spread benefits.[86]

To achieve policy results, conservatives may not need to be productive; the lack of new initiatives often has the practical effect of retrenchment or "policy drift," producing conservative outcomes by making previous liberal policy less effective.[87] Conservatives may also pursue goals through budget reforms and cumulative appropriations decisions, rather than regular lawmaking.[88] Yet studies of the federal budget also find that many more agencies and budget areas are added than subtracted over time. Government typically finds new things to do or revises what it is already doing, but rarely decides not to do something it has done in the past.

Previous research is strangely silent about the implications of this asymmetry. If significant policy change is more likely to be liberal than conservative, each ideological group and political party is in a fundamentally different strategic position. First, conservatives will more often be on the opposition side of efforts at major policy change. Liberals will be much more dependent on government's capacity to enact new policies to achieve their goals. Second, when conservative or Republican politicians are involved in substantial policymaking, they will likely be enacting liberal policies or policies that strike a balance between expansion and contraction (e.g., Bush's promotion of Medicare prescription drug coverage). Both liberals willing to compromise and conservatives willing to find places where they want to expand government will be more involved. Third, any equilibrium under a liberal policymaking regime (or universal Democratic control of government) is likely to look quite different from the conservative or Republican version. Policymaking in one era will not be a mirror image of the other, even when a new governing majority takes shape.

This requires a significant adjustment of our view of status quo bias: the idea that the current policy is the most likely outcome of any policy debate and the proponents of policy change have a harder road than advocates of no change. Proponents of policy changes to expand government are worse off than their competitors that want no change but better off than proponents of alternate policy changes that contract the scope of government. This may be why conservatives and liberals both feel that they are losing their battles to better armed opponents. Liberals complain that proposed policies to address social problems are too easy to kill; conservatives complain that policies that do pass are much more likely to expand government. Both groups are correct. There is a conservative bias in each individual policy debate (toward no action) but a liberal bias in the collective actions of government in most periods (toward expansion). Even successful contractions of government are sold as reforms of existing programs and often require participation from some of the initial coalition that favored the programs undergoing reform.

Policy theories should not treat the expansion and contraction of government as the products of similar dynamics. A shift toward Republicans or Democrats in the electorate should not be expected to have the same type of effect. Similarly, policy research should not divide development into two categories of incremental expansion and dramatic policy change. Significant policy change often relies on previous policies and moves in the same direction, but can hardly be dismissed as a simple expansion. When the Clean Air Act is renewed and dramatically expands what is regulated, it can be just as important as writing a new act. Additionally, scholars are too quick to ascribe idiosyncratic motives to important political figures on the American right that are associated with expansions of government (such as Nixon and Bush). To the extent that those figures want government to get something done, they are often engaged in a mixture of liberal and conservative policy advocacy. The slow growth of government has been an important trend at all levels of government and nearly all places in the world. This must be a starting point for any theory of policy change, rather than an afterthought.

INSTITUTIONALIZED ENTREPRENEURS

My next key point of emphasis is on the actors most likely to influence policy. Lindblom argues that the most important actors in policymaking are proximate decision-makers, including legislators, executives, and others with direct authority. Policy is usually an outcome of their structured interactions, although there is no obvious link between their pre-existing ideological preferences and their final decisions because they can be influenced by each other as well as by interest groups and activists.[89] Yet the common view of policy entrepreneurs excludes these actors or focuses more attention on outsiders.

Kingdon's focus on outsiders is curiously disconnected from his own studies of health and transportation policy. *Agendas, Alternatives, and Public Policies* begins by identifying all of the important actors that develop policy ideas and ensure political feasibility, according to interviewees in these policy communities in the 1970s. Kingdon's data shows the important role of administrators, interest groups, and congressional staffers in developing workable policy ideas and clearing them with key constituencies. Yet his interviewees confirm that the most important institutional actors (including the president and congressional leaders) play the largest roles in policy change in both issue areas.

The people I call "institutionalized entrepreneurs" have the same skill set emphasized in the accounts from Mintrom and Kingdon but also have the institutional position to play a major role in policy change. Not all policymakers play this role. In the US Congress, Richard Fenno finds that members differ in the relative importance they ascribe to re-election, power within their chamber, and good public policy. Some members are more interested in playing a policymaking role and this is reflected in their assignment to committees and their behavior.[90] Political observers describe some members as "show horses" who seek publicity and others as "work horses" who seek policy influence; there is evidence that this distinction appears in practice.[91]

In *America's Congress*, David Mayhew finds considerable variation in the extent to which members engage in leading legislation or in taking public stands on issues.[92] He identifies several "major congressional entrepreneurs" that have left their names on important legislation.[93] He also finds that senators are involved in ten times as many actions of importance as House members. There is thus considerable variation in the extent to which actors that are in a position to play a policymaking role actually do so, governed by both the strength of their official role and their personal skills and interests.

Consider several examples of the most frequent policy leaders of the twentieth century. The first is Daniel Patrick Moynihan. In addition to long-time service as a US Senator, Moynihan served in the Kennedy, Johnson, and Ford administrations. He authored a famous and controversial report on race, family, and poverty. Generally seen as a liberal, Moynihan was willing to lead domestic policy efforts for Nixon and embrace conservative changes to welfare policy. Historians partially credit him with Great Society programs, transportation investments, many social welfare policy changes, and important bureaucratic organizational reforms.

One of Moynihan's staffers, Ralph Nader, became an important consumer advocate and interest group innovator (well before his role as a leftist gadfly in the 2000s). After publishing an important book on automobile safety in the 1960s, Nader helped found dozens of organizations to pursue environmental, energy, health, economic, and transportation policies as well as civil rights. He is known mostly for inspiring a generation of liberal advocates to build public interest groups with close connections to Congress. He is partially credited by historians for seminal policies such as airline deregulation, the Freedom of Information Act, and pension reform.

The prize for the most successful liberal activist of the twentieth century, how-ever, should go to Edward M. Kennedy. Although he never won the Democratic nomination for president or served as a floor leader in the Senate, Kennedy is credited with passing more significant policy changes than all but two presidents (see chapter 3). He played an important role in passing legislation on civil rights, labor, science, crime, education, health, energy, transportation, immigration, and housing over five decades. Kennedy was known as a workhorse senator will-ing to partner with Republicans in the Senate and the White House.

Republicans were also active policy entrepreneurs, but not usually in efforts to contract the scope of government. Jacob Javits served as a US Senator from New York for 24 years. There is no elected Republican currently in national office as liberal as Javits. He was known as a supporter of civil rights and the Great Society, but historians also partially credit him with tax reform, labor poli-cies, education grants, cancer research funding, and job training programs. He also played an important part in the creation of the National Endowment for the Arts. His willingness to ally with liberal presidents and to help broker com-promises allowed him to play a central role, despite his membership in a dying moderate faction of the Republican Party.

Bob Dole served the more traditional role as the leader of the Republican Party in the Senate for more than a decade. Another unsuccessful presidential aspirant, Dole was nonetheless influential in Congress. He helped enact legisla-tion in science, welfare, crime, health, labor, environmental, and budget policy and is also credited with influencing Reagan-era executive orders. Although initially viewed as a conservative within Republican circles, Dole eventually became the moderating influence on the Republican revolution of 1994, help-ing to negotiate compromises that earned the support of Bill Clinton and the House of Representatives.

This is not a complete list of important policymakers in the second half of the twentieth century, but it can serve as the basis for some modifications of tradi-tional notions of policy entrepreneurship. First, these are hardly peripheral actors taking actions in the shadows. They were each widely recognized as among the most important political figures of their times. They are each associated with a few initiatives that consumed them over a long period before becoming law, but they are also known for brokering compromises at the end of a process. Second, the policymaking action is in Congress, with other branches playing supporting roles. Most non-presidents that serve as regular policy entrepreneurs are sena-tors with influence on multiple administrations. Third, the examples I use here fall into two ideological categories (consistent with my discussion of ideological asymmetry): they are either liberal leaders willing to find partners in compro-mise or they are liberal to moderate Republicans willing to work toward expan-sions of government. Fourth, each was well known as a negotiating partner who could deliver. They possess direct political power but are known for working with others to enact policy. The concept of policy entrepreneurs emphasizes the role of individual skill, but scholars should not lose sight of relationships and reputations for political power built over time.

INTEREST GROUPS

In addition to presidents and legislators, interest groups can also play important roles in policy development. Rather than trying to exchange money or votes for policymaker support, the interest groups with the most potential to drive policy change become regular and active partners in coalition and compromise with institutionalized entrepreneurs. Compared to legislators, the interest group advantage is that they can pursue policy change in all branches of government over long periods. As Baumgartner and Jones argue, they are well positioned to select venues amenable to their concerns as well as shift the jurisdictions of their legislative and administrative allies.[94] The disadvantage is that they rarely have direct decision-making power.

In my first book, *The Not-So-Special Interests*, I argue that some advocacy organizations with substantial longevity, large scale, and formal ties to public supporters become institutionalized into serving two semi-official roles in government: they serve as stakeholders for policy positions and representatives of broad public constituencies.[95] These institutionalized interest groups take up a sizable proportion of the opportunities for influence; they are substantially more involved in all branches of government and more prominent in all types of media. Meanwhile, most interest groups are left out of political debate and policymaking venues.

The NAACP, for example, is known as the representative of African Americans. Even when policymakers question whether its leaders are faithfully representing member concerns, they act as if they take its role as representative stakeholder for granted. The NAACP is incorporated in nearly all discussions of civil rights policy (see chapter 2) and serves as the assumed spokesperson for African Americans in many other policy areas. Its acquiescence is viewed as useful for stimulating wider political consensus. Likewise, the National Association of Manufactures, a business association, was the main vehicle for advancing the economic interests of corporations in national policy for much of the twentieth century. Its endorsement of policy was seen as an authoritative seal of approval by American business. The U.S. Conference of Mayors, an intergovernmental lobby, was viewed as the voice of cities by mid-century policymakers. All three interest groups were active across many different policy areas for decades, developing reputations for influence and entrepreneurship akin to policymakers.

GOVERNING NETWORKS

I use governing networks to understand the organizational and individual actors involved in policymaking and their relationships. The idea that the structure of relationships among actors is an important component of policymaking has a long pedigree. The use of social network analysis is the contemporary incarnation of the trend—it formalizes our view of the relationships among political actors.

Networks are also seen as an alternative to other theories of the policy process (deserving their own section in Sabatier's *Theories of the Policy Process*). Although I view these policy network research traditions as important antecedents of my approach to policymaking, I do not intend to draw primarily from them. The most important place where I differ is in the kinds of networks I study and the resulting difference in my definitions of network membership and ties. I am not primarily interested in the relationships among coalitions of actors outside of government that seek policy change in the same area over an extended period (such as advocacy coalitions).

Rather than start with a community of actors who care about a particular issue area, I focus only on actors who help pass legislation or bring about executive orders, administrative agency rules, or court decisions. I include elected and appointed government officials and interest groups and activists in the same networks. My approach does not presume that networks all have issue boundaries; the same actor may be prominent in many different issue areas. As long as identifiable actors are credited with policy enactments, I analyze their shared responsibility for policymaking.

Governing networks are instantiations of the actors and relationships that led to policy change in each issue area and time period. The network itself cannot be viewed as a cause of policy change because it is a combined view of the different coalitions and compromises that produced successive policy changes. The network is a description of many causes, rather than an independent cause. It is a way of aggregating the many instances of coalition and compromise that helped cause the enactment of specific policy changes. The governing network provides a view of the proximate patterns of cooperation that led to collective policy output.

Actors in governing networks cooperate with one another for different reasons. Some relationships involve social ties developed through long-term friendly interaction. Others reflect long-term information exchanges and ongoing channels of communication. Some invoke formal alliances or working coalitions. Other ties involve arrangements of convenience among typical opponents behind moderate policy positions. Still others are the product of a joint desire to achieve something and have names attached to the effort. In many instances, the line between coalition and compromise is not bright: multiple actors want to achieve something but do not begin with agreement on what; they debate, compromise, and respond to one another's concerns until some proposal gains wide support.

Although many different types of governing networks produce policy change, a particular type was associated with the policymaking success of the Long Great Society. The network was a product of sustained cooperation among institutionalized entrepreneurs across a wide range of policies for four consecutive presidential administrations. The network was large and mostly liberal, but only a small subset of actors was consistently and widely involved. This included prominent interest groups, long-serving legislators, presidents, and executive branch officials, including several who were active in all three branches of government. Compared to other networks, two features set it apart: (1) it was driven by a core of established actors who pursued a wide program to expand government across many different domains and (2) the relationships in the network were sustained throughout the sixteen-year period, surviving a substantial conservative shift in opinion and elections. The relationships in the governing network were only the proximate causes of policy change during the era. A convergence of numerous institutional and social trends alongside entrepreneurial actions enabled sustained cooperation. Yet the governing network was not an epiphenomenon of a liberal epoch or a mere reflection of public mood; it was the product of ties among institutionalized entrepreneurs that enabled the substantial liberal policymaking of the era.

Comparing Theories of Policymaking and Democratic Government

The chapters that follow assess my claims and compare them to previous theories. Chapter 3 assesses whether policy change is consistently associated with changes in the public agenda or whether it arises mostly through institutional dynamics of cooperation in government institutions. Chapter 4 tests whether policy productivity and ideological direction follow changes in partisanship and ideology or whether the specific historical factors associated with the Long Great Society era offer a better account of policy history. Chapter 5 evaluates the appropriateness of issue typologies that categorize some issues as driven by public mobilization in comparison to my view that each issue area differs subtlety from the universal policy process of elite interaction. Chapter 6 assesses whether any actor-centered approach to explaining policymaking success makes sense in light of the multiple precursors to policy change and the way that observers differ in analyzing their relative importance.

The book will also assess the utility of my points of emphasis. I demonstrate the ideological asymmetry of policy change and show its consistent effects on participation and policymaking. I assess whether the most influential circumstances for policymaking are internal or external to government and whether the actors involved are insiders or outsiders. I illustrate the usefulness of governing networks in understanding the *Long Great Society* and differences across issue areas. The analysis is only one step in the collective scholarly effort to disentangle the policymaking process but I am hopeful that it can change the focus of future scholarship.

My comparison of empirical theories of policymaking also has repercussions for our normative ideas about what American democracy should entail. The focus on governing networks and elite-level policy debates is inconsistent with the broadly shared expectation that democratic governance ultimately derives from the preferences of the people. Although the theoretical perspective offered here is open to the influence of many different factors on the policy process, it sees only a limited role for the American public.

The essence of *macro politics* models is that policy change derives from changes in public opinion and the results of elections. If policymaker preferences drive outcomes, those preferences usually change with electoral results or as policymakers fear future electoral defeat. A central idea of *agenda setting* theories is that public concerns help to drive policymakers toward solving particular problems. I expect the partisan and ideological composition of political institutions to play a role, but not a definitive one. I expect public opinion polls and expressed public concerns to have even less impact. If I am correct, both political scientists and public observers have overemphasized the role of the public in the policymaking process.

The overemphasis is born from a normative gloss: Americans want the public to be influential. Democratic theory suggests that the citizens should ultimately control government or at least be able to hold government accountable for its decisions through elections. American government is supposedly "of the people," by the people," and "for the people." Our view of democracy suggests that the government's ideas about what problems are important and what policy should entail should come from the people.

Yet there is no reason why we should begin empirically with a public-centered model of the policy process. Starting with the assumption that democracy fulfills its ideals is not a useful way to construct empirical theory. It is analogous to beginning a policy analysis with the assumption that policy will achieve its goals. Government by the people is but one possible model for the policy process, and it may not be a likely one.

This book assesses several prominent attempts to build models of policymaking based on public opinion. I challenge the idea that the public is empowered to decide what topics policymakers should address. I contest the claim that aggregated trends in public opinion predict the ideological direction of policy-making. I find that no type of issue is systematically conducive to influence by public opinion. In all respects, I argue that most policymaking is far removed from public influence. The need for coalition and compromise among elites to enact policy change leaves the political system largely insulated from grassroots public pressure. The result is that the American national policymaking system is unlikely to live up to our expectations about the central role of the public in the democratic process.

Our current collective view of the policy process is too focused on public opinion and elections and too confident that a small number of variables can explain policy change over a prolonged period. The political science concentration on roll-call votes and survey data also misses the most important components of policymaking. Pundits, scholars, and citizens pay too much attention to events like the 35 votes to repeal Obamacare and too little attention to bipartisan agreements to expand government, like the prescription drug bill. A reevaluation of past models is certainly in order. The policy process is unlikely to be simple, but a focus on the patterns of coalition and compromise among policy-makers is likely to be the best starting point.

CHAPTER 2

Aggregating Policy History

The 2008 Democratic presidential primary campaign featured a debate about responsibility for civil rights policy change. After Barack Obama repeatedly referenced Martin Luther King, Jr.'s dream of ending segregation, Hillary Clinton sought to credit Lyndon Johnson, rather than King: "Dr. King's dream began to be realized when President Johnson passed the Civil Rights Act...It took a president to get it done."[1] The candidates eventually reached agreement that both figures played a major role, but the debate over the relative importance of public mobilization and government machinations continues. Even crediting both King and Johnson leaves out a considerable array of factors important to the story.

In times of disagreement over credit and responsibility, "let history be the judge" is a common refrain. The notion suggests that, given time to reflect and investigate all angles of a story, historians will reach a collective judgment that is better than any contemporary account. This book relies on historical judgments to build composite histories of public policy change. As the Obama-Clinton debate suggests, some historical debates are perennial. Rather than apportion credit between King and Johnson, this book reaches the same conclusion as the two candidates: it simply credits both. In order to assess the relative importance of each actor and political circumstance to policy change, this book expands the analysis to review the historical evidence on many important policy enactments. I assess how often Johnson and King, along with other actors and political circumstances, influenced significant policy enactments.

I use a content analysis of secondary sources of policy history to compile information on hundreds of different instances of policymaking, which I call policy enactments. These qualitative histories cover the totality of the policy process in a particular issue area over an extended period. Reading all 268 of the policy histories and examining each of their narratives would provide plenty of case studies, including existence proofs that almost any factor and any type of person can have an effect on policy outcomes. Aggregation of policy histories provides a comparison of the relative importance of each actor and political circumstance. It teaches how often something matters, not just that it has mattered sometimes.

Any aggregation of these policy histories necessarily sacrifices some of the texture of their contextualized storytelling, but it leads to a dataset that offers much more than examples. Aggregating histories from different periods creates a timeline, a chronology of major policymaking events. It also provides a catalog of the political circumstances that historians judged important to policy change. In addition to listing relevant factors, the aggregation categorizes them and finds trends in their relative importance across time and issue area. It also produces a compendium of the people and organizations credited with policy change. Since the histories tie specific actors to particular policy changes, I use the accounts to explore the patterns of cooperation among the actors involved in policy change. This provides information not only on how often Johnson and King influenced policy, but when they did so together and who else assisted.

The best way to see how I conducted the content analysis, compiled the data, and analyzed the results is to use an example. This chapter is thus constructed differently from the methods sections of most scholarly books. It focuses on the history of civil rights and liberties policy since 1945, starting with the example of the Civil Rights Act of 1964 but expanding well beyond it. For each type of analysis, I use the 28 policy histories covering civil rights and liberties that I coded to give the reader background on the research method and the results it provides. Wading through this history gives me a chance to substantively address the opening dispute between Obama and Clinton about the role of internal and external forces in civil rights policy change. The ultimate aim is simply to demonstrate how the research proceeds and how it can answer important questions about American politics.

I do not claim that the civil rights domain is a prototypical policy area; in fact, chapter 5 will demonstrate that it stands out in several ways in comparison to other domestic policy areas. Nonetheless, it serves as a less likely case for my ideas. If any policy area should be driven by public mobilization and external events, civil rights should be among the most likely. It is thus a hard case for a perspective built on the importance of institutions and internal negotiations over policy. Rather than settle the debate, this chapter seeks to apply the insights of policy history to a substantive problem: interpreting and evaluating the role of different political circumstances and actors in civil rights policy change. The main goal is to show and tell. Policy histories contain interesting data that can be used to assess the American policymaking system. My aggregate data analysis is designed to draw productively from them.

The Treasure Trove of Policy History

Policy histories are an underutilized information source on the evolution of American policymaking. Specialists in each policy area often review the political process surrounding policy development, producing narrative accounts of how, when, and why policy changes.

This source of data may be unfamiliar. It is atypical of institutional studies of lawmaking and distinct from the case studies common among policy researchers. It also differs from general political history, designed to tell the story of everything that happened in government over a particular period. In contrast, policy history is primarily geared toward chronicling the output of government: adopted public policy changes. Policy historians are interested in any and all political factors and personalities that contributed to public policy outcomes, but only as they relate to the policies that government selected.

Policy history offers several advantages compared to other literatures. First, it is not a search for confirming evidence of a preselected theory. Policy historians are not attempting to show that one factor matters more than all of the others; they are driven first to identify the most important changes and then to assess all potential contributing factors. Second, it is open to policymaking happening in any branch of government and led by any coalition. It does not start with particular actors' agendas and ask whether they were successful. Third, it does not intend to analyze the entire workings of the political system, only to explain particular policymaking events. It is not distracted from the task of explaining policy outcomes by synthesizing general political developments.

Policy history is an underdeveloped field. The writers I analyze do not always think of themselves as policy historians. They are often political scientists, economists, or sociologists interested in a particular topic. Just as often, they reside at schools of public policy where their colleagues are more interested in evaluating policy results than in understanding the political process behind policy development. A few are journalists or government officials who nonetheless undertake a substantial scholarly project. Some are even textbook writers attempting to set the context for students interested in pursuing a career in a particular policy area. Policy historians usually think of themselves simply as experts on their issue area; they may call themselves health policy or environmental policy specialists.

The most prominent previous use of policy histories in political science was by David Mayhew in *Divided We Govern*. He uses a portion of the literature that I analyze to develop a list of important policy enactments, just as I do. Mayhew limits the investigation to Congress and also adds contemporary judgments by journalists. Mayhew defended the policy histories as more conscious of the real effects of public policy and less swept up by hype from political leaders than the contemporary journalistic judgments.[2] Although contemporary observers and policy historians identify a similar list of important enactments, policy historians are more concerned with the content of policy. Compared to year-end accounts like those compiled by *Congressional Quarterly*, policy histories are more likely to include important changes that flew under the radar and are less likely to highlight symbolic actions that made no change in policy.

Most policy historians rely on their own qualitative research strategies to identify significant actors and circumstances. The books that I use quote first-hand interviews, media reports, reviews by government agencies, and secondary sources. These are expert judgments by specialists in each policy area; they have searched the evidence regarding policy change in their specialty and produced accounts sensitive to the context of each policy debate. I learn from their studies rather than trying to impose a universal standard of evidence across all cases in a new independent analysis. Although there are differences in the judgments of historians, I build a composite history based on the main threads of their assessments.

Compiling Policy Histories

I compile information from 268 books and articles that review at least one decade of policy history in a particular issue area since 1945, substantially expanding Mayhew's source list. Many policy histories begin with the period following World War II and most consider 1945 a good starting point for understanding contemporary politics. I end the analysis in 2004 to allow sufficient time for historians to report on recent events. Combined, the histories cover the 14 domestic policy issue areas identified by the Policy Agendas Project (PAP), covering the bulk of domestic policy.[3] Table 2.1 reports the contents of each issue area, provides examples, and matches them to PAP category numbers. Nearly all areas of domestic policy fit within one of the included categories. Using PAP categories also enables ease-of-comparison with previous data.

To compile policy histories, I use bibliographic and online searches of keywords from the topic lists and subcategories available at policyagendas.org as well as literature reviews in each issue area. Rather than sample, I attempt to construct a population of sources based on several exclusion criteria. I exclude sources that focus on advocating policies or explaining the content of current policy, rather than identifying important policy enactments and covering the political process surrounding them. I also exclude sources that cover fewer than ten years of policy history to focus on broad historical reviews that compare events to determine the most important policy changes. Rather than focus on only a single enactment or a single actor, these long-term analyses ensure that scholars consider short- and long-term causes and effects.[4]

I also exclude sources that analyze the politics of the policy process from a single theoretical orientation without a broad narrative review of policy history. This guards against a search for confirming evidence, where scholars emphasize

Table 2.1 **Issue Area Content Descriptions**

Issue Area Category (PAP No.)	Included Issues
Agriculture (4)	Farm subsidies and the food supply
Civil Rights and Liberties (2)	Discrimination, voting rights, speech, and privacy
Criminal Justice (12)	Crime, drugs, weapons, courts, and prisons
Education (6)	All levels and types of education
Energy (7)	All types of energy production
Environment (8)	Air and water pollution, waste management, and conservation
Finance and Commerce (5)	Banking, business regulation, and consumer protection
Health (3)	Health insurance, the medical industry, and health benefits
Housing and Development (14)	Housing programs, the mortgage market, and aid directed toward cities
Labor and Immigration (5)	Employment law and wages as well as immigrant and refugee issues
Macroeconomics (1)	All types of tax changes and budget reforms
Science and Technology (17)	Space, media regulation, the computer industry, and research
Social Welfare (13)	Anti-poverty programs, social services, and assistance to the elderly and the disabled
Transportation (10)	Highways, airports, railroads, and boating

Note: The table reports the issue area names and descriptions of the common subcomponents covered within each area. The numbers recorded are from the Policy Agendas Project. A full description of each issue area's contents is available at http:www.policyagendas.org.

factors that are central to their theory without fully assessing alternative factors.[5] To be included, a source had to attempt to explain when, where, and why a series of policy enactments occurred. The full list of sources, categorized by issue area, is in Appendix A.[6]

The 28 sources that cover civil rights and liberties policy history include eight general civil rights histories, several volumes on civil liberties, and specialized histories covering the topic of civil rights and liberties as it applies to religion, race, gender, sexuality, schools, employment, information, voting, affirmative action, abortion, and disabilities. The other 13 policy topic areas include similar diversity of sources and subtopics.

From Narratives to Data

The policy histories each include copious information, but I sought to focus on their explanations for discrete policy enactments. The first step was to identify significant policy changes in each book or article. With the help of research assistants, I read each text and identified significant enactments. I include policy enactments when any author indicated that the change was important and attempted to explain how or why it occurred. The relevant portions of the codebook and instructions are available in Appendix A. As a reliability check, pairs of assistants assessed two of the same books; their lists were identical or differed by only one or two enactments. Aggregating across all policy histories in each issue area provided a timeline of major policy changes.[7]

I instructed coders to find enacted policy changes: "You only need to analyze policy that was actually passed or issued, not legislation that never made it into law. You do not need to analyze policy that is mentioned in passing or mentioned in describing another event. You only need to include policy changes that the author of each book considers significant. We only want to include the author's history and their explanation of events, rather than your own."

The compilation identifies 790 significant policy enactments since 1945. It improves upon previous measures of policy output. First, it expands the analysis beyond Congress. Policy change occurs in all branches of government. Although Congress is the most important site for significant policy enactments, some actions by the other two branches set policy and are just as influential. My lists are not a full assessment of administrative and judicial activities but they include their policymaking actions. Agency rules and court constitutional or statutory interpretations are included if historians regard them as significant changes in policy. Second, the analysis covers a broad policy spectrum, including issue areas where important policy decisions may go unnoticed by contemporary journalists. In addition to tracking items in the news, scholars should pay attention to issue areas where the most important changes may generate less notice. Finally, the method enables using the policy histories to identify the people and circumstances responsible for policy change.

For each enactment, I code whether it was an act of Congress, the President, an administrative agency or department, or a court. I also categorize it by issue area based on the PAP issue area codebook.[8] For example, the Civil Rights Act of 1964 is considered a law passed by Congress in the area of civil rights and liberties. Figure 2.1 illustrates how this data can be used to explore changes over time in civil rights policymaking. It reports the number of significant civil rights and liberties policy changes that occurred within each branch of government during each presidential administration. The figure shows an early era where policy changes were restricted to judicial and administrative actions, an era beginning

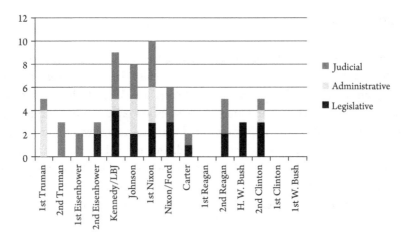

Figure 2.1 Civil rights policy enactments over time

in the 1960s when policy changes were widespread, and a later resurgence of policy changes. This type of time series enables periodization as well as comparison with other annualized data.

I also code each enactment as liberal, conservative, or neither; for this analysis, I followed Erikson, Mackuen, and Stimson, coding enactments as liberal if they expanded the scope or responsibility of government and conservative if they contracted it.[9] A liberal change is defined as one that expands the size or scope of government responsibility, funding, or regulation; it does not necessarily involve liberal actors. A conservative enactment contracts the size or scope of government responsibility, funding, or regulation (also regardless of the actors involved). Policy changes that involved no change in the scope of government responsibility or a mix of conservative and liberal provisions were coded as neither or both. Similar to Erikson, Mackuen, and Stimson, I made an exception if the conservative and liberal sides were understood differently, such as in the pro-choice and pro-life opinions on abortion. In these few cases, I use the commonly understood direction.

I also coded whether a policy change was large, medium, or small. A small change was defined as one that was not as significant, more incremental, and had little substantive impact on American policy. A large change was one that was non-incremental and had a substantial and enduring impact on American policy. Others were coded as medium. Because the large, medium, and small categories are quite subjective, this book only uses them to assess the broader applicability of other findings. All enactments included were considered significant by at least one policy historian. Finally, we coded each policy change based on whether it was thought to be important at the time of enactment or only later reported to be influential. The base category was important at the time, but some authors specifically mentioned that particular policy enactments only became important after they were adopted. Although there are limitations to any dataset built via human coding of historical sources, this compilation represents the most extensive attempt yet to draw quantitative data from historical accounts of policy specialists.

The civil rights and liberties policy histories identified 61 total significant policy enactments. Compared to other areas, a much higher percentage of civil rights policy changes took place in the courts. Most civil rights changes were liberal; they expanded the scope of government responsibility. Most fell in the medium-size category and were recognized as important at the time they were enacted.

Of the 790 significant domestic policy changes since 1945 across all issue areas, 64.4% were laws passed by Congress, 9.1% were executive orders by the president, 10.1% were administrative agency actions, and 15.8% were judicial decisions. These new data reveal similar patterns of policymaking to their closest previous analogs but show more pronounced changes over time. My new time series of total significant policy enactments per biennium is correlated with Mayhew's measure at .71 but shows substantially more enactments in each period and more variation over time. The series is also correlated with several other previous measures of policy productivity at higher than. 6.[10]

In addition to simple counts of the number of policy changes per time period, the data can also be used to assess change over time in the ideological direction of policy. In total, 56.6% of significant policy enactments were liberal, 8.9% were conservative, and the remaining were both or neither. This finding is not a product of any tendency by policy historians to be less likely to highlight conservative policy changes. Krehbiel criticizes the year-end summaries of journalists for being too liberal, arguing that the policy historians help correct their biases.[11] The Erikson, Mackuen, and Stimson measure, which is based only on contemporary judgments from journalists, coded an even smaller share of laws as conservative.

To judge change over time, I use the measure from Erikson, Mackuen, and Stimson: the number of liberal policy enactments minus the number of conservative policy enactments.[12] My new time series of liberalism per biennium is also correlated with their previous Congress-specific measure at .72 but my average score was nearly three times as high as theirs and more than twice as variable across time. Adding enactments in other branches of government makes aggregate policy history appear consistently more liberal and makes the ideological trends in each direction more pronounced.

In the chapters that follow, I use these data on when policy changes occurred and in what ideological direction they ventured. From this information alone, I can connect policy changes to other events taking place at the same time. For example, I divide time periods by presidential administrations, congresses, and other periods. Any time series data meant to be associated with government action can potentially be connected to my new data. This enables tests of *agenda setting* theories (in chapter 3) and *macro politics* models (in chapter 4). The evidence in each chapter relies on a different data structure. Chapter 3 analyzes the correlates of policy enactments with cross-sectional time-series data; the cases are each biennium in each issue area. Chapter 4 uses the time series of policy productivity and ideological direction to assess the factors governing change over time in total policy output.

An Example Policy History: The Civil Rights Act

The content analysis of policy histories is designed to provide more than just a list of important policy enactments. It also seeks to draw from historical accounts regarding why policy change occurred and who should be held responsible. For every policy enactment mentioned by each author, I sought to draw from their accounts by accumulating all of the political circumstances and actors credited with generating policy change.

Return to the example of the Civil Rights Act of 1964. Eighteen different sources pointed to this act as a significant policy change and attempted to explain how and why it occurred. Most explanations of how the act came about involved multiple factors, such as the one offered by Tracy Roof: "The reaction to Kennedy's assassination, President Johnson's commitment, and mounting pressure placed on Congress by the civil rights movement and public opinion outside the South all built momentum behind passing a comprehensive and effective civil rights act in 1964."[13]

Reports about the Civil Rights Act from policy historians pointed to many different circumstances. They included references to several congressional factors, such as a change in the relative balance of Democrats and Republicans after 1960, leadership by congressional committee chairs, congressional party leaders, and other individual members, an agreement between the House and Senate, and key votes in committee and on the floor. The accounts also pointed to a supportive president as well as supportive cabinet officials and agency heads. They cited the influence of related government reports, court rulings, and state government actions. Many mentioned pressure from interest groups, including nongovernmental organizations, corporations, and unions. They pointed to particular examples of congressional lobbying and constituent pressure.

This was not entirely an internal story, of course. The historians also cited media coverage and news articles, changes in public opinion, issues raised in election campaigns, focusing events, and many protests. Some emphasized that the act was an extension of earlier policies and that earlier policy choices made it more likely, referring to civil rights acts and executive actions adopted in the 1950s and early 1960s. They also pointed to important ideas and frames, including the role of the Cold War and international opinion. In short, several trends and political circumstances converged to allow the Civil Rights Act to pass into law.

The sources also credited 45 specific actors for helping to bring about the Civil Rights Act of 1964. These included presidents Kennedy and Johnson and several members of Congress, such as Ted Kennedy, Everett Dirksen, Charles Goodell, Emanuel Celler, Hubert Humphrey, Katherine St. George, Margaret Chase Smith, Philip Hart, and Ralph Yarborough. The list includes Democrats and Republicans and members of each chamber. Credited actors also include administration officials such as Burke Marshall, Nicholas Katzenbach, and Robert F. Kennedy.

Outside groups and activists were also credited with the policy change. Responsible national interest groups reportedly included the National Urban League, the Leadership Conference on Civil Rights, the AFL-CIO, and the NAACP. Social movement groups such as the Southern Christian Leadership Conference, the Student Nonviolent Coordinating Committee, and the Mississippi Freedom Democratic Party were also credited. Individual activists including Cesar Chavez, Malcolm X, Martin Luther King, Jr., A. Phillip Randolph, Aaron Henry, Bayard Rustin, and Pauli Murray were also given their due.

Quite a few individuals and organizations played important roles to allow the act to pass, alongside supportive political circumstances. I seek to comprehensively assess the circumstances and actors that play a role in policy change, compiling similar narrative historical reports for other policy enactments. Most do not involve anywhere near this range of important circumstances or actors; the Civil Rights Act is atypical in the breadth of its coalition and the political factors necessary to enable passage. Yet the composite histories of each policy change take the same form as the one I just outlined. They have fewer noted circumstances, but each explanation points to some subset; they involve fewer actors, but nearly all explanations tie specific individuals or organizations to policy change. This book's task is to compile and analyze the information from these reports.

Explanatory Factors in Policy Change

I code all policy histories for the factors that each author judged significant in each policy enactment. To capture their explanations, I have coders ask themselves

61 questions about each author's explanation of each enactment from a code-book. Based on these questions, I record dichotomous indicators of whether each author's explanation included each factor for every significant change in policy that they analyze. These factors include all of those listed above in the explanation for the Civil Rights Act of 1964 and many others. Appendix A includes the relevant factors included in the content analysis classified into the categories used in this book. Coders of the same volume reach agreement on more than 95% of all codes.[14]

In most results, I aggregate explanations across all authors, considering a factor relevant when any source considered it part of the explanation for an enactment. I use this minimal standard because many policy histories did not include substantial explanatory material on some of the policy enactments that they viewed as significant. Further analysis (in chapter 6) reveals that author differences do not substantially change the relative frequency of the explana-tory factors associated with each issue area or time period. Attempts to use other standards, such as requiring majority or universal agreement across authors, yielded comparative results that were similar (even though every factor was con-sidered important less frequently).

I categorize the factors associated with each policy change. Congressional fac-tors include references to the influence of individual leaders, institutions, or votes within Congress. Administrative factors include references to the influence of the president or administrative officials or government reports. Judicial factors include references to the influence of court cases or fear of court intervention. State and local factors include references to state or local policies that served as models or influence by state and local officials. Media factors include references to general media coverage or specific reports. Public opinion includes factors related to polls, public mood, election results, campaign discussion, protests, or constituency calls to Congress. The interest group category includes references to the advocacy or influence of particular groups or general congressional lobbying. International factors include references to international events, opinion, or laws or to competition with other nations. The event category includes references to focusing events, wars, economic downturns, or budgetary changes. The research category includes references to academic studies, the influence of scientists, data on social problems, and private or government reports. Path dependence includes references to past policies that new policy built upon or that changed the options available to policymakers. The ideas category includes references to posi-tive or negative frames used in a policy debate or a reluctance to oppose an idea.[15]

Aggregating data to the category level allows an investigation of which types of factors matter the most in the policymaking process as a whole and within specific issue areas, time periods, and institutions. For illustration, table 2.2 reports the percentage of policy enactments within the civil rights and liberties domain that reportedly involved each category of circumstances. The results show that interest

Table 2.2 **Reported Circumstances Associated with Civil Rights and Liberties Policy Enactments**

Factors	Civil Rights Policy Enactments Involving Each Factor (%)
Congressional Factors	39.3
Administrative Factors	47.5
Judicial Factors	44.3
State and Local Factors	24.6
Media Factors	21.3
Public Opinion	34.4
Interest Groups	67.2
International	11.5
Events	23.0
Research	23.0
Path Dependence	42.6
Ideas	9.8

Note: The table reports the percentage of enactments that involved each factor, according to policy historians. N = 61

groups were involved in more than two-thirds of civil rights policy changes since 1945. Other categories that often play important roles include the administration, the judiciary, and path dependence. Public opinion plays a role in just over one-third of the cases. The influence of international factors is comparatively rare.

To increase the usefulness of this type of information, this book disaggregates these factors (in chapter 3), compares the factors relevant to each policy area (in chapter 5), and predicts when each type of factor makes a difference in policy change (in chapter 6). From the initial report, it is clear that interest groups are a significant part of the story of how civil rights policy evolved. Every type of factor played some role, but there was a clear hierarchy in the reported frequency of the impact of different political circumstances.

Actors Responsible for Policy Change

Policy historians also provide substantial detail regarding the actors involved in policymaking. Rather than just report who was president or who controlled Congress at the time of each enactment, they analyze the people who made a difference in each policymaking episode. To draw from the accounts, I record every individual and organization that policy historians credit with bringing about policy change. For each policy enactment mentioned by each author, I catalogue all mentions of credited actors (proponents of policy change that were seen as partially responsible for the enactment). The typical explanation credits the few actors most responsible for each policy change, rather than everyone who played any role. I then combine explanations for the same policy enactments, aggregating the actors that were associated with policy enactments across all authors.[16] Coders of the same volume reached agreement on more than 95% of actors mentioned as responsible for each enactment.[17]

Combined, the policy histories identify 1,306 actors that they partially credit with at least one policy enactment. I code which branch of government (if any) each actor represented. I also note whether each actor is an interest group as well as whether they are a government organization. I categorize the actors ideologically, based on whether they were Democrats (or liberal organizations) or Republicans (or conservative organizations), or neither.[18]

In the civil rights and liberties domain, there were 210 actors credited with policy change since 1945, including 63 individual members of Congress, 52 interest groups, and 16 government organizations. The specific actors credited with policy change most often in this area were the NAACP, the American Civil Liberties Union, and Lyndon Johnson. Despite the central role Barack Obama gave Martin Luther King, Jr. in this area, he was tied for eighth place on the list of actors, credited with four significant policy changes.

Several reliability checks increased confidence in the method of relying on policy history for compiling these data. First, different authors mention similar distributions of political circumstances and actor types for the same enactments. Second, authors covering policy enactments outside of their area of focus (such as health policy historians explaining the political process behind general tax laws) cite similar distributions of political circumstances and actors as specialist historians. Third, although there were idiosyncratic differences across authors, they were not generally explained by whether the authors used interviews, quantitative data, or archival research, whether the authors came from political science, policy, sociology, economics, history, or other departments, or how long after the events took place the sources were written. I investigate the role of each of these characteristics of authors more thoroughly in chapter 6.

Building Governing Networks

To understand the structure of relationships among the actors credited with policy change, I use social network analysis. I build what I call governing networks consisting of actors reportedly responsible for policy change. Rather than define only some communities as networks, this flexible approach enables analysis of how patterns of cooperation change over time and across issue areas, using a comparable method and data source. The use of governing networks is also driven by the structure of available data. I rely on secondary sources to analyze hundreds of policy processes over many years in more than a dozen issue domains. Many do not go into great detail about the patterns of relationships among advocates, but nearly all credit specific actors with particular policy enactments. The types of relationships that policy historians point to are those necessary to produce policy change.

In its simplest form, I can use the lists of actors credited with each policy enactment to create two-mode networks. Figure 2.2 illustrates this form of

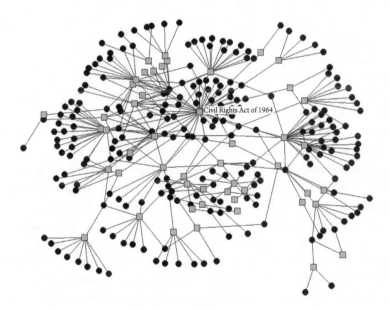

Figure 2.2 Two-mode network of credited actors and policy changes in civil rights and liberties

Squares are policy enactments; circles are actors credited with policy enactments. Links connect actors to the enactments for which they were credited.

network for the civil rights and liberties domain. In this network, grey squares represent specific policy changes like the Civil Rights Act of 1964. Black circles represent actors credited with policy change and lines connect the actors to the policy changes for which they were reportedly responsible. In other words, all of the actors listed earlier in this chapter are connected to the square representing the Civil Rights Act as well as any other policy changes with which they were credited. Martin Luther King, Jr., for example, is represented as a circle connected to four squares and Lyndon Johnson is represented as another circle connected to seven squares.

In chapter 4, I use these two-mode networks, but I connect actors with the issue areas where they are active, rather than the individual policy enactments. The strength of the connection between actors and issue areas is based on how many policy enactments each actor helped produce in each policy area. In other words, I analyze matrices with rows of actors credited with policy change and columns of the fourteen domestic policy issue areas; each cell contains the number of enactments credited to that actor in that issue area. Although this type of two-mode network is useful for some purposes, it does not allow for an investigation of cooperative relationships.

I use one-mode affiliation networks, which I also refer to as governing networks, to investigate the patterns of cooperation among different actors that helped drive policy change. These networks include all of the same actors (those that were partially credited with policy enactments). Rather than include the policy changes as separate nodes in the network, however, I use the ties (lines) to connect actors that were jointly credited with the same policy enactments.[19] This does not necessarily indicate that the actors directly worked together, but that they were both on the winning side of a significant policy enactment and that a policy historian thought they each deserved some credit. The affiliation network ties are valued as integer counts of the number of shared policy enactments between every pair of actors.[20] This analysis uses square matrices with the same actors in both rows and columns; cells contain the number of enactments for which each pair of actors is jointly credited.

To illustrate, figure 2.3 portrays the same data from figure 2.2 in an affiliation network form. In this figure, Democrats (or liberal organizations) are black; Republicans (or conservative organizations) are white; all other actors are grey. Circles represent actors in the legislative branch; squares represent actors in the executive branch; triangles represent nongovernmental actors; and diamonds represent judicial branch actors. Here, the number of shared policy enactments between each set of actors determines the width of the line connecting them. The size of each node is determined by the degree centrality, the total number of connections that they have to other actors.

Even though these data are taken from many different policy histories over a 60-year period of American policymaking, the figure shows a clear structure.

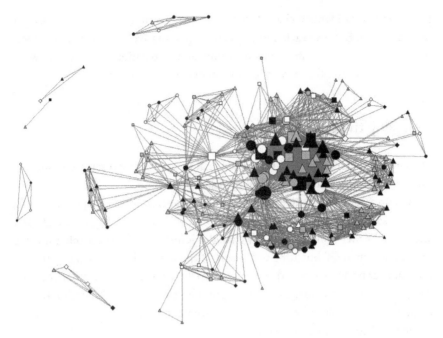

Figure 2.3 Affiliation network of actors credited with policy change in civil rights and liberties since 1945

Nodes are actors credited with policy enactments. Links connect actors credited with the same policy enactments. Democrats are black; Republicans are white; others are grey. Shape represents branch of government; circles are legislative; squares are executive; diamonds are judicial; triangles are nongovernmental. The size of nodes is determined by degree centrality.

There is one main component (group of connected actors) that is dominated by a central core of actors and several satellite clusters (groups of mutually connected actors with some ties to actors in the central core). The core actors are bipartisan, but the network as a whole has many more Democrats than Republicans. The core actors represent the legislative and administrative branches but also include many interest groups. The most central actors are the NAACP, John F. Kennedy, and Martin Luther King, Jr. Even though Johnson was responsible for more total policy changes than King, he is connected to fewer actors in this network.

Each governing network that I build and analyze enables an investigation into the patterns of cooperation that made policy change possible. Rather than build one network of all actors in all time periods and issue areas, I subdivide the data by issue area and time period. Chapter 5 analyzes the features of affiliation networks in fourteen different issue areas, allowing a comparison with the kinds of compositional and structural features present in the civil rights network. Chapter 4 divides the data by time period. In some cases, I build networks for policymaking during each presidential administration. In others, I use a broader periodization to identify characteristics of the governing networks for longer historical eras. Because each network can be quantitatively described in numerous ways, I can investigate trends over time and associations between network characteristics and other aspects of the policymaking process.

Assessing the Civil Rights Story

The limited data presented so far already enables an initial assessment of the history of civil rights and liberties policymaking. We cannot definitively discount the Clinton or Obama side of the argument that began this chapter. After all, policy historians credit both King and Johnson with the Civil Rights Act of 1964 and several other significant policy changes. Johnson was responsible for more total policy changes, but King was a part of the national policymaking process for a shorter period (in part due to his untimely death). The data also show that King is connected to more total actors, providing support for the notion that he helped bridge the gaps between social movement activists, traditional interest groups, and government officials.

Both sides of this argument also leave out considerable components of the story. The courts were more active in civil rights and liberties policymaking than either of the other two branches, suggesting that neither the social movement nor presidential leadership narratives are complete. Additionally, traditional interest groups appear to play a dominant role, both in early policy changes concerning African Americans and in the long period that saw extensions of civil rights and liberties protections to many other minority groups.

Yet the general picture is more consistent with Clinton's story of insider maneuvering than Obama's narrative of change from the power of public mobilization and ideas. In the case of the Civil Rights Act, both played an important role. In the broader expansion of civil rights and liberties throughout the latter part of the twentieth century, political circumstances inside government institutions and coalitions among interest groups seem to have played a more frequent role. Public opinion, media coverage, and ideas all played some role, but not nearly as often as institutional factors, path dependence, and interest group advocacy.

The initial analysis of governing networks also provides a potential middle ground in this discussion. Although many actors were involved in the struggle for civil rights and liberties, only a few actors were repeatedly involved and well connected to other important actors. Both Johnson and King played these roles, but so did interest groups like the NAACP. Fundamental policy change required repeated alliances of members of Congress, administration officials, interest groups, and social movement activists. The patterns of cooperation surrounding this overwhelmingly liberal advance of civil rights policy also involved some Republicans and many nonpartisan actors. Both supportive political circumstances and the repeated and cooperative actions of a few major participants in government helped bring about the civil rights revolution in American politics.

Although the aggregation of policy history cannot resolve long-standing debates among scholars of civil rights, it does address some fundamental questions about social movements and policy change. Some scholars emphasize that existing institutional actors such as interest groups and elected allies provide critical resources for movement leaders to access, whereas others claim that movements mostly gain by stimulating political responses to rebellion following perceptions of threat.[21] Much of the empirical evidence surrounding this debate consists of close observation of the American civil rights movement. Policy historians in this area regularly mentioned protests and occasionally referenced riots, but their collective story was more consistent with the emphasis on allies among traditional political leaders and interest groups. In particular, the administration and the courts were active in early civil rights policy before substantial protest mobilization and their role in expanding rights to new groups continued well past the decline of peak protest activity.[22] The network analysis also illustrates how interest groups like the NAACP and mainstream protest leaders like Dr. King connected newly mobilized activists to political leaders in the halls of Congress and the White House. Policy change required more than a widely held dream (as Obama insinuated) but did not always necessitate "a president to get it done" (as Clinton claimed). In this area, the artists of the possible included presidents, legislators, interest groups, and protest leaders working in cooperation.

Data Limitations and Objections

Like all social science data and research designs, the aggregation of policy histories has clear strengths and weaknesses. The analysis details hundreds of cases of policy change over a long history. It assesses the influence of dozens of broad political factors, as well as specific individuals and organizations, on policy change. The assessments are based on the close and contextualized analysis typical of case studies. The aggregation of these assessments allows an investigation of the frequency of the influence of each factor. A case study can document that leadership by an administrative official, a protest, and a lobbying campaign jointly led to the expansion of affirmative action in government contracting; the aggregation, meanwhile, can show that the influence of the lobbying campaign was more typical of all civil rights policy changes. I can also conduct large-N statistical analyses of the relationship between changing political circumstances and policy enactments.

The main limitation is that all of the analyses are dependent on the validity of the assessments of policy historians. If historians get the story wrong, I will replicate their mistakes. If they miss the importance of a political circumstance or incorrectly attribute a role to a particular official, my analysis will do the same. The aggregation across policy historians means that an occasional error will not be fatal, as long as it is not widely shared. It also enables me to test how and why historians' assessments differ.

Any biases that are widely shared among policy historians, however, will show up in all of the book's subsequent analyses. Biases in identifying significant policy enactments will be the most deleterious to my investigation, but biases concerning attribution of the circumstances and actors responsible for the enactments will also impact some conclusions. It is important to assess what these biases might entail, even if I cannot be sure about their severity or direction. I therefore want to address these likely biases, as well as the main objections associated with my reliance on policy historians.

DOES THE ANALYSIS LACK CASES OF NO POLICY CHANGE?

The book relies on analysis of policy enactments to assess the causes of policy change. That means I do not conduct any detailed studies of potential policy changes that were not enacted. This would include bills introduced in Congress that failed to pass, proposals made by the president or administrative agencies that were scrapped, or court decisions that made no change in precedent. The analysis also leaves out proposals made by interest groups or activists that failed to stimulate policymaker action, as well as the near infinite possible combinations of policy tools that society could collectively imagine to address social problems.

The practical reasons are twofold. First, policy historians do not consistently analyze potential enactments that fail to pass. When they do assess such alternatives, it is usually those that make it furthest before reaching a roadblock; this subset is a poor basis of comparison because it is the most likely policy changes among all those that failed. Second, the population of cases of failed policy initiatives is difficult to conceptualize and locate. Any policy proposal made by any participant in policymaking could conceivably be thought of as a failed case. Many of these proposals may move policy in the same direction as those that are enacted. They may be incorporated in policy in revised form or stimulate proposals to address similar problems; almost no policy change proceeds through government without modification.

There is also a theoretical reason to avoid specifying a clear denominator of potential policy changes in my analysis of policy enactments. Most previous attempts to do so have used all the proposals on the agenda of a particular actor. One of my central theoretical claims is that the importance of the step from proposal to consideration is overstated. I also allege that using the agenda of any particular actor as a starting point privileges their role in the policy process. If I am correct, it makes little sense to use actor agendas as the set of proposals from which enacted policies emerge. To test alternative views, I do incorporate measures of the issue agenda of each institution (in chapter 3) and the agendas of central policymakers (in chapter 4) but I do not present a list of potential enactments based on my own sources.

Instead of specifying a set of failed policy proposals as zero cases, I use alternative methods. I assess the influence of various factors on the number of enactments over time and in each issue area. The zero cases in these analyses are the time periods or issues areas where no change occurs. These analyses also compare times and places with little policy change with others where much change occurs. This method is the same as those used in previous analyses of *macro politics* and *agenda setting* theories. Because all issues and time periods are included, there is no selection bias or threat associated with selecting on the dependent variable.

Threats to causal inference are more severe in conclusions about the influence of specific circumstances and actors on policy change. Many of the circumstances that policy historians cite, or the actors that they credit, might also have been involved in many failed proposals. Nonetheless, the aggregation of policy history is not analogous to selecting policy changes and assessing the presence or absence of a potential causal factor. Rather than chronicling every actor present or every political circumstance that was contemporaneous with each policy enactment, policy historians attempt to home in on the factors most responsible for policy change. They do this through traditional qualitative methods: they assess whether a potential cause is consistent with the sequence of events, indicators of other effects, and implied mechanisms linking a cause to an effect. In doing so, they often envision shadow cases of potential alternative enactments or times or venues where no change occurred.

When a policy historian is assessing the causes of expansion of affirmative action in government contracting, they do not produce a list of every actor involved in Congress, the administration, or the interest group community; they highlight those that seemed to play the most critical and consistent role. They do not list every political circumstance; they highlight those that actors considered important at the time and seemed to repeatedly influence their behavior. If a historian lists lobbying but does not list public opinion in their explanation for the decision, it does not mean that there was no public opinion and there was some lobbying; it means they did not find evidence that the policymakers responded to public opinion but there were several signs that they responded to the lobbying. My analysis is reliant on whether they get the story correct and is open to criticism for making these assessments via qualitative research. To the extent that these assessments are possible, the analysis is an aggregation of evidence accumulated by policy historians of influential factors in policy change.

ARE THESE DATA ONLY DESCRIPTIVE?

The analysis relies largely, though not entirely, on descriptive data analysis. I present information on the frequency of circumstances and actors responsible for policy change as well as differences across issue areas and over time in their characteristics. This use of descriptive data does not imply that the evidence is merely of correlation. I am descriptively analyzing the causes of policy change according to policy historians. Because they have made assessments of causal influence in their narrative accounts, I am aggregating the frequency of their reported causes. This is challengeable on the grounds that one cannot make causal inferences with the kind of data that qualitative historians have at their disposal, but not on the basis of its use in descriptive statistics.

Similarly, many scholars view network analysis of the kind used here as fundamentally descriptive and incompatible with tests of causal theory. The network analyses provide a picture of the relationships among actors and descriptions of how their relationships differ across time and issue, but do not assess how or why those relationships developed. Yet inclusion in the governing networks used in this book is an indication that a policy historian viewed the actor as influential in bringing about a policy enactment. A connection to another actor indicates that they were credited with policy change alongside that other actor. The networks thus again constitute descriptive data analysis of causal assessments made by policy historians, in this case attributions of credit to specific individuals or organizations. The work is again susceptible to all critiques of qualitative assessments, but not because they are used in a network analysis.

In the case of network data, I make the additional assumption that if two actors both influenced a policy enactment, their cooperation played a role in the change. This is a potential problem with my analysis, rather than with the initial policy histories. In some cases, the policy historians pointed to compromises between multiple actors or credited coalitions among them, but in other cases they simply viewed both actors as influential and did not assess their interdependence. For this reason, I regularly refer to "patterns of cooperation" or "compromises and coalitions." The evidence that I use to establish ties between actors is certainly open to critique, though most lists of jointly credited actors did note some form of specific cooperation. Policy historians judged the individual actors influential, but the importance of their connection is my supposition.

The evidence from the civil rights example shows that Dr. King is central to the governing network, especially in connecting social movement activists with legislators and interest groups. This indicates that he was involved in multiple influential arrangements with these actors behind different policy enactments, even though these actors usually did not ally with one another to produce policy change absent King. I make the additional inference that King's role in the process was to connect these actors. That role is not taken directly from the historians: it is a claim based on analogous positions in social networks.

The research as a whole is susceptible to the same difficulties in casual inference that apply to nearly all observational social science. Observers cannot rerun history to establish that a policy change would not have occurred in each counterfactual. There is substantial covariation in political circumstances and actor involvement across time and place that makes it difficult to single out causes or important conjunctions. Like all other social science findings, the aggregate causal assessments of policy historians need to be regularly verified with other kinds of analysis. Readers should see them as qualitative attempts to assess causal influence.

In the civil rights example, assessments by policy historians more often point to interest groups, the administration, and the courts than to events or public opinion. This evidence does not mean that, absent the civil rights movement, the United States still would have pursued a major expansion of civil rights and liberties, but it is more consistent with a story involving some independent role for interest groups operating through courts and administrative agencies. The notion that movement activists worked with policymakers and interest groups is more plausible than the view that they succeeded through shifts in opinion or universal response to protests.

WHAT ABOUT DISAGREEMENT AMONG HISTORIANS?

Not all historians agree on the circumstances and actors credited with policy enactments. Policy historians rarely assess the completeness or accuracy of one another's explanations. They often report different actors or circumstances, but rarely explicitly dispute the importance of an actor or circumstance viewed as influential by someone else. In chapter 6, I show that no measure of differences in author research method, scholarly discipline, or time period explain the main differences across issue areas or time periods that I rely on in the book, but variation in author judgments remains. The main difference is in the scope of explanation: some policy historians identify a large number of precursors to policy change whereas others point to only a few; the same is true for the specific actors that they identify.

The variation in the emphasis authors put on each factor is not associated with enough similarity in their language to code it categorically. The variation that provides leverage for my analysis is that few factors are considered important across many enactments. If a policy historian credits public opinion with one enactment and interest groups with five, I conclude that interest groups were more commonly influential. Although I treat policy changes equivalently across enactments of very different scope by using frequencies from the population of all enactments, the results are largely similar if I include only large enactments.

BIASES IN IDENTIFYING ENACTMENTS

Because the analysis aggregates the judgments of policy historians, it is dependent on their accuracy. The most critical judgment is which enactments were significant policy changes. Aggregation was helpful in this regard, as it combined assessments of different subtopics and time periods to create a more comprehensive list. Nevertheless, policy historians may collectively make different judgments than other observers.

Previous analysis of Mayhew's lists of major enactments found some differences between his list drawn from year-end journalist reports (what he called "sweep one") and his list based on policy history (what he called "sweep two"). Some subsequent work showed that the list based on journalist reports varied more with political characteristics such as divided government.[23] Mayhew argues that the journalists might be caught up in the news agenda of each year, producing reports of important action even if little changed; policy historians instead look at the impact of policy enactments, judging with sufficient time for reflection.[24]

To evaluate how this critique applies to the new dataset, I use my indicator (from the historians) of whether a policy change was considered significant only in retrospect, rather than at the time of enactment. Exclusion of the policy changes that were not immediately considered important did not seem to change any major findings. I also compare my list of policy enactments with other lists but do not find systematic differences in the enactments included. My list of domestic policy enactments is more extensive than Mayhew's; it includes many changes that he found only in journalists' compilations and many that he found in neither sweep. The bias of my list seems to be in the direction of inclusiveness.

The main difference from previous lists is my addition of administrative and judicial policy changes. Yet policy historians may be less likely to notice policy-making in administrative agencies and lower courts compared to laws passed by Congress. Although I lack evidence about the direction of the bias, policy historians seem to consider many actions by Congress, the Supreme Court, and the president as significant policy changes and comparatively few by the more numerous agencies and lower courts. This is, to some degree, a reflection of their relative policymaking role. Nevertheless, I sense that some authors might apply a lower standard of significance to acts of Congress, even if new laws had little influence on policy in practice.

BIASES IN JUDGING THE INFLUENCE OF CIRCUMSTANCES

Policy historians might also have collectively pointed out the importance of some circumstances more readily than others in their explanations for policy change. I observe some minimal differences in explanations by discipline and background in chapter 6. Issue area specialists are more likely to mention the influence of scientific research than political scientists, possibly because their colleagues are involved in producing some of the research. Political scientists, meanwhile, seem to point to path dependence less often than historians (likely due to their disciplinary training).

Policy historians may also collectively focus less on some features of policy-making, such as those that remain constant for long periods. Histories rarely discussed control of Congress by the Democrats as a significant factor in policy change, likely because that control was constant for most of the years they cover. Similarly, they did not usually discuss relatively constant differences in interest group mobilization, such as those between the rich and the poor.

Nevertheless, I did not notice any collective tendency to leave out any category of explanatory factors. Most policy historians that covered many policy changes included a factor from most categories in at least one of their explanations. Historians rarely covered a long list of policy changes and never referred to interest groups or events, for instance, even if they referred to congressional or executive branch factors more often.

BIASES IN CREDITING ACTORS

As with judgments of the importance of circumstances, policy historians may be more likely to include some actors in explanations for policy change than others; these are unknown biases. It is possible, but not apparent, that the relative visibility of actors in the news media could have affected their prevalence in historical accounts. Many important congressional or administrative staffers may be left out if their actions were behind the scenes. The tendency to mention the role of the president frequently may reflect this bias or true judgments of influence. The main difference across policy historians was in breadth and specificity; some mentioned long lists of legislators and interest groups, some mentioned only a couple of actors, and some referred vaguely to constituencies rather than specific legislators or groups.

No category of actors seems to be systematically excluded. Collectively, historians credited actors in nearly all congressional committees and administrative departments. Nearly half of the actors mentioned had no official role in government, with the others distributed mostly in the legislative and executive branches. Only a few state, local, or international actors were credited. Many individual activists were mentioned, but usually not for more than one or two enactments. Historians may have underestimated the role of judges; they credited few Supreme Court justices while crediting many interest groups with the Court's decisions. It is difficult to say if these are biases or reasonable judgments of influence.

Even though it is impossible to assess these collective biases with the data from policy history, it worth reflecting on how it might affect the results. In the civil rights case, policy historians might be more likely to credit King and Johnson than administrative agency officials or backbench legislators. They may be more likely to mention the NAACP, if they brought a legal case, than the median justice that actually decided the case. There may be unsung heroes in lower-tier positions in Congress, the administration, or advocacy groups. The aggregation helps alleviate this problem, as long as at least one author pointed to the significance of the less prominent officials. Yet most of the evidence will reflect policy historians' shared biases. Despite these difficulties, this book's analysis is the most extensive effort to date to draw quantitative data from the vast information collected by policy historians.

Differences across Time, Policy Area, and Historian

The composite history of civil rights and liberties policy is an illustration of the kinds of analyses made possible by compiling information from policy histories. The aggregate story from policy history can help evaluate when and where policy change takes place, what actors are responsible, and what political circumstances helped bring it about. Answers to these questions add nuance to traditional stories of policy change, such as those told by politicians like Clinton and Obama.

I use these data to provide a sense of the most important aspects of policymaking and how each part of the system fits together. Chapter 3 investigates the number of policy enactments in each policy area in each branch of government and analyzes the most common circumstances invoked to explain policy change. Chapter 4 uses aggregate measures of policy productivity and ideological direction to investigate changes over time in the policymaking process. Chapter 5 investigates differences across policy areas, compiling information on all aspects of policymaking.

Chapter 6 investigates the data from policy histories in a somewhat different form. Both as a robustness check on the findings from the other chapters and as an analysis of whether different types of authors emphasize different aspects of the policymaking process, I investigate each explanation of each policy change as a separate case. The majority of the book uses the 790 policy enactments as cases, aggregating across author explanations. Chapter 6 uses nearly 2,000 individual explanations for specific policy changes to investigate the circumstances under which each type of political circumstance affects policy change. Although I find some intuitive and important differences across types of authors, the central thrust of the analysis shows that characteristics of issue areas, policymaking venues, and time periods are better predictors of what matters than the characteristics of policy historians.

Without discounting differences of opinion, the aggregation of policy histories offers a useful method of understanding the most important aspects of American policymaking and how they change across issue areas and time periods. The upside is to take advantage of hundreds of painstakingly conducted and varied case studies of the policy process. This aggregation leaves a role for every component of policymaking, but tells an important story about what matters most.

CHAPTER 3

Does the Issue Agenda Matter?

With the single stroke of a pen, President Barack Obama signed two major policy changes into law on March 30, 2010. The first finalized an overhaul of the American health care system and had been the center of the government's attention for months. The second nationalized the student loan program, ended subsidies for private insurers, vastly expanded federally insured student loans, and created new loan forgiveness policies. In the event accompanying the signing, Obama celebrated the twin achievements:

> The debate on health care reform is one that's gone on for generations, and I'm glad—I'm gratified that we were able to get it done last week. But what's gotten overlooked amid all the hoopla, all the drama of last week, is what happened in education—when a great battle pitting the interests of the banks and financial institutions against the interests of students finally came to an end.[1]

Both events were consistent with the premise that policy problems must be on the agenda before they result in new policies. Obama had discussed both issues during the presidential campaign and each addressed a prominent concern of a segment of American society. The events are less consistent with the broader assumption that this premise masks: that the agenda setting process is a key to understanding policy change and that government acts after it prioritizes problems. Health care reform was clearly put on the agenda by political elites in 2009, but it was equally high on the agenda of presidents Truman, Johnson, Nixon, and Clinton. Higher education, meanwhile, was an issue regularly on the backburner of American elite and public concern. In fact, part of the story of student loan reform was the lack of attention to its provisions because of the overwhelming attention to health care reform.

Even more strikingly, neither policy change is consistent with a view of democracy that seems to underpin policy scholarship on agenda setting: the idea that the public agenda helps determine the direction of policymaker interests. The American public in 2009 was overwhelmingly concerned with general economic problems, and rightly so; the United States was in the midst of its most severe downturn since the Great Depression. Media reports, public protests, and campaign ads criticized policymakers for diverting their attention from the economy to focus on health care. There were no precipitating events or clear media narratives preceding either significant policy change.

In the context of scholarship on public policy, what are we to make of these stories of policy change? They do not invalidate any existing theory directly. Few scholars claim outright that policy change addresses the most prominent issues of each time period or that elite action always follows public priorities. Yet these stories of policymaking put much of *agenda setting* theories in perspective.[2] Scholars collect and analyze evidence about agenda setting because they assume that its determinants are connected to those of eventual policy enactments; they expect policymakers to respond to public concerns, or at least their own problem prioritization.

Agenda setting theories may obscure the more common components of policymaking by focusing attention on the ways that problems are prioritized rather than how groups of actors coalesce around and jointly enact policy proposals. I argue that patterns of entrepreneurship, coalition, and compromise among institutional actors matter more to the policymaking process than the agenda setting dynamics that have been the focus of previous research. A small number of actors are responsible for the bulk of policymaking, largely independent of public concerns.

To present this new perspective, this chapter begins by reviewing the development of *agenda setting* theories. Second, it argues that agenda setting, especially when conceived as a stage in policymaking, is not a useful starting point for understanding policy change. Third, it demonstrates that measures of the public and elite agenda are poor predictors of policy change in different issue areas since 1945 in all three branches of government. Fourth, it reports how often each political actor and circumstance influences policy change and analyzes the list of the most commonly influential actors. Put in this context, Obama's twin achievements come to look like typical products of policymaking based largely on the outcome of internal struggles among policymakers themselves, rather than public concern or problem prioritization.

Agenda Setting and the Policy Process

Agenda setting is an important focus of contemporary policy research, attracting the attention of its most prominent scholars, journals, and conferences. This attention is long-standing and linked to the idea that the process by which issues make their way onto the government agenda says something important about the functioning of democracy. As Roger Cobb and Charles Elder put it, public agenda setting is a primary source of democratic control:

> The agenda building perspective…encourages inquiry into the rela-
> tionship between mass participation and elite decision-making. It raises
> important…questions that may be critical to the vitality of the democratic
> polity, suggesting that public participation in political decision-making
> may extend well beyond the mere selection of the governing elite to selec-
> tion and resolution of the major issues that a government will confront.[3]

Once this agenda makes its way from the public to the policymakers, according to Cobb and Elder, policy change may be almost a foregone conclusion: "Pre-decisional processes often play the most critical role in determining what issues and alternatives are to be considered by the polity and the probable choices that will be made. What happens in…formal institutions of government may do little more than [codify them]."[4]

Contemporary scholars present a much more moderate version of this view. Frank Baumgartner and Bryan Jones begin *Agendas and Instability in American Politics* by proposing "a punctuated equilibrium model of policy change in American politics, based on the emergence and the recession of policy issues from the public agenda."[5] Although they do not see policy change as inevitable following each change in the agenda, they argue that agenda setting is the main determinant of significant, non-incremental policy change: "Policy action may or may not follow attention, but when it does, it will not flow incrementally."[6] The updated version of the punctuated equilibrium model focuses on disproportion-ate processing of information about some policy areas, but still contains this idea:

> Most issues most of the time are far from the national political agenda,
> far from the front page of the newspaper, relegated to the various com-
> munities that exist in all areas of public policy, and subject to subsystem
> equilibrium processes. If and when these issues have won the attention
> of the primary policymaking institutions, errors have often accumu-
> lated, and punctuations must occur to "catch up" with changing reality.[7]

Most issues, at any given time, are off the agenda and subject to an agreed upon equilibrium position among participants, in other words, and a few rise to prom-inence and are associated with major changes in policy.

Scholarship in this area typically takes two forms. The first uses case studies to demonstrate that an increase in policymaker attention surrounding an episode of public or media concern led to an important change in policy. The second uses distributions of time series data on government agendas, budgets, or enactments to prove that policy development is typically incremental and occasionally dramatic. Jones and Baumgartner do not attempt to model government attention or policy outcomes as a function of the public or media agenda, but they do find what they call "truly impressive convergence" between the extent that the public rates an issue as the most important problem and the attention that Congress pays to that issue in hearings.[8] Jones and Baumgartner also claim that public opinion about social problems helps drive lawmaking, even if congressional hearings are less associated with new laws.[9]

In a recent update, Bryan Jones, Heather Larsen-Price, and John Wilkerson argue that the relationship between public concerns and government agendas constitutes a form of representation that may be on par, in its importance to democracy, with the congruence between public and elected representatives' views on policy.[10] They find correlations between when an issue is viewed as the most important problem by more people in the United States and the number of congressional bills introduced on that topic. They report correlations with other indicators of agendas and outcomes, arguing that representation by issue prioritization occurs across all three branches of government.

John Kingdon's Independent Streams theory of the policy process also incorporates a primary role for agenda setting. Agendas and alternatives are set, Kingdon claims, by some combination of events and real-world problems, ideas and evidence generated by policy specialists and scientists, and public opinion and election results.[11] Rather than necessarily proceeding in order, however, all three processes need to converge at the same time to enable policy change: the streams of problems, policies, and politics meet in a window of opportunity for significant policymaking. Kingdon investigates health care, transportation, and environmental policy in the late 1970s, cataloguing when the policymaking participants that he interviews view each policy topic within these areas as prominent.

Although Kingdon does not systematically investigate whether public opinion drives government agendas and policy outputs, he does argue that the public agenda severely constrains the policymaking process:

> The mood-elections combination has particularly powerful impacts on the agenda. It can force some subjects high on the agenda, and can also make it virtually impossible for government to pay serious attention to others. But once the item is on the agenda, the organized forces enter the picture, trying as best they can to bend the outcomes to their advantage.[12]

Individual policy entrepreneurs, interest groups, and policymakers are empowered to pursue their preferred policies by the convergence of policy problems on the agenda and public political mood: "Entrepreneurs once again appear when windows open."[13]

Although it places less emphasis on agenda setting, the Advocacy Coalition Framework (ACF) also assumes that policymaking follows from changes in the issue agenda made possible by public opinion and events external to government. Paul Sabatier and Christopher Weible list (1) socioeconomic change, (2) public opinion change, (3) electoral change, and (4) policy feedback from unrelated issue areas as the four types of unstable events that can alter the relatively stable parameters of the policymaking system and the constraints and resources of each issue area's policymaking community: "In fact, the ACF hypothesizes that change in one of these dynamic factors is a necessary condition for major policy change."[14] The main paths from these external factors to policy change involve learning based on experience and information from the real world or shocks from major political or socioeconomic events: "These external shocks can shift agendas, focus public attention, and attract the attention of key decisionmaking sovereigns."[15] Updating the ACF, Sabatier and Weible argue that focusing events like natural disasters and negotiated agreements between major factions within an issue area may also lead directly to major policy change.

All three theories explain policy change by looking for changes in the government agenda, usually stemming from public opinion or real-world events. A comparison of the frameworks reaches this conclusion: "Multiple-streams, punctuated-equilibrium, and advocacy coalitions point to similar types of events and factors that set the stage for major policy change. These factors include dramatic events or crises, changes in governing coalitions, and administrative and legislative turnover."[16] None of the three theories is solely concerned with issue agendas; they each point to many other factors important to policymaking, including the endogenous relationships among policymakers and interest groups emphasized here. The shared underlying focus, however, is that we can learn about the likelihood of significant policy change in each issue area by looking at shifts in public and government agendas.

How the Stages Model Sent Scholars Astray

Many theories share an emphasis on agenda setting dynamics because they were developed in reaction to the stages model of the policy process. The stages model cut the policymaking process into a series of steps: policymakers developed an agenda of actionable problems, considered potential alternative solutions, adopted and implemented a policy, and then evaluated its results. Rather than a theory to be tested, the stages model usually served as a guide for division of labor among policy scholars; some focused on analyzing potential solutions, others on implementing them in the bureaucracy, and still others on policy evaluation.

The stages model could charitably be described as a standard against which the real policymaking process was judged. Policymakers should prioritize problems, focus on the most important public issues, and respond to popular concerns, but that does not mean that they do so reliably. Given that public policy has always been an applied science, this standard is not surprising. Most public policy school faculty members evaluate the results of past policy and assess options under consideration, with an eye to improving outcomes. *Agenda setting* theories analyze the political determinants of policy in the shadow of this larger policy research enterprise. As a result, scholars have sought to modify the stages model so that it comports more with the real policymaking process.

Each *agenda setting* theory rejects the strong form of the stages model, but it continues to inform how each set of scholars thinks about the policy process.[17] Sabatier says that the stages model is a heuristic that inappropriately assumes linearity. Jones and Baumgartner criticize the stages model, emphasizing how policymakers are boundedly rational and search for nearby solutions rather than assess all alternatives. Yet both argue that agenda setting is a critical step in policymaking. The assumption that agenda status precedes enactment, derived from the stages model, makes the issue agenda a worthwhile dependent variable on its own.

Scholars do find that some stages are combined, occasionally skipped, and may not go in the order proscribed. Most famously, Kingdon argues that solutions often come before problems. Advocates identify policy proposals that they support and then look for problems where they can attach their proposals and call them solutions. Nevertheless, even Kingdon argues that policy proponents have to wait for a problem in need of addressing to present itself and a supportive public mood before policies can be enacted.

There are two assumptions associated with *agenda setting* theories that reflect the concerns of the original stages model. The first is that policymakers enact policy where they focus their attention. The second is that their prioritization draws from the concerns of the public and the media as well as nonpolitical events. The first assumption is an expansion of the premise that proposals must be on the docket in order to pass, made possible by the equation of agenda setting with problem prioritization. The second assumption stems from the idea that deciding what problems to address is a potential form of public representation.

This chapter assesses each assumption and advocates an alternative view. Policy enactments may not follow reliably from the relative focus of policymakers in each issue area in each time period. Public opinion, media coverage, and events may all be inputs to the policy process that are only sometimes important and infrequently serve as the primary catalysts for policy change. Policy

enactments may be a function of the internal negotiations and coalition building dynamics of policymakers and interest groups, rather than of changes in
the issue focus of officials or inputs like public priorities and media coverage.
To assess these ideas, I conduct a re-evaluation of existing evidence on policy
agendas as well as a new overview of the important factors in policy enactments
identified by policy historians.

Agenda Setting Measures and Policy Enactments

The best source of data on American federal policy agendas comes from the
Policy Agendas Project (PAP). At policyagendas.org, this project makes available data on the topics of congressional, presidential, and judicial activity for
most years since 1945 along with indicators of the importance of each topic in
public opinion and media coverage. This dataset is used primarily to present case
studies of policy development or conduct analysis of distributions.[18]

Using this data, Jones, Larsen-Price, and Wilkerson report separate correlations between public views of important problems, government agendas, and
policy outcomes over time for each topic area.[19] They find that public opinion is
associated with policymaking in only some issue areas and argue that the relationship is mediated by path dependence and lack of public attention to policymaking.[20] They do not attempt a baseline global model of the determinants of
the policy agenda or policy enactments.

To pursue the first known analysis of this type, I created a new
cross-sectional time-series dataset with cases for every domestic policy topic
area for every biennial congress since 1945. The dataset has 420 cases covering 14 domestic policy areas in 30 two-year periods. For each biennium and
topic, I record the number of associated congressional hearings, public laws,
Congressional Quarterly legislative summaries, executive orders, State of the
Union address mentions, Supreme Court cases, *New York Times* articles, and
important laws (based on *Congressional Quarterly* attention). All of these data
are publicly available at policyagendas.org. To this dataset, I append my new
measures of significant policy enactments in each branch of government and
in total (from the policy histories). I am thus able to predict when, where,
and on what topic important policy changes are enacted, using measures of
the public, media, and elite agenda in each branch of government. The goal
is to see whether important policy changes follow reliably from public and
government agendas.

I use this dataset to present several models of policy enactments in each
branch of government, using one dependent variable from the PAP and one new
measure. For each set of models, the first model includes no fixed effects for

issue area or congress, the second model includes only issue area fixed effects, and the third includes issue area and time fixed effects. This is similar to comparing three panel models: one with random effects, one with one-way fixed effects, and one with two-way fixed effects.[21] For both sets of models, the third is most appropriate and fits the data best. Nonetheless, it is helpful to see which independent variables account for only variation across issues and which account for variation only across time.[22] The models each include contemporaneous attention to the issue in government as well as two variables from the previous biennium: the importance of the topic in public opinion and its level of news media discussion.[23]

Do Agendas Drive Policymaking?

As a starting point, table 3.1 reports bivariate correlation coefficients for each pair of measures of the policy agenda and policy enactments. The first eight measures derive from the PAP and the final four measures derive from the content analysis of policy histories. The table highlights correlations above .3 but these are relatively rare. The number of hearings in an issue area per congress is correlated with the number of related articles in *Congressional Quarterly*, the total number of laws, and the number of *New York Times* articles, but not as highly with the most important laws or number of significant policy enactments. The public agenda is not highly correlated with any measure other than mentions in the State of the Union address. Unsurprisingly, the president tends to emphasize issues of public interest in his address to the nation. No indicator predicts the number of significant policy enactments well, except for the three components of the measure and *Congressional Quarterly* articles. Significant executive branch policy changes are not highly associated with attention indicators. The number of significant judicial policy changes is correlated with the total number of Supreme Court cases.

Overall, these correlations are lower than one would expect based on *agenda setting* theories. They are also somewhat lower than Jones and Baumgartner find in their analysis, which looks at each issue separately for all years.[24] They find that the time-series relationship holds for some issue areas but not for others. Similarly, Jones, Larsen-Price, and Wilkerson find correlations between public opinion and policy agendas across time in some issue areas, but they find that the relationships with policy outcomes are substantially less strong than the relationships with agenda indicators.[25] In their analysis, only three of sixteen issue areas show significant correlations between public opinion and executive orders, another three show correlations between public opinion and laws, and four issues show correlations between public opinion and Supreme Court decisions.

Table 3.1 **Correlation Coefficients among Policy Agenda and Enactment Measures**

	Hearings	CQ Articles	Public Laws	Exec. Orders	State of Union	Supreme Court Cases	Public Opinion	NY Times Articles	CQ Most Import.	Signif. Laws	Signif. Exec.	Signif. Court
CQ Articles	**0.66**											
Public Laws	**0.45**	**0.42**										
Exec.Orders	0.10	0.13	-0.02									
State of Union	0.14	0.10	-0.10	0.13								
Supreme Court Cases	0.17	0.23	0.16	0.24	0.00							
Public Opinion	0.15	0.22	-0.09	0.06	**0.60**	0.07						
NY Times Articles	**0.49**	**0.42**	0.28	0.09	-0.08	**0.38**	-0.05					
CQ Most Import.	0.08	0.24	0.12	0.03	0.09	-0.13	0.21	0.01				
Signif. Laws	0.25	**0.35**	0.18	0.09	0.07	-0.01	0.07	0.06	0.29			
Signif. Exec.	0.11	0.22	0.05	0.14	-0.04	-0.04	-0.02	0.02	-0.04	0.12		
Signif. Court	0.08	0.17	0.05	0.06	-0.10	**0.42**	0.05	0.14	-0.01	0.12	0.08	
All Sig. Policy	0.27	**0.41**	0.17	0.14	0.00	0.13	0.07	0.11	0.20	**0.85**	**0.48**	**0.49**

Notes: Table entries are correlation coefficients. The dataset covers domestic policy areas in the Policy Agendas Project dataset for all biennial congresses since 1945. Bolded coefficients are above .3. There are a total of 420 possible cases (14 domestic policy areas in 30 biennial congresses) but data is sometimes missing for the earliest or latest years.

This analysis provides a broader perspective. Public opinion is not highly correlated with measures of policy output. It is not a good guide to when and on
what topic significant policy change will be enacted in any branch.[26] The government agenda and policy output are more closely tied, but not for executive
branch outcomes.

Moving to a multivariate approach, table 3.2 reports models to predict the
number of legislative enactments by topic area and congress. The first three
models predict the number of significant new laws, using the measure based on
the collective judgments of policy historians. The second three models predict
the total number of laws passed, regardless of their importance. The first model
indicates that a one-standard-deviation increase in congressional hearings in an
area is expected to increase the number of significant laws in that area by 33.5%
(calculated separately). In the model with fixed effects for issue areas, however,
the size of the estimated increase is cut to 23%. This pattern of results suggests
that Congress consistently spends more time on some issues and legislates more
on those issues; beyond this, there is a smaller relationship between their issue
focus and their significant lawmaking.

The first model for lawmaking shows a statistically significant effect for media
coverage, but in the opposite direction of expected influence (with more media
coverage leading to less policy). Public opinion has no significant effect. The
model with fixed effects for both topics and time shows no significant effect
for either measure of the public agenda. The fit of the initial model is poor;
it improves substantially with fixed effects for issue areas and time periods.
Together, public and elite agendas are not good predictors of significant enactments. Some issue areas and some time periods are just consistently associated
with more activity.

These models assume that media and public attention would be associated
with a one-congress lag to affect lawmaking, rather than acting concurrently.
Replacing the lagged variables with concurrent measures of public opinion and
media coverage produces similar results, with the same pattern of statistical significance. Readers might also suspect that the public and media agenda influence the congressional agenda. In this case, their impact on lawmaking would
be soaked up by their indirect effect through the congressional hearings measure. Removing the congressional hearings measure from these models, however, produces the same lack of association. In the most forgiving scenario, using
a non-significant estimate of concurrent public opinion's effect, removing all
other variables and fixed effects, a one-standard deviation increase in the portion
of the public citing an issue as the most important problem increases significant
laws by only 7.5%. The bivariate estimated effect of concurrent media coverage
in the same forgiving scenario (also statistically insignificant) is similar in mag-
nitude. The public agenda does not appear to influence significant lawmaking.

Table 3.2 **Models Predicting Legislative Enactments by Topic and Congress**

	Significant Legislative Policy Enactments			All Public Laws		
		With Issue Area Effects	With Issue and Time Effects		With Issue Area Effects	With Issue and Time Effects
Congressional Hearings	.40*** (.08)	.29*** (.09)	.27* (.12)	.44*** (.05)	.34*** (.05)	.44*** (.05)
Importance in Public Opinion (t-1)	-.00 (.01)	-.01 (.01)	-.00 (.01)	-1.42*** (.33)	-1.59*** (.30)	-.74* (.35)
Coverage in News Media (t-1)	-2.56* (1.5)	1.81 (2.9)	2.8 (2.7)	.09 (.06)	-.07 (.05)	-.08 (.07)
1st Congress of Presidential Admin.	.27** (.11)	.27** (.11)	-.05 (.32)	.09 (.06)	.08 (.05)	.08 (.15)
Constant	-.37	-.54	-.34	2.28	2.72	2.33
Pseudo R²	.03	.07	.15	.04	.10	.17
N	392	392	392	420	420	420

Note: Table entries are negative binomial regression coefficients, with standard errors. Congressional hearings and news articles are measured in the hundreds. Public opinion is measured as the percent of the public that identifies an issue area as the most important problem times one hundred. Issue area fixed effects are included in the second and fifth columns, but not reported. The excluded issue area is macroeconomics. Biennial congress fixed effects are included in the third and sixth columns, but not reported. The excluded congress is the fifth in the series. *p < .05; **p < .01; ***p < .001 (two-tailed).

The models predicting all public laws in each issue area and time period also fail to demonstrate responsiveness to public opinion or media coverage. Public opinion is a statistically significant predictor of laws passed, but the direction of causality suggests that Congress passes fewer laws associated with the issues of public concern. Replacing the lagged public opinion measure with a concurrent measure also produces negative coefficients but the estimates do not reach statistical significance. Removing the congressional attention variable to allow for any indirect effect of public opinion through congressional attention reverses the sign of the coefficient but the relationship is not statistically significant. This pattern of results suggests no strong relationship.

Congressional attention is a consistent predictor of the total number of laws passed in each issue area and congress. A one-standard-deviation increase in congressional hearings in a topic area is expected to produce a 4.4% increase in the total number of laws passed in that area. This estimate is robust even after including fixed effects for issue areas and time periods. It also remains after controlling for contemporary, rather than lagged, public and media attention. Congress, therefore, does legislate more in the areas where it holds more hearings but the laws produced by their increased attention do not correspond to the public agenda. The fit of the models predicting total public laws is poor, but better than for those predicting significant laws.

Table 3.3 uses the same types of models to predict the number of executive policy enactments by topic area and biennium. The first three models predict the number of significant executive orders and administrative agency decisions, using the measure based on policy history. The second three models predict the total number of executive orders, using PAP data. For each dependent variable, the table again includes one model with issue area fixed effects, one model with issue and time fixed effects, and one model without them. The fit of these models is generally poor. Most of the explained variation comes from the fixed effects rather than the agenda variables. Some time periods and issue areas are associated with more executive orders and significant executive branch enactments, regardless of the content of the policy agenda.

The models for significant policy enactments show no effects for the presidential agenda, the public agenda, or the media agenda. Executive enactments are difficult to predict from the agenda measures. The same results hold if I analyze significant executive orders and significant executive agency rules and decisions as two separate dependent variables. Neither seems to follow from public or elite prioritization of problem areas.

The results for the models predicting all executive orders do demonstrate a relationship between media coverage and outcomes. A one-standard-deviation increase in media coverage is expected to increase the number of executive orders in the following two years by 26%. In the models including fixed effects for issue

Table 3.3 **Models Predicting Executive Enactments by Topic and Congress**

	Significant Executive Policy Enactments			All Executive Orders		
		With Issue Area Effects	With Issue and Time Effects		With Issue Area Effects	With Issue and Time Effects
State of the Union Mentions	-.27 (.48)	-.16 (.51)	.18 (.54)	.38 (.26)	.46* (.22)	.87* (.26)
Importance in Public Opinion (t-1)	-.01 (.01)	.00 (.02)	-.26 (1.7)	.18 (.73)	1.02 (.65)	.26 (.75)
Coverage in News Media (t-1)	-.44 (2.7)	9.4 (5.8)	9.3 (5.3)	.21* (.10)	.40*** (.09)	.36* (.15)
1st Congress of Presidential Admin.	.16 (.21)	.18 (.20)	1.3 (1.1)	.15 (.11)	.16 (.09)	-.37 (.31)
Constant	-1.17	-1.30	-2.7	.80	-.05	.51
Pseudo R^2	.00	.07	.14	.01	.09	.12
N	392	392	392	392	392	392

Note: Table entries are negative binomial regression coefficients, with standard errors. State of the Union mentions and news articles are measured in the hundreds. Public opinion is measured as the percent of the public that identifies an issue area as the most important problem times one hundred. The excluded issue area is macroeconomics. Biennial congress fixed effects are included in the second and fifth columns, but not reported. Issue area fixed effects are included in the third and sixth columns, but not reported. The excluded congress is the fifth in the series. $^*p < .05$; $^{**}p < .01$; $^{***}p < .001$ (two-tailed).

areas, State of the Union mentions are significantly associated with executive orders in each issue area. A one-standard-deviation increase in this measure of the presidential agenda is expected to produce a 27% increase in executive orders. Given that the president regularly discusses some issues more than others, therefore, disproportionate attention in any two-year period is associated with more actions. Based on the results of previous models, these actions are likely of the insignificant variety. The executive branch may be better positioned to unilaterally adopt responsive but minor policy changes.

Policymaking in the wake of the December 2012 shootings at Sandy Hook Elementary School provides a window onto this process. Following the shootings, gun control became a central matter of public debate and consumed media attention for months. President Obama responded quickly, issuing a list of 23 executive actions on January 16, 2013. These included modifying restrictions on gun violence research, requesting consumer product standards on gun safety, and providing grants for school resource officers. More significant action required legislation and hit substantial roadblocks. Bans on "assault" weapons and high-capacity magazines made little progress in Congress. Even a bipartisan bill to expand background checks to gun purchases on the Internet and at gun shows failed to clear the Senate. More significant proposed executive actions also produced uproar in Congress, becoming embroiled in oversight and slowing approval of administrative appointments.[27]

What about policymaking in the courts? Table 3.4 predicts the number of significant judicial policy enactments recorded by policy historians and the total number of Supreme Court decisions per biennium in each issue area. In this case, there is no measure of the agenda available other than the total output measure, the actual cases taken up by the Supreme Court. That likely accounts for the fact that the fit of the models predicting significant judicial enactments is better than for the other two branches.

The results indicate that Supreme Court cases are significant predictors of significant policy enactments by the judiciary. Including controls for time period makes this relationship insignificant. The courts were simply more active in all issue areas in some years (particularly during the 1960s and 1970s); this is reflected in both their total output of decisions and their significant enactments. In the second set of models, the media agenda is a significant predictor of total Supreme Court cases, but only in the models lacking fixed effects for each time period. The media were covering more policy issues at the time the courts were more active. The results of models substituting contemporaneous public and media attention are substantially similar.

No branch of government shows consistent issue agenda effects. Public attention to policy problems is a poor predictor of policymaking in all branches. It does not substantially alter the government agenda, increase total policymaking

Table 3.4 **Models Predicting Judicial Enactments by Topic and Congress**

	Significant Judicial Policy Enactments			Supreme Court Cases		
		With Issue Area Effects	With Issue and Time Effects		With Issue Area Effects	With Issue and Time Effects
Total Supreme Court Cases	2.2*** (.32)	2.6*** (.65)	.82 (.71)	—	—	—
Importance in Public Opinion (t-1)	-.00 (.01)	.01 (.02)	.01 (.02)	1.61 (.92)	-.29 (.45)	.90 (.47)
Coverage in News Media (t-1)	-1.8 (2.8)	-8.7 (5.7)	-6.7 (6.1)	.97*** (.16)	.86*** (.09)	.11 (.09)
Constant	-1.73	-2.62	-1.95	2.17	1.52	.91
Pseudo R²	.09	.14	.24	.02	.16	.22
N	392	392	392	406	406	406

Note: Table entries are negative binomial regression coefficients, with standard errors. Supreme Court cases and news articles are measured in the hundreds. Public opinion is measured as the percent of the public that identifies an issue area as the most important problem times one hundred. Issue area fixed effects are included in the second and fifth columns, but not reported. The excluded issue area is macroeconomics. Biennial congress fixed effects are included in the third and sixth columns, but not reported. The excluded congress is the fifth in the series. *p < .05; **p < .01; ***p <.001 (two-tailed).

in related areas, or lead to significant policy enactments. This does not necessarily indicate that policymakers address issues that concern no part of the public, only that they fail to disproportionately address the "most important problem" that the public specifies on public opinion polls. Although used in many previous studies, this measure may not appropriately represent the diversity of public concerns. Policymakers may instead respond to "issue publics," concerned subsets of the public associated with each area, or focus only on the concerns of the most financially well off citizens.[28] Yet even the government agenda is an unreliable guide to significant policy enactments. Government attention to issue areas is somewhat associated with new laws and executive orders, but it is not associated with significant executive enactments. Even accounting for all three types of agendas, none of the models produces a good fit. This suggests that there is a long series of steps between agenda setting and policy change and that an issue does not have to be high on the agenda at any given time to be associated with significant policy development.

Reported Determinants of Policy Change

The collective knowledge of policy historians can help elucidate why agendas are untrustworthy guides to significant policy change. Policy historians are not necessarily tied to the view that agenda setting factors are the first step in the policy process. Aggregating the findings from their narrative histories of policy development may help explain the puzzle of significant policy change that is not a reflection of the prioritization of policy problems. Policy historians often point to circumstances related to entrepreneurship and bargaining inside of government institutions, rather than factors related to agenda setting.

Table 3.5 reports the percentage of policy enactments associated with each institutional factor, using the judgments of policy historians. It lists the frequencies with which each factor reportedly played an important role out of the total 790 significant policy enactments since 1945. Most policy enactments involved more than one factor. The bolded factors are categories; the most prominent types of explanatory factors within each category follow each label. A factor is counted as important when any policy historian judged it as important.[29]

Executive branch factors are the most commonly credited sources of significant policy change (in nearly 60% of enactments). Presidential leadership was a common component of explanations. Presidents sometimes encourage their co-partisans to adopt a position that is normally contrary to their ideological preference. One important case was President George W. Bush's efforts in support of No Child Left Behind, a policy that "was far more pervasive and coercive than one [the Republican Party] had opposed in 1994."[30] On other occasions,

Table 3.5 **Institutional Factors Contributing to Significant Policy Enactments**

	Policy Enactments (%)
All Congressional Factors	**48.61**
Change in Party Control of Congress	17.97
Supportive Individual Member(s) of Congress	33.16
Ability to Reach Agreement between House and Senate	19.11
Success in a Key Vote on the Floor of the House or Senate	12.41
Success in a Key Vote in a Congressional Committee	7.85
All Executive Branch Factors	**59.75**
Supportive President	47.34
Supportive Agency or Department Director	31.39
All Judicial Branch Factors	**18.10**
Court Ruling Required Action	14.43
Fear of Court Ruling	3.92
Threats of Lawsuits	3.80
All International Factors	**8.73**
Foreign Example	1.77
International Pressure or Competitiveness	6.71
International Government Agreement	2.03
All State and Local Factors	**12.53**
Example Taken from State Action	9.87
Example Taken from Local Action	2.66
Modeled on State or Local Plan	3.16
All Interest Group Factors	**48.73**
Supportive Advocacy Group(s)	33.80
Supportive Corporation(s)	19.75
Congressional Lobbying	16.08
New Interest Group Mobilization	6.08
Financial Advantage of Proponents	1.65
Role of Political Parties	
Republican Coalition	4.43

(Continued)

Table 3.5 **Continued**

	Policy Enactments (%)
Democratic Coalition	8.48
Bipartisan Coalition	29.37
Change in Political Party Strength or Balance of Power	17.97

Note: The table reports the percentage of significant policy enactments that reportedly involved each factor. Within each category, it reports the most common explanatory factors. There were 790 total significant policy enactments since 1945.

presidents are credited with designing bills that stimulate consensus among diverse factions and dampen controversy.[31] Sometimes, the executive branch can adopt policy on its own. Secretary of Education Lamar Alexander used discretionary funds to develop national education standards and offer incentives to localities to adopt them.[32] On other occasions, multiple executive branch actors are credited with congressional action. The Secretary of Labor and President Bill Clinton, for example, were jointly credited with passing the 1996 increase in the minimum wage.[33]

The president often works with congressional leaders to support policy change; their joint involvement is sometimes decisive. According to one policy history, the 1983 amendments to Social Security were made possible because President Ronald Reagan and Democratic Party leaders intervened with an appointed blue ribbon panel: "The White House gave up its strategy of letting the commission come up with the solution on its own and decided instead to work closely with the group of five to see whether a compromise agreement couldn't be reached."[34] Sometimes, as in the Social Security example, the internal negotiation within policymaking institutions is the subject of great public and interest group debates. On other occasions, important policy change is the product of policymaker negotiation that may go largely unnoticed. One policy history provides an example: "The origin of [the Employee Retirement Income Security Act], then, was largely a top-down effort by a handful of politicians. The law expanded government's role in company pensions well beyond what major business groups favored."[35]

Internal factors within Congress also often help produce significant enactments (48.6% of the time) because institutionalized entrepreneurs play roles in brokering compromises that appease different interest groups, parties, and factions. For example, the Fair Housing Act of 1988 was made possible by a compromise position forwarded by Representative Hamilton Fish: "The Fish compromise, which won jury trial safeguards for Republican-leaning constituencies—builders, realtors, appraisers, lenders, apartment landlords—was embraced with relief by all parties."[36] Congressional compromises may also involve logrolling: "a succession of two classic legislative log-rolls between rural lawmakers and urban liberals secured passage of the Food Stamp Act of 1964 and set the template for further legislative reforms over the next decade."[37]

Factors related to interest groups were also quite commonly associated with significant policy enactments (48.7% of cases). Many particular interest organizations were singled out for their role in developing a proposal, publically calling for policy change, or lobbying Congress. For example, the United Mine Workers was credited with the Coal Mine Safety Act of 1969, beginning a pattern of government intervention to assist those with disabilities.[38] Social groups well represented by interest groups were also referenced as important components of policymaking. One policy history explains a specific benefit for veterans: "This politically powerful group had strong claims on the nation's gratitude and conscience; objections to special treatment for veterans were easily made to appear churlish and even unpatriotic."[39] Other explanations, such as one for the National Mental Health Act, relied on lobbyists: "The bill had friends in Congress... in the affected agency, among interest groups, and in the press.... The new element which seemed to fill the gap... was a full-time, single-minded, paid lobbyist."[40]

Many stories of significant policy change involve a combination of interest groups and policymakers. Take one description of the passage of the Family and Medical Leave Act:

> It was [Henry] Hyde, an influential figure among House Republicans, who was persuaded two years earlier to support the bill because it may reduce abortions. While this image may serve as a description of what happened in the end, an explanation of how it all came about might be found in the statement of two key antagonists: "It hurt us to see it referred to as 'watered down' but it helped with the numbers," explained Donna Lenhoff of the Women's Legal Defense Fund, describing the proponents' legislative strategy to capture more votes. On the other side, Mary Tavenner of the Concerned Alliance of Responsible Employers said, "if we had not been there, family leave would have passed as written. We made them change it. The bill became more and more 'reasonable' until inevitably some businesses were neutralized."[41]

Interest groups and policymakers on both sides often feel that they gave significant ground in order to pass a bill they could accept.

Political party politics also play a role in policy change, though policy historians focused on political parties in a minority of cases. Bipartisan coalitions were more commonly involved in policy change than coalitions of only Democrats or Republicans; bipartisanship was an important factor in approximately 30% of significant policy enactments. Democratic coalitions were more common than Republican coalitions, reflecting Democratic dominance in Congress over the latter part of the twentieth century. In approximately one-in-five cases, a change in political party strength or the balance of power between the parties reportedly contributed to policy change. Factors related to the judicial branch were also apparent in nearly one-in-five enactments. International, state, and local government factors were less common.

What about factors outside of government institutions that are often the focus of *agenda setting* theories? Table 3.6 reports the percentage of policy enactments associated with other factors considered important in studies of policymaking. One-in-four policy changes is reportedly associated with some factor related to public opinion, though often alongside institutional factors. For example, policy historians credited the "Don't Ask, Don't Tell" decision on gays in the military to Bill Clinton's leadership, the 1992 election, media attention, and interest group pressure.[42] Historians viewed media reports as influential less often (in 18.2% of enactments). One policy history explains the Tax Reform Act of 1986 as, in part, the product of media attention: "As gross abuses of the system became more and more commonplace in the media, the demand for 'tax reform' become harder and harder for even Republicans to ignore."[43]

Events were more commonly referenced in explanations for policy change (34% of enactments), although only a minority of these cases were singular focusing events. The majority of events referenced involved ongoing wars or economic recessions. Nevertheless, focusing events were mentioned even in unrelated issue areas. The 1957 Soviet launch of Sputnik helped pass the National Defense Education Act, giving related interest groups a competitiveness argument to push for federal education intervention.[44] The 1956 war between Israel and Egypt stimulated oil import restrictions.[45] The assassinations of Martin Luther King Jr. and Robert Kennedy helped pass the Gun Control Act of 1968.[46] In all three cases, events helped push along ongoing policy discussions by shifting the calculus of policymakers seeking a compromise that could be enacted.

According to policy historians, factors related to research were also common explanations for policy change (in 37.1% of enactments). Rather than sift through academic reports, policymakers rely on data and summary reports from government agencies, scientists within government, or interest groups. Scientists at the National Institutes of Health repeatedly drove increasing federal expansion into mental health.[47] Government reports summarizing the risks of smoking led to restrictions on smoking on airplanes and federal buildings.[48]

Factors related to path dependence and issue framing were also credited with significant minorities of policy changes. Policy historians did not generally use

Table 3.6   **Other Factors Contributing to Significant Policy Enactments**

	Policy Enactment (%)
All Public Opinion Factors	**25.44%**
Constituent Pressure	9.37%
Protest/Demonstration	2.91%
Supportive Public Opinion	11.14%
Issue Raised in Election Campaign	11.52%
All Media Factors	**18.23%**
General Media Coverage of Problem	16.96%
Specific Media Report	7.09%
All Event-Related Factors	**34.05%**
Event Highlights Problem	19.62%
Affected by Ongoing War or Military Event	7.85%
Affected by Economic Downturn	13.80%
All Research-Related Factors	**37.09%**
New Data Arises on Problem	19.11%
Supportive Academics/Scientists	10.63%
Government Report Issued	18.23%
Report Issued by Interest Group	9.11%
All Path Dependence	**42.41%**
Change Extends Earlier Policy	32.41%
Affected by Early Policy Choice	21.01%
Earlier Policy Choice Eliminated a Policy Alternative	2.41%
All Issue Framing	**20.38%**
Proponents had Compelling Argument/Frame	16.46%
Opponents Lacked Compelling Argument/Frame	3.67%
No One Wanted to Oppose	3.04%

Notes: The table reports the percentage of significant policy enactments that reportedly involved each factor. Within each category, it reports the most common explanatory factors. There were 790 total significant policy enactments since 1945.

this theoretical language; they simply reported that significant policy changes were extensions of earlier policies (categorized as a form of path dependence) or that proponents of a policy change forwarded an argument that most accepted as compelling (categorized as a form of issue framing). Path dependence was substantially more common (present in 42.4% of enactments), but mostly reflected built-in features of congressional policymaking. For example, many significant policy changes were made possible by the reauthorization of past bills (such as No Child Left Behind as an update of the Elementary and Secondary Education Act). This provides some insight as to how institutions set their agenda. Agriculture may be on the agenda, after all, simply because the farm bill is regularly up for reauthorization.

Path dependent explanations do not imply that political coalition building is absent. Instead, policymakers often build patterns of regular cooperation based on expansions of previous policy. One example comes from repeated expansions of Social Security:

> The 1958 amendments...showed how the program could expand even in mildly adverse economic and political circumstances. Over time, the collaboration between [Wilbur] Mills and the bureaucrats in the Social Security Administration became practiced and smooth. Although there were things on which they disagreed, such as Medicare, they nonetheless worked together to produce social security benefit increases. After 1958, therefore, the program enjoyed true bipartisan backing in Congress and at least the tacit support of the White House.[49]

Specific Actors Responsible for Policy Change

Particular individuals and organizations, like Mills and the Social Security Administration, were often credited in explanations for significant policy change alongside circumstantial factors. Table 3.7 lists the individuals and organizations credited with the most significant policy enactments since 1945 (out of the 790 total enactments). I also include the number of issue domains in which they were active (out of the 14 total) and highlight which actors were Democrats or liberal organizations (D), Republicans or conservative organizations (R), or neither.

In the vast majority of cases, these actors were credited alongside others for their roles in each policy enactment. Rather than policy entrepreneurs toiling outside government, the most productive actors in policymaking are the most well-known elected officials, interest groups, and government departments. Every president from Harry Truman to Bill Clinton made the list, many near

Table 3.7 **Actors Credited with Most Significant Policy Enactments**

	No. of Policy Enactments	*No. of Issue Domains*
Lyndon B. Johnson (D)	55	6
Richard Nixon (R)	50	4
John F. Kennedy (D)	39	5
AFL-CIO (D)	36	6
Bill Clinton (D)	32	5
Edward M. Kennedy (D)	32	5
Ronald Reagan (R)	31	4
Dwight D. Eisenhower (R)	26	7
Environmental Protection Agency	25	1
Harry Truman (D)	25	4
Jimmy Carter (D)	24	3
NAACP (D)	22	5
George H. W. Bush (R)	20	5
Department of Justice	18	3
House Ways and Means Committee	18	2
Wilbur Mills (D)	18	1
Department of Agriculture	16	5
Department of Health, Education and Welfare	15	3
Gerald Ford (R)	15	2
U.S. Conference of Mayors	15	4
American Civil Liberties Union (D)	13	2
Bob Dole (R)	13	6
Edmund Muskie (D)	13	1
David Stockman (R)	11	3
Hubert Humphrey (D)	11	5
Department of Labor	11	3
Wilber Cohen (D)	11	2
Daniel Moynihan (D)	10	3
Ralph Nader (D)	10	3

(Continued)

Table 3.7 **Continued**

	No. of Policy Enactments	No. of Issue Domains
Jacob Javits (R)	10	5
John Blatnik (D)	10	1

Note: The table reports the number of significant policy enactments that were partially credited to each individual or organization out of 790 significant policy enactments from 1945 to 2004. The table also reports the number of Policy Agendas Project issue domains in which each actor contributed to at least one policy enactment. Actors with (D) next to their name were coded as Democrats or liberal groups. Actors with (R) next to their name were coded as Republicans or conservative groups.

the top. Long-serving members of Congress who held many positions of leadership also helped produce many policy changes. Prominent interest groups made the list, as did the largest domestic policy administrative departments.

A small proportion of the 1,306 policymaking actors were involved in a sizable fraction of policy enactments since 1945. Only 11 actors, mostly presidents, were involved in more than 3% of all significant policy changes. Broad participation across issue areas is even less common, with only one actor involved in policymaking in at least half of the domestic policy issue areas. This suggests that, although participation in policymaking is broad, the number of actors who are relevant to a substantial fraction of decisions in any time period is quite small. The involved group usually includes the president and a few major interest groups, legislators, and administrative agencies. In terms of partisan composition, the only Republicans on the list of most credited policymakers are the presidents, two moderate senators, and Reagan administration official David Stockman. Another notable feature is that many of the actors listed held multiple positions; three presidents who were also active legislators top the list.

Most of these top performers were active in American governance over an extended period. Figure 3.1 depicts the longevity of different actors. The length of the lines indicates the number of years that each actor was partially responsible for policymaking, from the first policy change in which they were credited to the last. I have removed the government organizations from the previous list, but it includes most of the same actors. They are now ordered based on the earliest year in which they were involved. Some actors are credited with policy after they leave office. Many of John F. Kennedy's initiatives did not become law until after his death; policy historians nonetheless thought he deserved credit.

The results reveal that few actors play important roles in policymaking for longer than a decade (the figure includes only 32 active participants out of 1,306 total). The actors with longevity tend to be broad interest groups like

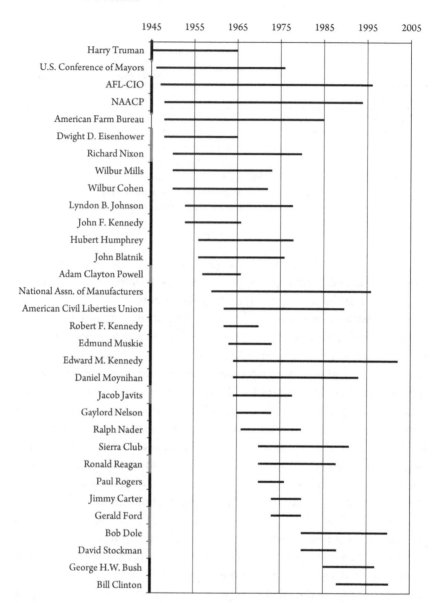

Figure 3.1 Involvement of individuals and interest groups in policymaking across time

The figure depicts the time period in which each actor was involved in policymaking, based on the first and last policy enactment in which they were credited. Actors next to a black line were coded as Democrats or liberals; actors next to a grey line were coded as Republicans or conservatives.

the AFL-CIO and the National Association of Manufacturers. The American Farm Bureau and the NAACP were also important for many years, though for a smaller range of issues. This comports with the view of interest groups in my first book, *The Not-So-Special Interests*: only a small subset of groups known for representing broad constituencies and concerns have regular opportunities for influence.[50] Likewise, only a small number of legislators were responsible for policymaking over a long period, especially Edward M. Kennedy and Daniel Patrick Moynihan. Liberal actors dominate the list for most of the period. Beginning in the 1980s, a group of conservative actors becomes more prominent, just as some of the long-serving liberal actors drop out of the policymaking process.

Internal and External Factors in Policy Change

Significant policy changes are usually the product of combinations of important factors rather than one factor alone. Table 3.8 reports a cross-tabulation based on two variables that combine different types of explanatory factors. The row variable divides the 790 policy enactments based on whether they were associated with any explanatory factors related to the internal machinations of at least one of the three branches of government. The column variable divides the policy enactments based on whether they were associated with any explanatory factors related to agenda setting, including public opinion, media coverage, or events.

Table 3.8 **Distribution of Internal and External Factors in Reported Determinants of Policy Change**

	No Factors Related to Public Opinion, Media Coverage, or Events	Factors Related to Public Opinion, Media Coverage, or Events
No Factors Related to Internal Dynamics of Government Institutions	*120* Enactments (15.2%)	*44* Enactments (5.6%)
Factors Related to Internal Dynamics of Government Institutions	*271* Enactments (34.3%)	*355* Enactments (44.9%)

Note: Table entries are cross-tabulations of two variables combining two types of explanations for policy change. The first includes all factors related to Congress, the administration, or the courts. The second includes all factors related to public opinion, media coverage, or events. Factors related to interest groups, research, path dependence, framing, or international, state or local government are not included in either category.

Factors related to research, path dependence, issue framing, interest groups, and international, state, and local governments are not included in either aggregate category.

According to policy historians, the vast majority of enactments (79.2%) are partially a product of the internal dynamics of government institutions. In contrast, just over half of policy enactments are partially explained by factors related to agenda setting. A substantial share of policy enactments involve factors related to both agenda setting and policymaking institutions. Relatively few policy enactments (5.6%) involve agenda setting factors but no factors related to the internal processes of government institutions. The average policy change involved 2.4 distinct factors related to government institutions but only 1.2 factors related to agenda setting as well as 1.2 related to interest groups. Factors related to agenda setting were typically part of explanations that also involved institutions and groups. On average, the policy changes partially credited to agenda setting factors also involved 3.4 factors related to institutions and 1.7 factors related to interest groups. In other words, agenda setting factors were partially responsible for policy changes that required quite a few explanatory factors. Agenda setting factors rarely produced policy enactments without help from institutional factors and interest groups.

The policy histories point to some examples of the related dynamics. Competitors in Congress may channel and use public opinion, as in the case of the National Environmental Policy Act. Henry Jackson used the public demand for new policy to challenge Edmund Muskie's previous environmental statutes.[51] Twenty years later, President George H. W. Bush responded to environmental issues raised in the presidential campaign but it took a lot of steps between election results and a policy enactment:

> Declaring that he wished to be the 'environmental president,' Bush focused on air pollution [in the campaign].... Once elected, Bush was committed to press for amendments to the Clean Air Act. He devoted significant time and energy to drafting the bill; even more important, he committed substantial political capital to getting the legislation through Congress.[52]

Policymakers also can choose to act in the face of uncertain or even opposing public opinion. One policy history reports that "democratic institutions negated the impact of the public at large on immigration policies. In the end, a coalition of well-organized interests and public officials, empowered by the nation's political institutions, successfully pushed for a significant liberalization of U.S. [immigration] policies" in 1990, against the public's wishes for more restrictive policies.[53] According to an example from a tax policy history, unclear public opinion also opens the way for policymakers to compromise: "With voters sending mixed messages…contradictions riddled budgetary policy. As a consequence, Congress and the President reached a clumsy compromise that…provided deficit-increasing tax relief and overall deficit reduction at the same time."[54]

Events can also provide politicians with excuses to do what they already want to do. The Job Creation and Worker Assistance Act of 2002 provides an example: "The terrorism threat combined with the economic slowdown…to give Congress and the president excuses to throw budgetary caution to the wind.…The administration wanted to show it was still concerned about the economy. Once again, tax cuts were its chosen vehicle."[55] Events may also help to push actors toward compromise, as in the case of the Railroad Revitalization and Regulatory Reform Act of 1976: "Only billions for 'revitalization' in an environment of inflation and unemployment and the threatened shutdown or nationalization of part of the railroad system had brought William Coleman, Brock Adams, President Ford, and railroad labor and management that far."[56]

Policymakers can also use heightened media coverage to guide them toward modifying their positions, temporarily aligning their interests with others in support of policy change. One example comes from the National Traffic and Motor Vehicle Safety Act of 1966: "The press was a crucial factor in passage of the bill.…Support for the bill sprang from the political maintenance needs of two senators—[Abraham] Ribicoff, who had a new forum [his subcommittee's investigations of General Motors' attacks on Ralph Nader,] and [Warren] Magnuson, whose staff urged him to change his pro-industry image and broaden his base of support."[57]

Agenda setting factors are hardly irrelevant to the policy process, but they typically serve to enhance the possibility for change in the internal dynamics of government: they help enable coalitions sufficient to enact significant new policies. Events, public opinion, and media reports are but a few of many factors that can play this role, including research or interest groups. Either way, the internal processes of coalition building are of primary importance.

Institutionalized Entrepreneurs in Policy Change

The evidence from the collective judgments of policy historians and from the models designed to predict policy enactments via measures of agendas combine to paint a revised portrait of the policy process. Agenda setting factors rarely lead to significant policy change on their own. It appears unnecessary for an issue to rise dramatically on the public or elite agenda to result in significant policy change. Public and media concerns are rarely a good indication of the likelihood of a policy enactment. Just because gun control gains public and media attention following a school shooting, that does not mean important new restrictions are forthcoming. Even the government agenda is usually a better predictor of insignificant executive orders, rather than the most significant policy changes since 1945 (though contemporaneous hearings are associated with significant new laws).

The lack of correspondence between agendas and policy change is a challenge for *agenda setting* theories, including three of the most common ways of analyzing public policy. The issue agenda should play a more constrained role in the Punctuated Equilibrium, Independent Streams, and Advocacy Coalition frameworks. Each theory nonetheless contributes valuable insights. The emphasis on venue shopping and jurisdictional change in Punctuated Equilibrium theory can explain how policymakers and interest groups bring about policy change, even if it follows no upsurge in public concern. The policy entrepreneurs highlighted by Independent Streams theory still take advantage of windows of opportunity, even if those involve internal coalitions rather than a joining of public concern with policy proposals. The dynamics of cooperation and compromise within Advocacy Coalitions influence their ability to advance potential new policies, even if they must build ties to dominant policymakers beyond their subsystems.

Policy history suggests that all issues may stay on the agenda consistently enough to lead to significant policy changes at any given time and that issues may become the center of public and elite attention without leading to policy change. These patterns explain the twin cases that begin this chapter: Obama's student loan and health care reforms. An issue can reach the agenda several times and only result in policy change one of those times. As Suzanne Mettler argues, explaining how health care reached the agenda without explaining the path to enactment is ignoring most of the story:

> Health care reform hit the political agenda in 2009 as it has approximately every 15 years since 1920. Each time, the issue has consumed the attention of policymakers and the media for months of intense drama, protracted battles, and deal-making between the political parties and with interest groups. That health care reform would require Herculean efforts by the president and congressional leaders was a given; that such efforts would guarantee success was anything but.[58]

Based on conventional notions of agenda setting, the case of student loan reform is even more difficult to understand. It passed as an add-on to the health care legislation without higher education becoming a major issue of public or government concern. As the patterns in this chapter reveal, the likely explanations for both are the ability of policymakers and interest groups to reach agreement on a proposal, rather than in their prioritization of problems.

The evidence is consistent with a more circumscribed role for agenda setting. Congressional attention to a topic area is associated with the laws that Congress passes, including many of significance. About half of significant policy changes involve some factor related to agenda setting. Yet the role of agenda setting is small in comparison with internal bargaining and entrepreneurship by politicians and groups. Research and path dependence also were reportedly quite influential. Agenda setting factors like focusing events and public opinion usually require some combination of these other factors to produce significant policy change.

Although they incorporate attention to endogenous change, *agenda setting* theories serve to focus attention away from the internal machinations of policymaking institutions and toward public concerns and the prioritization of problems. Coalitions of policymakers and interest groups must converge around an acceptable policy proposal for policy change to move forward. This appears to require entrepreneurship by important officials, coalitions among diverse actors, and compromise among factions in each policy debate. It does not appear to require their collective prioritization of a public concern. Internal processes matter much more than the agenda setting dynamics that are the focus of prior theory.

The results also have important implications for Americans' views of democracy. Agenda setting dynamics are cited as an example of the close connections between government and citizens. Agenda setting was supposed to offer another route for ongoing representation and responsiveness after elections of public officials. If government responded to public concerns and changed its priorities when the public agenda shifted, citizens in a democracy would have another route to influence decision-making. If the outcomes of policymaking follow from internal struggles among policymakers, rather than their efforts to respond to popular concerns, agenda setting cannot offer a route to enhanced representation. Political institutions may be more insular and less responsive than commonly assumed. At least when it comes to the sources of significant policy change, scholars and citizens may need to adjust our expectations accordingly.

CHAPTER 4

The Long Great Society

The 1996 Republican Party Platform promised to "abolish the Department of Education" and "end federal meddling in our schools."[1] Just five years later, newly elected conservative President George W. Bush led the drive to dramatically expand the department's role. The No Child Left Behind Act was widely viewed as the largest federal intervention in education policy since the law it renewed, the Elementary and Secondary Education Act of 1965. Bush's dramatic intervention in education was not accompanied by many other policy changes of the same ilk. In most respects, twenty-first-century policymaking has been far removed from the government expansion of the 1960s and 1970s—though it has never quite matched Republican platform rhetoric emphasizing limited government.

Perceptions of acceptable policy ideas change over time. In the 1972 State and Local Assistance Act, Richard Nixon and Congress sent $30 billion to state and local governments with few strings attached—and they called it a conservative reform. The idea of a Republican president proposing general revenue sharing today is quite far-fetched. Policy changes that are commonplace in one era may be inconceivable in others.

Differences in the ideological mood of policymakers sometimes—but hardly always—reflect election returns. In the 1964 election, Lyndon Johnson won all but six states and the Democrats gained 37 seats in Congress. The following congressional session produced a legendary trove of new laws in dozens of policy areas, expanding the scope of government and ushering in the Great Society. By 1968, Democrats had lost 52 seats in the House and 8 in the Senate; they won only 13 states in the presidential election. Yet neither gridlock nor a backlash reigned; the following congressional session saw landmark new liberal laws in environmental, health, labor, education, transportation, and urban policy. By the time Nixon signed general revenue sharing into law, the American state had dramatically expanded in size and scope.

Students of American government are accustomed to hearing stories where public sentiment and new elected officials seem to drive policymaking. Scholars are drawn to explanations for policy that begin with exogenous variables like party control, election results, and public opinion. Some evidence seems to support this view. *Macro politics* studies of American policymaking since 1945 show over-time patterns relating political inputs to aggregate policy output. Erikson, Mackuen, and Stimson find that the ideological direction of landmark laws follows trends in public opinion and election results.[2] In turn, this aggregate policy direction has important consequences, helping to determine who wins and loses in the American economy.[3] McCarty, Poole, and Rosenthal find that party polarization significantly reduces the quantity of lawmaking and produces more conservative policies.[4]

Yet this sort of story fails to explain American policy history. Mandate elections do not always bring immediate policy change.[5] After Ronald Reagan won 49 states and the Republicans gained 16 seats in the House in 1984, government could muster few landmark pieces of legislation; one was later ruled unconstitutional. The period of policy change we associate with the Great Society actually began before any public mandate. Congress passed the Clean Air Act, the Civil Rights Act, the Food Stamp Act, and a major tax cut before the 1964 election. Regardless of electoral shifts, policy development sometimes builds on itself. The height of liberal policymaking continued into the early 1970s after Johnson had left office. The national policymaking system then underwent a broad transformation that produced less extensive and more conservative policymaking in the mid- to late-1970s.[6]

David Mayhew, the author of the original measure of landmark laws used in most *macro politics* analyses, found a period of substantially increased lawmaking lasting from 1961 to 1976. In this chapter, I show that this period effect still helps to explain policy output since 1945 no matter how policy is measured or what covariates are included. I find that the period effect has an even more substantial impact on the ideological direction of policymaking. The effects are not limited to Congress; they extend to all branches of government.

I label the period from 1961 to 1976 "the Long Great Society" to emphasize that it reached its height with Johnson's broad and liberal domestic policy agenda but that it extended well beyond his presidency. Conceiving of the Long Great Society as a uniquely activist period enables a re-evaluation of past research. I argue that this transformational period in American policy history was made possible by its unique governing network. The community of actors involved in policy change was large and diverse. Yet a core of central actors sustained a policy drive across many policy issue areas over the entire period. The period effect is not accounted for by changes in partisan control of government, policymaker ideology, or public opinion. It was made possible by a sustained pattern of advocacy, coalition, and compromise among long-serving members of Congress, prominent interest groups, large executive departments, and four

experienced presidents active across the domestic policy spectrum. The governing network of this era held together across four bipartisan administrations, featured a core set of actors across many issue areas, and stood out in comparison
to the networks that preceded and followed it.

This chapter investigates American domestic policymaking since 1945 with
attention to this distinct era. First, I compare *macro politics* models and periodizations of activist eras and reintroduce my own perspective. Second, I analyze
trends in new measures of policy output and ideological direction in the three
branches of government and I show that the Long Great Society period effect
helps explain trends in policy output and ideological direction in all branches
of government. After accounting for this period, the evidence no longer sup-
ports a dominant and consistent role for partisanship, ideology, or public opinion. Third, I show that the network of actors that enacted policy in that era held
together over sixteen years and featured a unique cross-issue core-periphery
structure, including the active participation of the presidents. Finally, I explore
the implications of this period for views of American policymaking.

Macro Politics Models

In *Divided We Govern*, Mayhew produces a list of important enactments for
each biennial congress from 1946 to 2002 based on the judgments of journalists wrapping up each congress (sweep one) and, up to 1990, the retrospective
judgments of policy area historians (sweep two).[7] He predicts the number of
these landmark laws passed by each congress, including a period effect dummy
variable that he calls "activist mood" for each congress from 1961 to 1976. This
variable predicts substantially more lawmaking: each congress during the period
produced 8.5 additional landmark laws. The only other variable that predicts the
number of landmark laws is whether the congress is in the first two years of a
presidential administration. Rather than dwell on the period effect, Mayhew
focuses on the null finding regarding the influence of divided government.

William Howell, Scott Adler, Charles Cameron, and Charles Riemann use
new measures of landmark laws derived from Mayhew's sweep one and a similarly constructed series to show that divided government may reduce the output of the most universally recognized important laws.[8] Joshua D. Clinton and
John S. Lapinski aggregate 19 different analyses of important laws to create a
new measure of importance for each new law.[9] Nolan McCarty uses measures
from these authors to reanalyze the amount of lawmaking per congress.[10] He
finds that party polarization, rather than divided government, reduces legislative
productivity. Despite its explanatory power, Mayhew's period effect variable is
not included in the models used by McCarty or Howell et al.[11]

In *The Macro Polity*, Erikson, Mackuen, and Stimson use Mayhew's series of landmark laws to construct a measure of the liberalism of lawmaking, subtracting the number of laws that contract the scope of government responsibility from the number that expand it for each congress.[12] They predict this policy liberalism measure using Democratic Party control of government (coded from 0 to 3 based on party control of the House, Senate, and presidency) and measures of public opinion on policy (called public mood). They find that lawmaking is responsive to partisanship and public opinion: more Democrats and more public liberalism equal more liberal policy. They also neglect to include the period effect variable for 1961 to 1976.

The Long Great Society as an Activist Liberal Era

Mayhew credits Arthur Schlesinger, Jr. and Samuel Huntington for the notion that 1961-1976 constituted a unique era featuring an activist orientation. These scholars saw it as a period of government-wide liberalism rather than legislative productivity. Schlesinger understood the era as part of a cyclical periodization:

> As the private interest of the 1920s had led to the public action of the 1930s, the 1950s now led into the 1960s and a new rush of commitment: Kennedy and the New Frontier; Johnson and the Great Society; the racial revolution, the war on poverty.... By the later 1970s Americans were once more, as they had been in the 1950s and 1920s, fed up with public action and disenchanted by its consequences.[13]

Schlesinger saw the period arising and ending with elections, but recognized that Richard Nixon and Jimmy Carter did not match the formula; he credited Nixon with a long list of liberal actions and called Carter "the most conservative Democratic President" of the century.[14]

Huntington labels the period from the early 1960s to the mid-1970s the "fourth major creedal passion period since independence," comparable to what he calls the Revolutionary, Jacksonian, and Progressive eras.[15] He viewed it as an age of protest, not a part of a cycle:

> [The awakening of the early 1960s] produced a politics from the mid-sixties to the mid-seventies that makes those years a clearly identifiable period in American political history. The agenda of politics, the tone of politics, the issues, the intensity, the cleavages, the actors, the forms of political activity—all took on distinctive characteristics.... The distinctive profile of politics from 1960 to 1976 is dramatically revealed

in the horseshoe bulge that recurs during these years in a variety of important quantitative indicators of political activity.[16]

As part of this bulge, he points to the rise and fall of lawmaking, protests, and riots.

Both Schlesinger and Huntington pointed to changes in public and elite ideological moods, but they saw the moods as relatively constant over the period, rather than reacting thermostatically to changes in policy. There were some differences in their views: Schlesinger popularized the notion of the imperial presidency; Huntington believed presidential power was eroding. Huntington emphasized social movements; for Schlesinger, it was public opinion.

The more typical explanation for the policymaking bulge in this era focuses on the Great Society itself. With large Democratic majorities, public sympathy surrounding the Kennedy assassination, and a large popular vote margin in 1964, Johnson was able to bring about what Sidney Milkis called a "transformation of political life no less important than the Progressive Era and the New Deal."[17] After urban unrest and social protest, a high-growth economy and a large new and active generation of young people enabled the government to commit to economic justice.[18] Kimberly Morgan summarizes the traditional account: "Some have characterized this period as one of the 'big bangs' in American social policy, a time when grand visions of social transformation were possible. Social spending dramatically increased in this period, and the determination of Lyndon B. Johnson and his administration to wage a War on Poverty signaled new federal commitment to social welfare policy."[19]

These explanations leave the length of the active period and its wide issue emphasis unexplained. Just two years after the 1964 election, Democrats lost substantial seats in Congress as public opinion moved decidedly against bigger government.[20] Nonetheless, policymakers in the 1970s accepted and expanded the programs of the Great Society and added many more tasks for national government.[21] In addition to social welfare, the program encompassed health care, the environment, and many other concerns.

The Policymaking System of the Long Great Society

Although Mayhew, Schlesinger, and Huntington identified a period of extensive liberal policymaking, they did not explain the mechanism for how changes in public and elite attitudes led to new public policy enactments. The factors that they identified, social protest and public mood, seem far removed from the proximate causes of lawmaking, executive branch expansion, and judicial activism.

Policy change came about in many different issue areas as a result of a sustained pattern of advocacy, coalition, and compromise among political elites.

Several electoral and institutional trends converged to enable policymakers and activists to enact policy across the issue spectrum in all three branches of government. By the early 1960s, Democrats won overwhelming congressional majorities and public opinion had shifted in favor of government expansion.[22] The number of issues on the public and elite agenda expanded dramatically starting in 1961 and remained elevated.[23] The national interest group community began to dramatically expand and diversify.[24] Social movements and mobilization by disadvantaged groups brought new demands for government action.[25] Presidents were empowered to serve entrepreneurial policymaking roles by the expansion of the administrative state and the presidential branch.[26] In the US Senate, member staff expanded and seniority norms declined in importance, enabling individual senators more latitude to pursue policy goals.[27] Procedural changes to the rulemaking process and the in the federal courts provided access to new litigants, expanded the types of permissible evidence, and enabled group representation in legal proceedings.[28] No single change was sufficient to enable the network of actors responsible for significant policy change to take shape. Many of the trends continued long after the productive period of liberal policymaking ended. The combination of all of these changes near the beginning of the period opened the potential avenues available to institutionalized entrepreneurs to build coalitions in multiple issue areas and venues.[29]

Important transformations in American policymaking may only be visible from looking at the system as a whole, including secular trends within each institution and changes in the interactions among them. With its multiple branches, numerous veto points, and supermajoritarian institutions, the American government makes changing public policy quite difficult. As a result, policy enactments are nearly always the product of joint causation; no one can accomplish anything without support from, or at least acquiescence by, a large number of other actors. An era of productive policymaking requires cooperative arrangements addressing many different substantive concerns.

During the Long Great Society, a broad network of actors working with four consecutive presidents led liberal policymaking. Hubert Humphrey helped start the Peace Corps and raise the minimum wage with President John F. Kennedy; he worked on tax cuts, the Civil Rights Act, and immigration reform with Johnson. After losing the presidency to Richard Nixon in 1968, Humphrey went on to help pass minimum wage legislation and education reform under President Gerald Ford. Republican Jacob Javits helped pass civil rights laws and Great Society programs and create the National Endowment for the Arts during the Johnson administration; he went on to reform pension regulation and war powers under Nixon and Ford. Some interest groups also played outsized roles across the issue spectrum and regardless of the party of the president. The U.S. Conference of Mayors was involved in environmental and housing policy under Kennedy, the Great Society programs of Johnson, labor legislation under Nixon, and transportation reform under Ford. The AFL-CIO was critical in labor legislation for decades, but also enabled change in immigration, civil rights, and housing policy under Johnson, Nixon, and Ford. The coalition that enacted the Great Society saw it through to implementation and further development in administrative agencies and the courts during the 1970s.[30]

The successful liberal policymaking of the Long Great Society was made possible by many different trends, but the composition of involved actors, the breadth of their issue focus, and the structure of their relationships provided the mechanism for translating policy demands into results. As Shep Melnick writes, "The result [of the early part of the era] was a dense and eclectic network of reformers with impressive policy expertise, a bottomless agenda of proposals and demands, and ready access to government officials, congressional aids, and journalists."[31] A core group of closely connected actors including presidents, members of Congress, executive departments, and interest groups engaged in joint and sustained policymaking across issue areas. Before and after the period, a smaller, diffuse, and coreless community was responsible for policymaking separated by issue concerns.

The importance of the cross-issue and cross-branch governing network of this era has been noted by those who saw its demise. Jacob Hacker and Paul Pierson note that America veered suddenly away from its progressive orientation at the end of the 1970s; they attribute the transition to changing ideas and the rise of conservative interest groups.[32] Theodore Lowi argues that government expanded to accommodate myriad interest group demands, giving power to bureaucracies that were captured by constituent interest groups.[33] Hugh Heclo posits that policymaking underwent a transformation to separate issue networks of actors linked by expertise.[34] What all of these accounts miss is that they are describing the breakdown of a system that was only operational for 16 years. Sustained and similar links between branches of government in multiple issue areas should not be seen as the base state of governance; it is rare and difficult to reproduce.

ADVOCACY, COALITION, AND COMPROMISE

Regardless of supportive underlying political conditions, policy historians view the process of coalition building as instrumental to policymaking. The passage of the Elementary and Secondary Education Act (ESEA) of 1965, for example, was the product of successful political maneuvering:

ESEA went through Congress in 89 days and emerged from that process with only modest changes. That reflected both the strength of Lyndon Johnson's political position at the start of 1965 and the lengths to which the administration had gone to clear it with key legislators and interest groups before sending it to the Hill... its passage did not seem straightforward at the time. Rather, almost until the last, Johnson worried that it might come unstruck.[35]

When political conditions switch directions, policy does not always follow. Nixon first oversaw the growth of federal housing subsidies and benefits to their peak and later reformed the programs. The federal government eventually started community development grants, Section 8 housing subsidies, and a variety of formula grants to cities under Ford. This housing policy involved two administrations, compromises among many legislative proposals, and active participation by interest groups and a federal department.[36]

In *macro politics* models, the Elementary and Secondary Education Act of 1965 seems like an inevitable government expansion by a newly elected liberal majority. To policy historians, it was accomplished quickly only because it was the product of lining up supporters in Congress and the interest group community. The actors had to compromise and trade favors along the way; they worked to find the right arguments to satisfy concerns and the appropriate methods of coaxing reluctant supporters. Likewise, the Housing and Community Development Act of 1974 was not a simple reversal or expansion of Johnson administration policy. The compromises were not easy, but they were available because a coalition of legislators, interest groups, and administration officials had been working together for more than a decade.

Policy histories shed light on the multiple processes by which these patterns of cooperation are built. On some occasions, such as the 1971 increase in Social Security, policymakers reached an agreement of convenience: "Social Security policy issues were in rare alignment, such that policymakers at both ends of the political spectrum wanted to pursue the same specific proposal to meet their own goals."[37] On other occasions, such as the Higher Education Facilities Bill in 1963, it took substantial time to find a workable compromise to match the goals of different leaders with the same outcome.[38] In the judiciary, alliances among interest groups, foundations, lawyers, and policymakers laid the groundwork for decisions extending civil rights and liberties.[39] Even executive orders, seemingly individual actions of presidents, were the product of large-scale negotiations involving actors in multiple branches as well as interest groups. In the case of a water pollution order by Johnson, for instance, Ed Muskie and Henry Jackson in Congress shared Johnson's policy goals but not his view of the appropriate policy tools; no one saw themselves on the same side until a compromise was reached.[40]

During the Long Great Society, a network of important actors regularly found and executed these compromises across many issue areas. Policymakers in the era built a durable network across policy domains that are usually separated.[41]

PRESIDENTS IN POLICY HISTORY

The most important actors during the Long Great Society were the presidents.[42] A plausible factor linking the presidents of the era was congressional experience. Army general and university president Dwight D. Eisenhower preceded the era; farmer and one-term governor Jimmy Carter ended it. In contrast, in 1961, Kennedy entered office with 14 years of experience in both houses of Congress alongside Johnson, who had 24 years of congressional experience, much of it spent in leadership. Nixon had also served in both chambers of Congress and as Vice President. Even Ford, who played a less significant role, had spent 24 years in Congress, including in leadership. Changes in the presidential primary system following the 1968 elections allowed candidates without support from Washington officeholders to win party nominations, leading to Carter's presidency and coinciding with the end of the Long Great Society.[43] All of the presidents elected since that time have served a combined eight years in Congress.[44]

The congressional experience of the Long Great Society presidents assisted them in assessing the political practicality of their initiatives and in developing coalitions. The benefits of successive presidents with national legislative experience likely have increasing returns. Presidents are among the most important institutionalized entrepreneurs, but the constitutional system requires them to build and sustain networks that provide future presidents with the means to continue their agendas.[45] The Long Great Society presidents had worked with one another prior to their administrations and they knew the same congressional leaders and active interest groups. Cumulatively, this allowed them to develop a governing network that included many of the same actors across several issue areas, despite differences in party.

The road to the Employee Retirement Income Security Act of 1974, for example, included all four Long Great Society presidents. The proposal evolved from a pensions cabinet committee appointed by Kennedy; it was developed throughout the Johnson administration; Nixon reframed the legislation and extended its impact; Ford signed it into law.[46] Many of the same interest groups, administrators, and legislators were active in formulating the policy across four presidential administrations.

Nixon's election was a potential turning point for the ideological direction of policy. As Democrats controlled Congress, Nixon did not have full control of domestic policy and may have acquiesced in a desire to hold power. He had several high profile battles with the Supreme Court and Congress. Yet it is striking that Nixon presided over an expansion of the Great Society as well as new liberal initiatives to address environmental and consumer concerns. He proposed national health care and implemented wage and price controls and affirmative action programs. Political historians explain Nixon's liberal domestic policymaking as a product of his focus on foreign policy and unique aspects of his personality, rather than political trends.[47]

Significant Policy Enactments Since 1945

My compilation of policy histories enables a new look at changes in the level of policymaking since 1945, including the visible difference of the Long Great Society era. Figure 4.1 illustrates the number of policy enactments during each biennium, differentiating between laws passed by Congress, executive branch actions, and court decisions. The Kennedy administration began a substantial increase in lawmaking, which reached two peaks: the first during the Great Society and the second during Nixon's first two years. Judicial policymaking also expanded during the Warren Court, with extensive policymaking extending into the initial terms of the Burger Court. Executive policymaking was more variable, but hit peaks during Nixon's first term and Bill Clinton's first term.

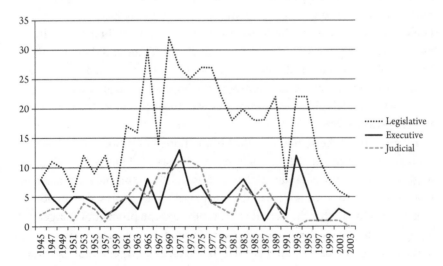

Figure 4.1 Biennial significant policy enactments in each branch of government

The figure depicts the number of policy enactments identified by policy histories during each biennial Congress. Each enactment is categorized based on whether it was a new law passed by Congress, a presidential executive order or regulatory rule, or a judicial decision.

The Long Great Society stands out as a highly productive period of policy-making, both in Congress and in the other branches of government. This is also evident in multivariate models. Table 4.1 uses the total numbers of significant legislative, executive, and judicial enactments per biennium as dependent variables. The legislative models include a dummy variable for Unified Government, the House Polarization measure from McCarty, Poole, and Rosenthal, and dummy variables for the first congress of an administration and the first congress of a new party's rise to the presidency.[48] This follows the variables in McCarty's analysis, also using negative binomial count models.[49] The second column for each branch adds the Long Great Society period effect. The third column adds a one-period lagged dependent variable to assess the possibility that policy productivity is self-reinforcing. The executive and judicial branch models follow the same format, but I replace the House polarization measure with a measure of the distance between the president and the House mean (from DW-Nominate) for the executive models and a measure of Supreme Court polarization for the judicial models.[50]

The Long Great Society period effect is a highly important predictor of policymaking in all branches of government; each two-year period during the era produced 1.7 times as many significant laws, 1.6 times as many executive branch enactments, and 2.7 times as many judicial enactments.[51] Unified government does not significantly increase enactments in any branch of government and the direction is inconsistent with the idea that divided government plays a substantial role in reducing policy output. Party polarization does not significantly reduce output, although its sign is in the direction anticipated by McCarty, Poole, and Rosenthal for the legislative and the executive branches.[52] In the models with a lag term, the legislative branch enacts more policy during the first half of a presidential administration and the executive branch enacts more policy when a new party takes control of the presidency. In all three branches, the fit of the model substantially improves with the inclusion of the Long Great Society period effect.

I corroborated the significant effect of the Long Great Society with several alternative measures that focus only on the legislative branch, including the original Mayhew list of landmark laws, measures based on only the most significant laws, and a measure based on aggregating 19 analyses of important laws.[53] I also found that the period effect is not simply a product of a larger policy agenda. It remains large and significant in models including Sarah Binder's measure of the size of the policy agenda (based on newspaper editorials) and in models including the total number of Supreme Court decisions to predict judicial policy enactments.[54] The period effect is also not a function of changes in the "gridlock interval;" models including Keith Krehbiel's measure did not alter the effect of the Long Great Society.[55] Finally, the period effect lasts longer than

Table 4.1 **Models Predicting Significant Policy Enactments in All Branches of Government**

	No. of Legislative Enactments			No. of Executive Enactments			No. of Judicial Enactments		
Unified Government	-.29 (.18)	-.29 (.16)	-.13 (.13)	-.1 (.23)	-.11 (.21)	-.14 (.22)	.15 (.28)	-.2 (.23)	-.13 (.23)
Ideological Polarization (in branch)	-1.1 (.67)	-.35 (.63)	-.38 (.5)	-.25 (.54)	-.3 (.51)	-.21 (.5)	7.3*** (2.08)	3.5 (1.9)	2.33 (2.1)
1st Half of Presidential Administration	.16 (.21)	.17 (.18)	.29* (.15)	.03 (.26)	.03 (.24)	-.12 (.25)	—	—	—
1st Congress After New Party in Presidency	.21 (.25)	.23 (.22)	.25 (.17)	.35 (.3)	.36 (.28)	.61* (.29)	—	—	—
Long Great Society (1961-1976 period effect)	—	.52** (.18)	.32* (.14)	—	.46* (.2)	.45* (.2)	—	.98*** (.21)	.77** (.26)
Lagged Previous no. of Enactments (in branch)	—	—	.04*** (.01)	—	—	.04 (.03)	—	—	.06 (.04)
Constant	3.45	2.84	2.15	1.66	1.54	1.26	-1.08	-.05	.11
Log Likelihood	-102.4	-98.6	-88	-71.06	-68.72	-64.24	-68.06	-58.61	-56.51
Psuedo R^2	.03	.06	.14	.02	.05	.07	.08	.21	.21
Maximum Likelihood R^2	.18	.36	.62	.07	.21	.3	.32	.64	.66
N	30	30	29	30	30	29	30	30	29

Note: Table entries are negative binomial regression coefficients, with standard errors in parentheses. Ideological polarization and the lagged dependent variables use branch-specific measures. *$p < .05$; **$p < .01$; ***$p < .001$ (two-tailed).

the Great Society itself; including only a four-year effect does not show a strong relationship or eliminate the effect of the 1961–1976 period.

The Ideological Direction of Policy since 1945

Similar historical patterns are evident in the cumulative ideological content of policy change. Figure 4.2 illustrates the time series of the number of liberal enactments minus the number of conservative enactments per biennium for each branch of government. This is the measure preferred by Erikson, Mackuen, and Stimson, excluding enactments that were not expansions or contractions of government. Although only 56.6% of enactments were coded as liberal (8.9% are coded as conservative and the remainder as neither), these measures of ideological direction are strongly associated with the total number of enactments in each branch and period; the correlations are .69 for legislative productivity and liberalism, .63 for the executive branch, and .8 for the judicial branch. When government is active in any branch, it is usually more liberal (at least since 1945). Scholars have traditionally studied policymaking productivity and ideological direction with separate theories and empirical models, but they are clearly linked. This finding is not a product of any tendency by policy historians to be less likely to highlight conservative policy changes. If there is any difference,

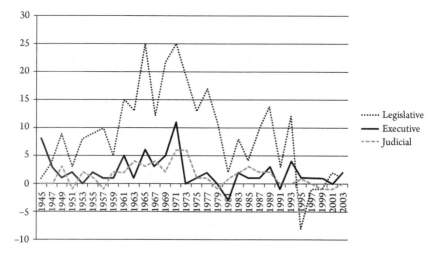

Figure 4.2 Biennial policy liberalism (liberal minus conservative enactments) in each branch of government

The figure depicts the difference between the number of liberal and conservative enactments during each biennial Congress identified in policy histories. Liberal enactments are those that expand the scope of government responsibility; conservative enactments contract it. Enactments that do not clearly expand or contract the scope of government are not included.

policy historians are more likely to identify conservative policy changes than contemporary journalists.[56]

Figure 4.2 shows that the Kennedy administration begins a period of liberal expansion that peaks during the Great Society and the first Nixon administration and declines until rising again during the second Reagan administration. Although broadly similar, there are important differences between the policy-making productivity and liberalism time series. The move toward conservative policymaking begins earlier in the 1970s than the trend toward less productive policymaking, indicating that the mid-1970s were a period of high productivity with a more mixed ideological direction. The first Clinton administration stands out as a period of productive oscillation: two years of productive liberal lawmaking are followed by two years of productive conservative lawmaking after the Republican takeover of Congress.

The associations in the ideological direction of policymaking among the branches of government are not as high as the associations in their productivity, but this is primarily true outside of the Long Great Society. Excluding 1961–1976, the correlation between legislative and executive branch liberalism is only .1; the equivalent correlation between legislative and judicial liberalism is only .25. The Long Great Society was thus a period of high productivity and liberalism in all three branches of government, but this pattern of three branches in sync with one another was not repeated before or after it. In many historical eras, administrative policymaking follows its own dynamics; it can respond to ideology, partisanship, and real-world events, and the effects are sometimes immediate and other times delayed.[57] Court decisions also often follow their own dynamics, but their policymaking role was ideologically aligned with the other two branches during the Long Great Society.[58]

Table 4.2 uses OLS regression models to predict liberalism in each branch in each biennium. The models include Democratic control of government and the ideological mood of public opinion in the previous four years, the two variables used in *The Macro Polity*.[59] I also include a measure of the ideology of each branch of government: the House mean for the legislative branch, the president's ideal point for the executive branch (from DW-Nominate), and the ideal point for the median Supreme Court justice for the judicial branch.[60] This should account for changes in the ideological preferences of the actors that are not reflected in party control of government. Ideology is coded with conservatism in the positive direction. For each branch, I again include a second model adding the Long Great Society period effect and a third model adding the lagged dependent variable.

The baseline model performs reasonably well only in the case of legislative liberalism. Although neither Democratic control nor ideology is a statistically significant predictor in the model, each is independently a strong predictor of

Table 4.2 **Models Predicting Biennial Policy Liberalism in Each Branch of Government**

	Legislative Liberalism			Executive Liberalism			Judicial Liberalism		
Democratic Control of House, Senate, Presidency	3.25 (1.9)	3.06 (1.89)	3.29 (2.31)	.23 (.79)	.29 (.80)	.91 (.77)	-.04 (.44)	-.07 (.41)	.44 (.52)
Ideology (house mean, president, median justice)	-37.29 (26.60)	-29.54 (25.31)	-55.38 (29.58)	-.08 (1.03)	.01 (1.05)	.43 (1.08)	.71 (.87)	.64 (.8)	-.4 (1)
Public Opinion			.21 (.39)			.19 (.15)			.02 (.13)
Public Ideology (Public mood in t-1, t-2)	-.44 (.37)	-.36 (.36)		.05 (.15)	.07 (.16)		-.07 (.11)	-.07 (.1)	
Long Great Society (1961–1976 period effect)	10.99** (3.2)	9.38** (2.71)	—	3.42* (1.48)	2.47 (1.32)	—	3.7** (1.25)	3.49*** (.82)	—
Lagged Previous Liberalism (in branch)	-.177 (.18)	—	—	-.28 (.21)	—	—	-.06 (.25)	—	—
Constant	25.6	20.8	-10	-2	-3.3	-10.3	4.5	4.3	-.28
R^2	.71	.69	.52	.35	.29	.18	.5	.5	.08
Adjusted R^2	.64	.64	.46	.19	.16	.06	.38	.41	-.05
N	26	26	26	26	26	26	26	26	26

Note: Table entries are OLS regression coefficients, with standard errors in parentheses. Ideology and the lagged dependent variables use branch-specific measures.
*$p < .05$; **$p < .01$; ***$p < .001$ (two-tailed).

legislative liberalism in bivariate models. Public opinion is never close to statistical significance as a predictor of liberalism in any branch; even models excluding the effects of Democratic control and ideology do not demonstrate effects. In the models for the ideological direction of executive and judicial policymaking, none of the three baseline variables are good predictors, even in combination.[61] Adding the Long Great Society period effect substantially improves the fit of the models for all three branches.

In the final models, each biennium during the Long Great Society was associated with 11 additional liberal legislative enactments (or 11 fewer conservative enactments), 3 additional liberal executive branch enactments, and 4 additional liberal judicial enactments. Replacing this variable with a period effect for only the Great Society (1964–1968) does not lead to a significant relationship or eliminate the effect of the 1961–1976 period. Krehbiel substitutes measures of public mood for Mayhew's period effect variable, arguing that it is a crude measure of public preferences; this conflation does not account for the changes in governance that took place during the Long Great Society. Whether predicting the amount of policymaking or its ideological direction, in Congress or other branches, the picture that emerges is of a distinct era of governance rather than a system moving consistently in response to public opinion or elections. Despite efforts to construct a *macro politics* model of public responsiveness, the categorization of the Long Great Society as an activist liberal period still offers more explanatory power.

Presidential Administrations and Governing Networks

Presidents clearly played a role in the extensive liberal policymaking of the era. The most frequently credited actors for policy enactments from 1945 to 2004 were presidents Johnson, Nixon, and Kennedy. Johnson was partially credited with 55 different policy enactments and Nixon with 50. Yet these presidents were not successful due primarily to the power of unilateral action. In nearly all cases, they were credited alongside members of Congress, executive agencies, or interest groups. Even their significant executive orders are rarely credited only to these presidents. No matter the branch of government that sets policy, presidents need other actors as coalition allies or partners in compromise to change policy.

Figure 4.3 illustrates each president's ties to other political actors. As a reminder, ties are formed when actors are jointly credited with the same policy enactment. The figure shows the number of members of Congress, interest groups, and other actors that jointly enacted policy with each president. Kennedy, Johnson, and Nixon are the most highly connected presidents, with

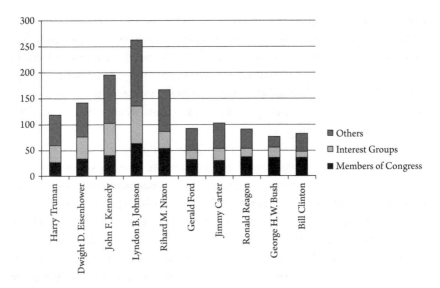

Figure 4.3 Ego affiliation networks by president

The figure depicts the number of actors jointly involved in policy enactments with each president. Each actor is categorized as a member of Congress, an interest group, or another type of actor.

Johnson and Nixon the most connected to members of Congress and Johnson and Kennedy leading in impactful connections to interest groups as well as other actors. The Long Great Society presidents were also connected with many of the same actors. All four presidents, for example, jointly enacted policy changes with Ted Kennedy, Hubert Humphrey, Jacob Javits, Abraham Ribicoff, the U.S. Conference of Mayors, the AFL-CIO, and the NAACP.

It was not only the presidents' ties that produced the policymaking era of the Long Great Society. The entire governing network held together for an extended time period. I test for this continuity of relationships by building affiliation networks for each four-year administration and then correlating them across time. A network correlation represents the level of association between two square matrices made up of the ties between all pairs of actors. Correlating the network from each four-year period with all of the others produces a set of associations between every two pairs of administration governing networks. The highest correlation between actor relationships among all administrations is between Nixon's first term and the Nixon/Ford term; the second highest correlation is between the Kennedy/Johnson term and Johnson's own term.

Quadratic assignment procedure regression, a technique based on 2,000 random permutations of network connections to correct for autocorrelation, can be used to predict correlations between each pair of networks.[62] The idea is to see what factors explain similarities among the ties between each pair of administrations. Table 4.3 reports the results of this regression model.[63]

Because the most important variable making governing networks similar is likely to be time, the model includes a measure of the years apart between each administration (measured from the center of the administration). This variable is significant, unsurprisingly indicating that administrations closer together in time produce similar actor associations. The model also includes dummy variables indicating whether administrations were tied to the same president or the same political party. It also includes a variable for difference in network size between administrations to evaluate whether administration networks are similar to one another simply by virtue of the number of actors they contain. Of these variables, the results show that only networks belonging to the same president are significantly more similar. Finally, the model includes a period effect variable that is coded one only if both administrations were during the Long Great Society and zero for all other pairs of administration governing networks. This variable is statistically significant and indicates that the strength of ties between actors in the four administrations of the Long Great Society was sustained.

In other words, dividing the Long Great Society network into smaller increments of time still produces evidence that the governing network hangs together over the entire period. The era's governing network is thus not a snapshot of connections during any one administration. Based on the model, this network was consistently tied together over time to the extent that it was not far from what would be expected from having a single president govern for the entire 16-year period. Whereas when a new president is elected—especially of a different party—they normally bring a new administrative and congressional coterie to Washington, the Long Great Society administrations relied on many of the same policymaking ties through four bipartisan administrations.

The Governing Network across Issue Areas

The Long Great Society governing network was also similarly active across many different issue areas. Figure 4.4 depicts a two-mode network connecting actors and issue areas during the full period. Grey circles represent actors and white squares represent issue areas. As a reminder, the strength of their connections depends on the number of policy changes in each issue area for which policy historians credited each actor. The network has a large number of actors, but a much smaller number are active in more than one or two policy areas. The network does not divide into three or four large components based on issue area types, as would be visible if separate groups were active in social policy and economic policy or any other subsets of the policy agenda. Instead, the network has a core of actors that are active in many policy areas.

Table 4.3 **Model Predicting Presidential Administration Governing Network Correlations**

	Administration Governing Network Correlations
Years Apart	$-.0005^{**}$
	(.0001)
Same Party	.0028
	(.0032)
Same President	.0482**
	(.01)
Long Great Society	.0303**
(1961–1976 period effect)	(.0084)
Network Size	.0
	(.0001)
Constant	.0179
R^2	.54
N	210

Note: Table entries are regression coefficients, with standard errors in parentheses. The dependent and independent variables are similarity matrices between pairs of presidential administrations. The test of statistical significance is a non-parametric test using quadratic assignment procedure. $^*p < .05$; $^{**}p < .01$; $^{***}p < .001$ (two-tailed).

The most central actors in the network are listed in figure 4.5, which depicts the core of the same network in figure 4.4 (with the layout readjusted after removing actors involved in fewer than four areas). The presidents are the most widely involved; one reason is that Kennedy, Johnson, and Nixon were all credited with policy changes that occurred before or after they left office. One idiosyncratic feature of this core is the role of the Kennedy family; John, Ted, and Robert were each active in producing policy change in at least four different issue domains, often together. Other central actors include several executive departments, a few interest groups, some liberal senators from both parties, and consumer advocate Ralph Nader. Some actors, like the Department of Justice and the NAACP, were active in all three branches of government during the period.[64] Despite the centrality of civil rights in the policy agenda of this era and the NAACP's organizational role, all of the individuals in the core of the Long Great Society network were white men. This core of actors was not always aligned when policy was initially developed, but it came together

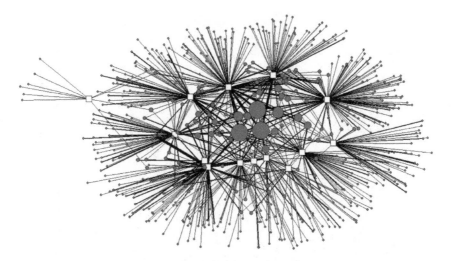

Figure 4.4 Full actor/issue governing network during the Long Great Society

The figure depicts a two-mode actor/issue network based on policy enactments from 1961 to 1976. Grey circles represent actors credited with policy enactments. White squares represent issue areas. The links connect actors that were credited with the enactments in each area (with the width representing the number of enactments where they were credited).

in the compromises and coalitions that made extensive liberal policymaking possible.[65]

The Long Great Society governing network was quite different than the ones that preceded and followed it. To compare, table 4.4 reports characteristics of four different networks of similar time periods corresponding to policies enacted from 1945 to 1960, 1961 to 1976, 1977 to 1992, and 1993 to 2004. The networks include all actors credited with policy enactments connected to the 14 domestic policy issue domains. The Long Great Society era had a much larger governing network; more than 600 actors were reportedly responsible for changing national policy during the era. The network reflects the increase in political mobilization during the 1960s and 1970s, with many new interest groups and government units engaged in policymaking.[66] The subset of involved actors contracted again at the end of the era. The other network measures listed in the table account for these differences in the size of the networks.

The two-mode network associated with the Long Great Society has a pattern of relationships that matches a core–periphery structure. The core–periphery model compares each network to an ideal type in which a central group of actors is closely tied to one another and surrounded by a periphery of less connected actors (a categorical distinction). The coreness statistic reports the extent to which each network fits this ideal type; the core density statistic reports the

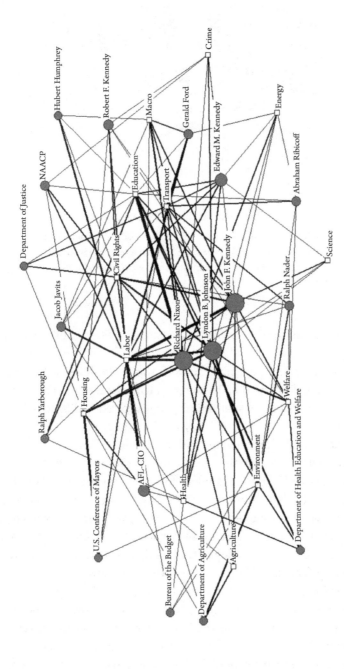

Figure 4.5 Core of actor/issue governing network during the Long Great Society

The figure depicts the core of a two-mode actor/issue network based on policy enactments from 1961 to 1976. The core includes the actors involved in at least four issue areas during the period. The links connect actors that were credited with the enactments in each area (with the width representing the number of enactments where they were credited).

average number of connections among the group of actors identified as the core of the network. High values here would indicate that a network is far removed from the "hollow core" that characterized some previous issue networks.[67] In all four of the networks, most actors lie outside the core of the network and are not involved in multiple issue areas. Yet the Long Great Society governing network most closely matches a system where one set of actors dominates policymaking in all issue areas. Authors studying many different issue areas credited the same set of actors for policymaking from 1961 to 1976 but did not do so for policy-making in other eras.

This structure did not arise primarily because of bipartisan relationships or alliances between liberals and conservatives. In fact, ties during the Long Great Society were more likely to be among co-partisans and co-ideologues. To see this, table 4.4 includes an External-Internal (E-I) Index for two ideological sets: liberal groups and Democratic politicians, on the one hand, and conser-vative groups and Republican politicians, on the other. The index is calculated by subtracting the number of ties within each subset from the number of ties between the two subsets and dividing by the total number of ties within and between the subsets. It measures the extent to which ties are disproportion-ately across groups (positive) or within groups (negative). Ties during the Long Great Society were the least likely to cut across party and ideological lines. This is primarily because most of the participants were liberal organizations or Democrats; Nixon, Ford, and Javits were prominent exceptions but they cooper-ated with larger groups of Democrats to expand government.

Table 4.4 also reports the most central actors, those that were credited with the largest number of policy enactments in each period. The most central actors were presidents during each era, but interest groups and members of Congress were also central. Johnson was central both as Senate majority leader and as president. Bob Dole was central in the latter two periods. Four out of five central actors in the first two periods were Democrats or liberals, whereas four out of five of the central actors in the 1977–1992 period were Republicans. The con-servative shift of the mid-1970s is thus reflected in the changing composition of the governing network in the following period, which produced much less new policy.

Reconciling the Long Great Society with Theories of Policymaking

General ideological and partisan trends in Congress do not fully explain the pat-terns of cooperation among policymakers or the ideological direction of policy output. Since 1945, the most significant phenomenon was a sustained period of

Table 4.4 **Characteristics of Governing Networks**

	1945–1960	1961–1976	1977–1992	1993–2004
Actors	295	601	401	201
Coreness	.108	.147	.112	.119
Core Density	.052	.174	.083	.015
E-I Index of Ideological Groups	−.123	−.265	−.198	−.156
Central Actors	1. Eisenhower	1. JFK	1. Reagan	1. Clinton
	2. Truman	2. LBJ	2. H. W. Bush	2. W. Bush
	3. NAACP	3. Nixon	3. Carter	3. Bob Dole
	4. LBJ	4. Ted Kennedy	4. Bob Dole	4. Chuck
	5. Wilbur Mills	5. AFL-CIO	5. David Stockman	Schumer
				5. Newt Gingrich

Note: The top three rows are characteristics of two-mode actor/issue networks associated with policy enactments in each historical period. The E-I index is based on the number of ties within each ideological group (liberals and conservatives) compared to the number of ties between the groups; it uses affiliation networks with ties governed by actors given joint credit for the same enactments. There is no useful measure of estimation uncertainty associated with the two-mode core-periphery model or the E-I index.

active liberal policymaking from 1961 to 1976. During the Long Great Society, presidents, administration officials, members of Congress, and interest groups jointly constituted a multi-issue governing network that produced a large bulge of policy in all branches of government, moving policy decidedly in a liberal direction. The exceptional character of this era, and its associated governing network, is a key to understanding both the productivity and the ideological direction of domestic policymaking since 1945. The analysis requires a reconsideration of theories of American policymaking.

First, the results are inconsistent with *macro politics* theories of policy change that focus on systematic patterns associating policy output with political variables changing over time, such as the ideological direction of public opinion, party control of the presidency, or polarization in Congress. Federal policymaking features complicated interactions among many actors and evolves as an entire system of interdependent parts, rather than a series of independent institutions.[68] Observed associations between political inputs and policy outputs may be dependent on the patterns of cooperation among policymakers. A small number of actors can have an outsized influence on policy results.

The role of governing networks hardly makes partisanship and ideological preferences unimportant. Democratic and liberal electoral victories may have long-term causal relationships with liberal policymaking that helped enable the emergence of the Long Great Society. Democrats controlled the House and the Senate throughout the era and a liberal shift in public mood preceded it. Public opinion began to move steadily in a conservative direction from the mid-1960s until 1980; if this contributed to the end of the period, it did so with a substantial lag. Likewise, partisan electoral change only somewhat matches the era's beginning and end; Democrats gained seats in House in the 1958, 1964, and 1974 elections but lost substantial ground in the 1966 elections and lost substantial Senate seats in 1968. The liberal gains in the House following the Watergate scandal empowered a new generation of legislators to change the internal rules of Congress, disempowering conservative committee chairs.[69] Curiously, the policy legacy of these reformed congresses was the Long Great Society's disintegration.

A numerical advantage of liberal ideologues and Democrats probably makes it easier to form coalitions to expand the scope of government. Ideological polarization and divided government likewise require changes in the patterns of cooperation necessary for policy change. But neither unified government nor ideological homogeneity makes policy change inevitable. Both sets of factors work through the mechanism of changing patterns of cooperation among political elites, and these patterns are responsive to many other factors beyond ideology and partisanship. The governing network of the Long Great Society illustrates how a largely liberal network can drive policymaking during periods of both unified and divided government. Democratic majorities and liberal politicians no doubt helped its emergence, but it survived a conservative electoral backlash and then began to reverse course even as the Democrats were in ascendance. Partisan and ideological trends are part of the political context that enables productive patterns of cooperation to emerge, but they do not lead unswervingly toward policy change. They make some historical eras more conducive to the necessary coalitions and compromises that political leaders still must build.

Second, there are lessons for the *agenda setting* theories assessed in chapter 3. Problem prioritization is seen as a response to a constrained policy agenda.[70] Yet some congresses have substantially larger policy agendas than others.[71] The results here show that the production of policy enactments across all branches of government varies even more dramatically. The system-level capacity to enable policy change also seems to be related to the ability of a governing network to tackle many issues at once, rather than to choose among their most important priorities. Government may be able to enact more policies when a core group of actors is responsible for moving policy forward on a variety of fronts, rather than by waiting for issues to rise on the agenda after being advanced in separate subsystems.

Despite building a theory of policymaking for many historical eras, Baumgartner and Jones understood the uniqueness of the Long Great Society. Most of the issue area transformations that they tracked in *Agendas and Instability in American Politics* coincided with the period. They highlighted how the system-wide features of policymaking had changed:

> The period of the late 1960s through the early 1970s was one of remarkable policy activity in the United States, one that affected governing arrangements from policy subsystems to the very structure of federalism. The positive-feedback systems that can occur for the individual policy communities... also occur for the grand secular trends.[72]

Aside from the role of agenda setting in their theory, my findings are highly compatible with their analyses—especially their empirical stories of policy change following the 1970s.

Third, my results are in some tension with equilibrium-based separation of powers theories. These accounts suggest that voting rules and institutional designs aggregate pre-existing preferences within each institution. There is also previous evidence that the branches rarely coordinate their actions.[73] Policy history suggests that the patterns of cooperation among political elites do not necessarily follow from their ideological preferences or institutional locations. The total policy output and ideological direction of policy in the three branches matches in at least one historical era. My analysis leaves out much of the activity of each branch, including many annual appropriations decisions in Congress and many non-policymaking actions in the executive and judicial branches. These activities, as well as symbolic actions like non-binding votes, may be easier to predict based on the partisanship and ideology of the actors. The aggregate preferences of the actors in each institution may also better explain the common success of the status quo over any policy change.

Nevertheless, individual leadership is important and does not always follow from ideological ideal points. After all, Johnson and Nixon, a southern Democrat and a Republican who were the primary enemies of the 1960s protesters and regularly vilified in movement materials, oversaw the period with the most liberal policy results since 1945. The point is not that their ideologies were misconstrued, but that their policy legacies turned out differently than one would expect from their viewpoints alone. The many signals that influence our impressions of political figures, including the symbolic politics of campaigns, public statements, and voting patterns, may not predict the likely direction of their policies. Policymaking in a large decentralized government requires individuals and organizations to coalesce around policy proposals that minimize opposition and then compromise and cajole many others to gain their acquiescence. That process is different from simply aggregating pre-existing preferences through institutional rules and procedures.

Studies of policymaking cannot ignore presidential leadership or condense it by focusing only on the president's partisanship. Idiosyncratic aspects of presidents, such as Nixon's view of the presidency, may have an independent influence on history. Nearly all observers of politics acknowledge this, but many political scientists resist it; presidency research suffers mightily from the "many variables, small-n" problem of causal inference. Several scholars have attempted to address this problem by grouping presidents into eras or regimes responsive to public mood, technological capability, or presidential practice.[74] The results in this chapter group presidents based on their congressional experience and their ties to other actors in the political system, which can build over contiguous administrations. The existence of a single era of presidential leadership does not imply that the process is cyclical or that a new era begins when another ends.[75] Instead, a linked era of presidential leadership may be preceded and followed by administrations that do not build on the networks of one another.

Fourth, the aggregate view from policy history also helps modify historical institutional perspectives, which tend to focus on path dependence and division by critical junctures.[76] The results here show that the amount and ideological direction of policy rarely build on that of the previous period.[77] Only the Long Great Society network featured a core of connected actors that remained major players for more than a decade. The end of a coherent period of policymaking may not coincide with the beginning of another. Policy historians show that the combined trends of each era come together in the cooperative actions of policy-makers. Some of the trends that helped to create the Long Great Society, such as the rise in social protest and riots, coincided with the period's beginning and end, but others, such as changes in Senate procedures and rules on standing in the federal courts, may have been helpful conditions for enabling it even though they did not end as the period drew to a close. Many of our existing qualitative views of the policymaking system come from observers in the late 1970s or stud-ies of policymaking in the late 1970s.[78] This era should be considered part of the breaking up of one policymaking system, but not necessarily the beginning of a well-developed alternative. Both before and after the 16-year period, policymak-ing lacks a sustained direction.

Even Schlesinger and Huntington, the originators of the Long Great Society period effect, underestimated the role of the patterns of cooperation among spe-cific institutional actors in creating and prolonging it. Both viewed policy change as a largely inevitable response to longer-term swings in elite and public moods. Absent attention to the patterns of cooperation that produce policy change, dis-tinctions about the ideological mood of entire eras may be no more helpful than *macro politics* models in predicting policy output.

Neither governing network composition nor structure constitute exogenous variables that arise independently of political trends or policy development. The era of social protest identified by Huntington, along with numerous institutional innovations and behavioral changes, provided the context within which the Long Great Society network developed. Early policy results allowed the same set of actors to build on their success. Governing networks provide a tool for understanding the patterns of coalition and compromise that are responsible for policy enactments. They do not demonstrate that pre-existing relationships among institutional actors were solely responsible for enabling productive eras. Instead, governing networks are a mechanism by which institutional and behav-ioral trends combine to produce policy change.

These networks are not automatic responses to electoral or ideological changes. A long era of consistent policymaking in one ideological direction is hardly the norm. The only such period that the United States has experienced since 1945 relied on a pattern of cooperation among a small group of actors active in many issue areas in all branches of government. Scholars cannot assume that political inputs lead inexorably to policy output either as a consistent func-tion of who governs or as an outcome of a public pendulum swinging from left to right. Instead, cooperation among policymakers is the necessary ingredient for policy change. The Long Great Society stands out in American policy history because of its coalitions and compromises, not just because favorable political conditions swept all policymakers along for the ride.

CHAPTER 5

Issue Politics and the Policy Process

President Obama announced the largest ever required increase in automobile fuel economy in July 2011. Although automakers generally opposed the new standards, the largest companies and the United Auto Workers union joined Obama for his announcement: "The Environmental Protection Agency and the Department of Transportation have worked closely with auto manufacturers, the state of California, environmental groups, and other stakeholders for several months [in preparing the new policy]."[1] The final rule will reflect several typical features of transportation policy: it involved administrative policymaking that was influenced by several agencies and many interest groups.

In January 2012, the US Supreme Court unanimously decided to restrict the ability of law enforcement to use Global Positioning System tracking systems on suspects without a warrant. The justices disagreed on their reasoning, with some referencing protections against search and seizure and others focusing on a right to privacy. Both areas of criminal justice policy were well-traveled ground for the judiciary, with courts issuing several important Fourth Amendment decisions each decade. Encountering a new technology, the courts also had to grapple with scientific evidence and data on users' expectations of privacy.

As Congress was engaged with other matters, these two branches were changing policy in issue areas that match their typical focus. When a new technology changed the context of policymaking, the branch that always handles criminal justice addressed it rather than requiring a restart of the policy process. When a new Republican majority was elected, it was still up to the Obama administration to issue requirements in transportation policy. The relative role of interest groups and research in policy development also turns out to be typical of these issue areas.

Although previous chapters have been assessing policymaking across all issues, it is unlikely that policymaking takes exactly the same form in all policy areas. Scholars seek to understand how the political system produces public policy, but the answers may differ across issue areas.[2] Although cognizant of these likely differences, scholars rarely consider them systematically. Across issue areas, does American national policymaking take place in the same venues with the same frequency? Is the relative importance of different political circumstances similar? Are the composition of participants in policymaking and the structure of the networks that connect them similar? If differences are widespread, can they be easily summarized?

Across the 14 domestic issue areas, neither the causal factors in the policy process nor the composition and structure of issue networks are universal. This chapter argues that each issue area is distinct from the others in a few ways, but typical in most respects. Categorizations that divide issues into types amenable to public participation and types destined for interest group negotiations are unlikely to correctly characterize influential factors. Separable types of policymaking do not follow from any known issue area categorization.

Investigations of policymaking are likely to focus on particular aspects of the policy process based on issue area case selection decisions, even though they seek generalized knowledge. The relevant circumstances and actors change subtly with the issue territory, as do the relationships among actors. Rather than assuming universality in policymaking or relying on typologies, scholars should be attentive to the few ways that each issue area differs from the others.

This chapter investigates these similarities and differences. First, I review ideas about issue area differences from *issue typologies* and studies of issue networks. Second, I argue that issue area differences should be seen as issue-specific exceptions to general patterns, rather than categorical distinctions based on one or two dimensions. Third, I review the record of significant policy enactments in each issue area and the explanations for policy change. Fourth, I analyze the networks associated with each policy area. Fifth, I search for underlying dimensions of issue area differences. Finally, I provide descriptions of the unique features of each issue area and their similarities to guide future scholarship.

Variable Politics by Issue Area

Theories of *agenda setting* and *macro politics* largely sidestep the question of differences across issue areas and are meant to apply to many domains. Although these theories are all applied flexibly to different issues, their applications tend to concentrate in particular areas. Among *agenda setting* theories, Punctuated Equilibrium studies focus more on budgets, the Independent Streams account draws more from transportation and health, and nearly 64%

of applications of the Advocacy Coalition Framework focus on environmental or energy policy.[3]

Issue area differences could help reconcile accounts of policymaking from different theoretical perspectives. For example, Punctuated Equilibrium accounts imply that significant policy change is driven by episodic agendas; other incremental policy changes are thought to be less important. In contrast, historical institutionalism argues that most significant policymaking is developmental; it relies on a path dependent process where early decisions constrain later decisions. Alternatively, some issue areas may be more episodic and others more path dependent.

A few theories of the policy process explicitly analyze issue area differences. They tend to involve issue categorization schemes that focus on one or two dimensions of variation associated with clear types. Theodore Lowi uses a three-category typology, categorizing policies as redistributive, distributive, or regulatory.[4] The idea is that scholars should expect to find differences in the politics of each issue area based on the kind of policy under debate and who has something to gain or lose from policy action. Applying Lowi's typology might categorize criminal justice and energy as regulatory issues governed by adjudication, transportation and health as distributive issues where policymakers seek to satisfy interest groups, and social welfare as a redistributive issue where conflict will be partisan and ideological.

Another famous typology comes from James Q. Wilson. He divides policy issues based on whether the costs and benefits of potential policies are concentrated or dispersed.[5] Energy might be categorized as a form of "interest group politics" where both costs and benefits are narrow. Environment and criminal justice might be governed by "entrepreneurial politics" where only costs are concentrated. Housing and labor could be seen as "client politics" areas with only concentrated benefits. Macroeconomics might be a quintessential form of "majoritarian politics" where both costs and benefits are broad.

These typologies have been difficult for scholars to follow, since most policy areas have elements of multiple types. They have not proved especially fruitful in understanding policy area differences, but new typologies have nonetheless proliferated.[6] The continued interest in typologies highlights the need to understand variation across issue areas in the venues where policymaking takes place and the factors responsible for policy change.

If differences across issue areas produce distinct politics, scholars should also observe different kinds of networks emerging in different areas. Policymaking in some areas may resemble "iron triangles" involving an alliance among client interest groups, an executive agency, and relevant congressional committees.[7] Issue areas like agriculture, energy, housing, labor, science, and transportation have these three associated institutions and are sometimes considered iron triangles. Hugh Heclo argues that, instead of iron triangles, "issue networks" now jointly govern many issue areas, led by experts who share knowledge rather than institutional position.[8] Both concepts involve a closely connected and allied leadership, but issue networks envision a kind of technocracy whereas iron triangles suppose that three institutions unite in favoring one public constituency. In contrast, scholars analyzing policymaker relationships in agriculture, energy, health, and labor policy find a "hollow core" with no central players arbitrating conflict among competing interests.[9] Others even argue that not all policy communities are large and broad enough to merit the label of issue networks.[10] Yet comparative analysis of issue networks is rare. Network studies feature the same strategy as *issue typologies*: they aim to find a few underlying dimensions on which to clearly differentiate issues areas.

Issue typologies, as well as ideal types of issue networks, provide a way to avoid characterizing policymaking as uniformly driven by factors inside or outside of government institutions. Scholars divide issues into types because they assume that some policy areas might be driven by trends in public opinion and election results whereas others are guided by institutional compromises among elites. In other words, perhaps readers do not have to choose between a policy process characterized by bargaining among policymakers and interest groups (like the one I propose in previous chapters) and one characterized by responsiveness to public concerns and opinions (like the one favored by *agenda setting* and *macro politics* theories). Perhaps some issue areas fall into each category.

Alternatively, if *issue typologies* do not usefully divide issues based on distinct types of policymaking, no issue area may be characterized primarily by public mobilization. Policy change across issues may be primarily the product of coalition and compromise in governing networks, with somewhat varying influence from external factors. Previous research has not uncovered typologies that successfully explain how the politics of policymaking or the character of networks differ across issue areas. Perhaps the differences are less stark than imagined.

Issue Area Differences as Exceptions to General Patterns

Kevin Smith advocates a move from typologies to taxonomies, classifying items "on the basis of empirically observable and measurable characteristics."[11] This chapter generally takes this approach, addressing two fundamental problems of *issue typologies*. First, typologies assume that differences in the politics of issue areas can be distilled into only a few important dimensions. Second, they assume that most issue areas will fall in a clear zone along these dimensions, enabling scholars to place them in boxes. Both assumptions may be unwarranted.

Issue areas may have broadly similar policymaking, with each issue area standing out in only a few important aspects. This perspective should apply to both the institutions and circumstances that make policy change possible and the actors responsible for policy change and their relationships. Whether scholars are looking at where and how often policy change occurs, the role of circumstantial factors in driving policy development, or the people and organizations that jointly bring it about, they should not expect issue area differences to conform to any typology.

Issue area differences manifest themselves in both obvious and subtle ways. It should be no surprise that criminal justice policy change happens more often in the courts compared to other areas; after all, a large proportion of court proceedings confront related issues. Learning that energy policy is less likely to be affected by public opinion than other areas, in contrast, may elicit more surprise. These differences are unlikely to be reducible to a few categories. Categorizing criminal justice as a court-centered issue area would miss all of the ways that it is similar to other issue areas while highlighting only one of its features. Similarly, categorizing energy policy as immune from public opinion would also put too much emphasis on a single aspect of its politics.

Issue network differences are also unlikely to allow categorization into separable types. In particular, the composition of networks (such as the partisan or institutional affiliations of its members) may vary independently of their structure. A large issue network bridging two branches of government may determine macroeconomic policy, but this may not correspond to a category that any other issue network fits well within. Issue area differences are thus unlikely to correspond to the characteristics that make typologies useful. Scholars should instead specify the differences between issue areas, even if they only amount to a series of exceptions to the typical policy process and the common features of governing networks.

Policy Enactments across Issue Areas

Policy is enacted in every branch of government and issue area, though hardly with equal frequency. Figure 5.1 depicts the number of significant policy enactments in each issue area in each venue since 1945, separating laws passed by Congress from executive orders by the president, administrative agency rules, and court decisions. Significant policy change has been much more frequent in environmental and health policy and less frequent in education, social welfare, housing, agriculture, and science. Differences in policy productivity across issue areas may be partially a product of category definitions, with areas like health more broadly defined than less productive issue areas like agriculture.

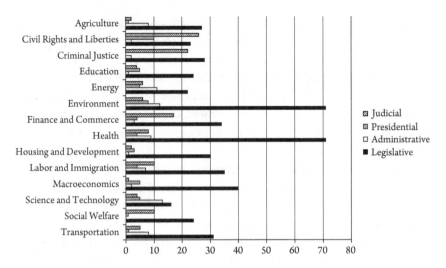

Figure 5.1 Policy enactments by venue and policy area

The figure depicts the number of policy enactments in each branch of government from 1945 to 2004, based on policy histories of each issue area.

Nevertheless, the productivity in health and the environment does reflect successful efforts to dramatically expand federal intervention into the economy and society since World War II. Health has been a constant concern, with new programs created to fund health research, care for the elderly and disabled, build hospital infrastructure, and regulate public health. The surge of environmental policymaking began later, peaking in the 1970s as activists for clean air and water joined forces with those concerned with conservation, climate, and biodiversity.

All other issue areas clustered between 34 and 61 enactments since 1945, averaging 0.8 significant enactments per year. The frequency of policy enactments across issue areas is partially a consequence of their relative prominence on the government agenda (which is relatively stable across time). The correlation between the total policy enactments in each issue area and the number of congressional hearings over the entire period is.49. Transportation is an exception: it is regularly on the agenda without producing many policy enactments.

Congress dominates policymaking in most areas but a few issue areas stand out for the extent to which policy enactments occur in other branches of government. In civil rights, criminal justice, and finance and commerce, policymaking occurs disproportionately in the judiciary. Compared to congressional lawmaking, policymaking in the federal courts is much more concentrated in a few issue areas. This distribution reflects the kinds of cases that the courts hear; these three areas are all associated with more total Supreme Court cases.

Enactments in the energy and science domains are more likely to come from administrative agencies. For example, the struggles over reformulated gasoline rules in the 1990s involved repeated discussions among interest groups, state regulators, and environmental organizations; all took place within the structure of informal consultations and official rulemaking at the Environmental Protection Agency.[12]

Policy changes also differ across issue areas in their ideological direction. Figure 5.2 illustrates the proportion of significant policy enactments that are liberal (expand the scope of government) within each policy domain over the entire 60-year period, with issue areas ordered from most liberal to most conservative. The vast majority of civil rights and housing policy enactments are liberal, but only one-in-three enactments are liberal in science and in finance. Civil rights policy saw a steady expansion of the federal role, whereas finance witnessed periods of both regulation and deregulation. For comparison, I include a measure of the liberal proportion of governing networks. In other words, this represents the proportion of all actors credited with policy change since 1945 in each issue area that are either Democratic officeholders or liberal organizations. There is less variation here, with liberals accounting for between 20% and 45% of participants in all issue domains. Many actors in the network are categorized as neither liberal nor conservative; liberals and Democrats almost always outnumber conservatives and Republicans across issue areas.

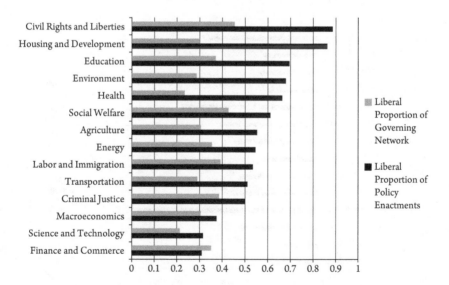

Figure 5.2 Liberalism of policy enactments and governing networks across issue domains

The figure depicts the proportion of significant policy enactments that expand the scope of government and the proportion of actors responsible for these policy enactments that are Democrats or liberal organizations in each Policy Agendas Project major policy domain.

The correlation between the measures of liberalism in enactments and governing networks is positive but modest ($r = .32$). Some policy areas, such as social welfare, involve liberals pursuing liberal policy changes; others like health involve fewer liberals but usually involve expansions of government. Areas like finance, in contrast, involve liberals and conservatives pursuing a mix of policy changes. Across issue areas, few significant policy changes contract the scope of government (with some exceptions in macroeconomics and finance). In most policy areas, the question is what actors ally around specific efforts to expand government. This does not seem to require overwhelmingly liberal coalitions.

Path Dependent and Episodic Policymaking

Issue areas also differ substantially in the extent to which their policymaking is path dependent or episodic. Figure 5.3 compares the percentage of policy enactments where policy historians referred to factors related to path dependence with the percentage of enactments where they pointed to particular events driving policy change. This does not mean that policy historians used the theoretical language of path dependence or focusing events; most did not. Instead, explanations involving path dependence include any statement that the enactment was an extension of an earlier policy, that an earlier choice made the enactment

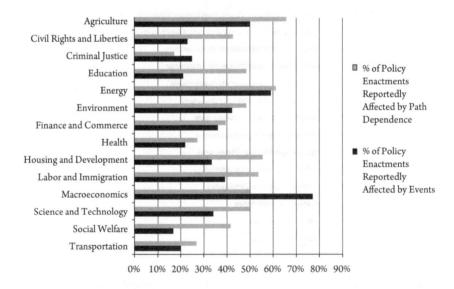

Figure 5.3 Developmental and episodic reported causes of enactments by policy area

The figure depicts the percentage of policy enactments in each issue area that were reportedly affected by path dependence (including earlier policy choices that made the enactment more likely or eliminated alternatives) and focusing events (including wars and economic downturns). The reports are based on policy histories in each area covering significant policy enactments from 1945-2004.

more likely, or that an earlier choice eliminated a potential alternative policy. Explanations involving events point to the effects of war, economic downturn, a government financial problem, a focusing event such as a school shooting, or a case highlighting problems in a previous policy.

The results show that policy enactments in agriculture, energy, housing, and labor are most likely to be path dependent. The regularity of farm bill updates provides a quintessential example. The 1948 version was passed because "the urgent need to replace terminating wartime measures sparked action within the [Department of Agriculture] and by agriculture committees in the Congress."[13] The 1990 version "represents only incremental change from the 1985 farm legislation, moving further in the direction."[14] Enactments in energy and macroeconomics are most likely to be associated with events, especially nuclear disasters and economic downturns. Several oil policy changes in the 1970s and 1980s were precipitated by wars in the Middle East and Iranian actions.[15]

These two categories of explanatory factors do not directly trade-off with one another. Some policy changes were not associated with either past policy choices or focusing events. Others were associated with both, such as reauthorization of an environmental statute in response to a natural disaster. Nevertheless, more episodic policy areas were associated with more congressional hearings. The number of hearings in each issue area is correlated at .46 with the difference between the percentage of enactments that were episodic and path dependent. Analyzing the issue agenda may thus track episodic issue areas while missing significant enactments in areas with more path dependence.

Reported Circumstances Responsible for Policy Enactments

Policy histories also point to somewhat different types of circumstances in explaining policy change in each area. Table 5.1 reports the percentage of policy enactments in each issue area associated with four categories of causal factors inside of government institutions. There is one category corresponding to each branch of government, but circumstances in each branch can also be cited in explanations for enactments in another branch. For example, a court ruling or executive action may contribute to a new law. The table also reports the percentage of enactments in each issue area that were the product of a bipartisan coalition or compromise, as reported in the policy histories.

Factors related to legislative branch bargaining, key votes, and congressional leadership were associated with a majority of enactments in education, housing, labor, macroeconomics, social welfare, and transportation; they were less common in civil rights, finance, health, and science. With the exception of science (where policymaking takes place disproportionately in the executive branch),

Table 5.1 **Reported Internal Government Circumstances Associated with Policy Enactments in Issue Area Histories**

	Legislative	Executive	Judicial	Bipartisan Coalition
Agriculture	42.11%	71.05%	5.26%	36.84%
Civil Rights and Liberties	26.23%	47.54%	44.26%	24.59%
Criminal Justice	30.77%	44.23%	23.08%	21.15%
Education	54.55%	75.76%	21.21%	36.36%
Energy	34.09%	65.91%	15.91%	34.09%
Environment	46.39%	65.98%	24.74%	28.87%
Finance and Commerce	25.86%	39.66%	32.76%	24.14%
Health	29.47%	52.63%	8.42%	20.00%
Housing and Development	50.00%	69.44%	5.56%	41.67%
Labor and Immigration	55.36%	58.93%	14.21%	44.64%
Macroeconomics	58.33%	83.33%	12.50%	54.17%
Science and Technology	18.42%	50.00%	15.79%	5.26%
Social Welfare	55.56%	58.33%	8.33%	38.89%
Transportation	57.78%	71.11%	8.89%	26.67%

Note: The table reports the percentage of enactments that involved each category of factors, according to policy historians.

all policy areas involved legislative factors in at least one-out-of-four enactments. Executive branch factors, such as presidential or administrative agency leadership, frequently contributed to policy change in most issue areas; the executive branch played a consistently important role in agriculture, education, macroeconomics, and transportation. Factors related to the executive branch were mentioned in a majority of enactments in most issue areas, with only finance, criminal justice, and civil rights as exceptions (the most popular areas of court concentration). The role of the judicial branch was again more variable across issue areas. Factors related to the judicial branch were credited with many policy changes in civil rights and finance and some in criminal justice, education, and the environment; most other areas showed comparatively little judicial influence.

Bipartisanship was a surprisingly common feature of policy changes in macroeconomics. One policy historian described the lead-up to the Tax Reform

Act of 1986: "During 1984 and 1985, while the deficit crisis mounted, both the Reagan administration and congressional Democrats, supported by Treasury staff, edged into a competitive scramble to occupy the high ground of tax reform. The consequence of this process was the passage of...the Tax Reform Act of 1986...the most dramatic transformation of federal tax policy since World War II."[16] Another historian reported that earlier tax policy was also bipartisan: "In the prosperity of the postwar years, tax policy...reflected the two-party acceptance of the New Deal, government intervention, and progressivity....Both parties endorsed an agenda of helping capitalism rather than fighting it."[17] Although we hear of repeated partisan fights over basic redistributive issues, macroeconomic policy enactments tend to involve bipartisan coalitions. Bipartisanship was also somewhat common in agriculture, education, energy, housing, labor, and social welfare. Bipartisan enacting coalitions may have been more evident than these estimates suggest; policy historians specifically pointed to Republican-Democrat cooperation only when they thought it contributed directly to the success or content of policy change.

Table 5.2 reports the percentage of policy enactments in each issue area associated with six categories of external causal factors. These categories correspond to those reviewed in chapter 3, though they are not mutually exclusive or exhaustive. The only external factors associated with a majority of enactments in any issue area were those related to interest groups and research. Not one issue area showed more consistent influence from public opinion and the media than from internal legislative and executive branch maneuvering. Factors related to interest group advocacy and lobbying are the only external circumstances that influence policy change as often as internal factors.

Media coverage was most commonly associated with policymaking in macroeconomics, the environment, social welfare, and transportation. Reports of pollution, poverty, and dilapidated infrastructure all play roles in policy development. The 1980 "Superfund" environmental cleanup law was "prompted by media coverage of the Love Canal incident and related events throughout the United States."[18] Another policy historian agreed: "Superfund was passed in 1980 in the wake of widely publicized concerns over toxic spills and waste problems at Love Canal, Valley of the Drums, and other sites."[19] Public opinion was a commonly reported cause of enactments in macroeconomics, civil rights, and labor and significantly less common in energy, finance, and science. Public concern over economic conditions was regularly credited with macroeconomic policy change.

Interest group influence was quite common in most issue areas, but was significantly more common in agriculture, transportation, the environment, and civil rights. Historians regularly credit lobbying by industry groups in agriculture and transportation as well as advocacy by public interest groups for civil

Table 5.2 **Reported External Circumstances Associated with Policy Enactments in Issue Area Histories**

	Media Coverage	Public Opinion	Interest Groups	International	State or Local	Research
Agriculture	18.42%	21.05%	63.16%	13.16%	0%	47.37%
Civil Rights and Liberties	21.31%	31.15%	67.21%	11.48%	24.59%	22.95%
Criminal Justice	25.00%	30.77%	30.77%	0%	9.62%	42.31%
Education	12.12%	27.27%	48.48%	12.12%	18.18%	42.42%
Energy	18.18%	13.64%	36.36%	13.64%	18.18%	31.82%
Environment	29.90%	25.77%	69.07%	12.37%	19.59%	54.64%
Finance and Commerce	10.34%	6.90%	36.21%	3.45%	5.17%	22.41%
Health	10.53%	11.58%	36.84%	7.37%	9.47%	38.95%
Housing and Development	16.67%	13.89%	58.33%	0%	19.44%	44.44%
Labor and Immigration	16.07%	30.36%	55.36%	10.71%	12.50%	37.50%
Macroeconomics	22.92%	41.67%	54.17%	14.58%	8.33%	41.67%
Science and Technology	7.89%	7.89%	36.84%	23.68%	2.63%	28.95%
Social Welfare	22.22%	22.22%	38.89%	0%	13.89%	36.11%
Transportation	22.22%	17.78%	57.78%	0%	6.67%	31.11%

Note: The table reports the percentage of enactments that involved each factor, according to policy historians.

rights and environmental protection. As Nadine Leher reports, even when farm groups lost influence over agriculture policy, interest group coalitions were still dominant: "Although the farm interest group bloc had begun to lose its exclusive status as primary keeper of farm policy, it was still able to reincorporate more traditional commodity provisions into the 1977 farm bill by teaming up with nutrition interests, who had grown accustomed to supporting commodity measures in exchange for food stamps."[20] Later reforms, such as the 1996 Federal Agriculture Improvement Act, were made possible by "the willingness of reform proponents to make strategic accommodations to farm interests."[21]

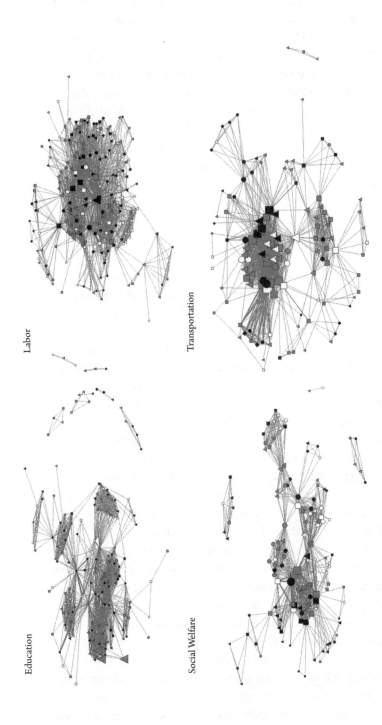

Figure 5.4 A sample of issue networks

Nodes are actors credited with policy enactments in each area. Links connect actors credited with the same policy enactments. Democrats are black; Republicans are white; others are grey. Shape represents branch of government; circles are legislative; squares are executive; diamonds are judicial; triangles are nongovernmental.

Science and technology policy registered the highest rate of international influence, with the Soviet launch of Sputnik serving as the most prominent example. State or local influence on policy enactments was most common in the areas of housing and civil rights but was significantly less common in science and agriculture. According to policy historians, factors related to research were commonly associated with policy change in most issue areas, with the exception of civil rights.[22] Policy historians regularly cite new data as well as summary reports from government agencies as factors in policy change. A 1983 report on the Strategic Petroleum Reserve, for example, helped produce policy changes designed to market oil from the reserve, with the support of Congress and President Reagan.[23]

The Diversity of Issue Networks

Policy histories also credit particular individuals and organizations with bringing about policy change in each area. Governing networks enable a visualization of the relationships among these actors. Figure 5.4 depicts a sample of networks for four issues. Nodes are actors credited with enactments; links connect actors credited with the same enactments. Black nodes are Democrats or liberal organizations; white nodes represent Republicans or conservative organizations; others are grey. Actors in the legislative branch are represented as circles; actors in the executive branch are squares; diamonds represent those in the judicial branch and triangles are nongovernmental actors.

There is remarkable variation in the composition and structure of networks across issue areas. Education has a core and several satellite clusters; labor has one dense large component; social welfare most resembles a hollow core; transportation features actors playing bridging roles, connecting outlying clusters to the central core. There is variation in the party and institutional composition of each network but all have substantial cross-party interaction.

Table 5.3 reports several characteristics of the composition of each issue area's network. Members of Congress dominate half of the networks and interest groups dominate two of the networks; others have a mix of central players. The civil rights governing network incorporates numerous national interest groups as well as less stable social movement organizations. The criminal justice network is smaller, but heavily reliant on interest groups to bring court cases. Despite infrequent lawmaking in social welfare and education, dozens of legislators are involved in both issue areas (perhaps requiring widespread agreement that is difficult to muster). Executive branch organizations are central in the transportation network, where each subset of industry groups is associated with a different regulatory agency.

Table 5.3 **Issue Area Governing Network Composition**

	Most Central (Degree)	Dominant Type	Congress Members No.	Links	Interest Groups No.	Links	Government Organizations No.	Links
Agriculture	Ag. Dept, Farm Bureau	Congress	17	9.9	8	9.9	6	6
Civil Rights and Liberties	NAACP, JFK, MLK Jr.	Int. Groups	63	20.4	52	4.9	16	23.1
Criminal Justice	ACLU, Bar Assoc.	Int. Groups	20	6.7	16	8.4	11	7.2
Education	Edith Green, NEA	Congress	54	19.5	27	16.1	15	16.1
Energy	Ford, Ted Kennedy	Congress	20	5.3	12	4.1	9	2.4
Environment	Ed Muskie, J. Blatnik	Mixed	36	13.1	34	7.2	33	13.1
Finance and Commerce	Eisenhower, LBJ	Congress	19	3.4	3	3	7	3.1
Health	Truman, Mary Lasker	Congress	46	9.7	31	9.9	26	8.7
Housing and Development	U.S. Conf. of Mayors	Mixed	39	9.7	29	14.6	22	9.5
Labor and Immigration	AFL-CIO, Labor Dept.	Mixed	76	14.8	63	17.4	24	16.5
Macroeconomics	Wilbur Mills, Treasury	Congress	42	11.6	12	15.2	16	20.4
Science and Technology	FCC, Nixon	Mixed	12	2.8	12	2.8	13	4.7
Social Welfare	Wilbur Mills, Social Sec	Congress	45	11.4	24	12.7	18	16.7
Transportation	Ford, Ted Kennedy	Gov. Orgs.	24	16.1	29	18.6	30	20.8

Note: The table reports characteristics of the actors credited with policy enactments in each issue area.

Table 5.4 **Issue Area Governing Network Structural Characteristics**

	Core-Periphery						E-I Index	
	Size	Density	Fitness	Core Density	Degree Centralization	Clustering Coefficient	Congress-Admin.	Bipartisan
Agriculture	49	0.17	0.7	0.88	9.50%	1.02	-0.11	-0.14
Civil Rights and Liberties	210	0.1	0.69	1.07	7.21%	1	-0.34	-0.28
Criminal Justice	83	0.08	0.52	1	10.52%	1.02	-0.5	-0.17
Education	170	0.1	0.47	0.62	9.83%	0.97	-0.14	-0.23
Energy	65	0.07	0.59	1	5.96%	0.91	-0.18	-0.28
Environment	144	0.09	0.68	4.39	7.74%	1.2	-0.21	-0.42
Finance and Commerce	54	0.06	0.48	1.05	4.34%	0.99	-0.03	-0.03
Health	141	0.07	0.49	1.17	6.60%	1.01	-0.28	-0.01
Housing and Development	119	0.1	0.48	0.87	15.50%	1	-0.07	-0.23
Labor and Immigration	211	0.1	0.49	0.84	14.18%	1.14	-0.06	-0.19
Macroeconomics	118	0.12	0.67	1.07	9.94%	1.06	-0.02	-0.01
Science and Technology	70	0.06	0.29	2	4.38%	0.98	-0.38	-0.29
Social Welfare	136	0.1	0.56	1.04	8.06%	1.07	-0.13	-0.24
Transportation	127	0.19	0.76	1.29	13.48%	1.12	-0.13	-0.15

Note: The table reports structural characteristics of the affiliation networks associated with policy enactments in each issue area.

Table 5.4 reports characteristics of the structure of each issue area's network.[24] Size is the number of actors. Density is the average number of ties between all pairs of actors. In this case, the interpretation is the average number of policy enactments for which each pair of actors in the network shared credit. As in chapter 4, the core-periphery model in table 5.3 compares each network to an ideal type in which a central group of actors is closely tied to one another and surrounded by a periphery of less connected actors. The fitness statistic reports the extent to which the network fits this ideal type; the core density statistic reports the density within the group of actors identified as the core of the network.

Degree Centralization measures the extent to which all ties in the network are to a single actor. The Clustering Coefficient measures the extent to which actors that are tied to one another are also tied to the same other actors.[25] Table 5.3 also reports two versions of the E-I (external-internal) index to track cross-branch and cross-party ties. The index measures the extent to which ties are disproportionately across groups (positive) or within groups (negative). The groups for the first index are actors in Congress and those in the executive branch; for the second, the groups are Republicans or conservative organizations and Democrats or liberal organizations.[26]

Governing networks differ in their structure across issue areas. Some networks are large and dense like transportation, whereas others are small and dense like agriculture. The health network is large but sparse but science is small and sparse. A large number of actors in a network may not inevitably reduce productive ties among participants; even though transportation actors differ in their focus on airlines, trucks, highways, trains, or boats, they seem to ally regularly. Even though a much smaller group was active in science, they did not form a stable cabal uniting disparate concerns in research funding and regulation. The issue networks that most resemble the core-periphery structure are civil rights and the environment; in these issue areas, there are clear insiders and outsiders. The most centralized networks are housing (around the U.S. Conference of Mayors) and labor (around the AFL-CIO); these peak associations tended to guide policy in their respective areas. Clustering is most evident in the environment, where alliances were consistent, and least evident in energy, where coalitions of convenience were more common.

The networks with the most ties between the legislative and executive branch are housing, finance, and macroeconomics. In finance, both microloans for the Small Business Opportunity Corporation and nondiscrimination rules for the Small Business Administration were initiated with the help of administrative agency officials and members of Congress.[27] The Federal Deposit Insurance Corporation Improvement Act was likewise credited to a consensus among legislators and executive branch officials.[28] The civil rights and science domains had the networks with the least common ties across Congress and the administration.

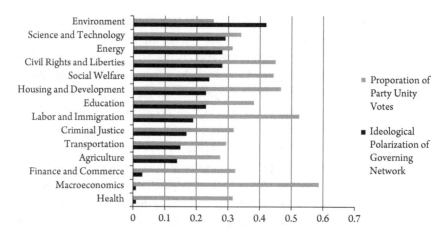

Figure 5.5 Governing network polarization and roll-call party unity across issue domains

The figure depicts the polarization of governing networks and the proportion of party unity votes in each issue area. Polarization is based on a reversed E-I Index for affiliation networks associated with significant policy enactments in each issue area. The index is constructed by subtracting the number of connections across the two partisan/ideological groups (Democrats/Liberals and Republicans/Conservatives) from the number of connections within the two partisan/ideological groups. The party unity data is based on all roll-call votes in each area, taking the average score from 1965 to 2004.

In these areas, different policy changes moved forward separately in each branch, with only a few legislators involved in executive branch decisions and vice versa.

Figure 5.5 provides a look at the degree of ideological polarization across issue areas. The issue areas are ordered from most to least polarized, as ranked by the governing network measure. The networks most polarized by partisanship are the environment and science. For comparison, I include an issue-specific polarization measure from Ashley Jochim and Bryan Jones.[29] Their measure is the proportion of party unity votes (with each party voting as a majority on each side) out of all roll-call votes in each area, taking the average score from 1965 to 2004. Many of these votes were not associated with bills that eventually became laws. The correlation between my measure (based on governing networks) and their measure (based on legislative voting) across policy areas is low and negative, suggesting that polarized voting patterns are not a good guide to the extent to which the coalitions that actually enact significant policy change are bipartisan.

Given the recent context, health and macroeconomics are the oddest cases. Polarizing policy changes such as the Affordable Care Act and the 2009 stimulus bill are not included in either dataset, but the results show that they may be outliers in their issue areas across the entire post-WWII period. The coalitions behind most health policy changes, including steady additions to Medicare and the National Institutes of Health, were quite bipartisan. Coalitions of important actors behind many of the Keynesian stimulus measures and war funding taxes that passed Congress in the macroeconomics category were also bipartisan, even though the measure using all congressional votes shows substantial polarization in this area. Sheldon Pollack explains one such instance in 1969: "Budget shortfalls forced Johnson, and later Nixon, to reluctantly take up the bill. The need to secure additional revenue to finance the prolonged military conflict in Vietnam forced Congress and the executive to embrace a conception of 'tax reform' consisting in closing revenue 'leaks' and reversing the 'erosion' of the tax base…Nixon expressed much the same mixed message on tax policy/tax reform as Kennedy had."[30]

The measures of polarization and ideology are based on very different data, so readers should not expect alignment. Nevertheless, it is striking that polarization in voting patterns does not appear to be associated with a lack of bipartisan coalitions when it comes to the significant policy changes that are enacted. Similarly, the liberalism of significant enacted policies does not necessarily imply that liberals successfully ally with one another to change policy. Although Republicans and conservatives are less frequently involved, significant policy changes usually require alliances across the parties as well as involvement by many non-ideological actors.

Dimensions of Issue Area Politics

To evaluate the number of underlying dimensions of issue area politics and to see where issue areas sit relative to one another on these dimensions, I use nonmetric multidimensional scaling. This provides two kinds of output: information about how well a model with each number of dimensions fits the data and a scale score for each case on each dimension. A typology that successfully made sense of the differences in politics across issue areas would require differences to be summarized by a small number of dimensions where the cases clearly separated into clusters.

Figure 5.6 depicts a multidimensional analysis of issue area dissimilarities, using the characteristics of policy change reported in figures 5.1, 5.2, and 5.3, the reported circumstances associated with policy change from tables 5.1 and 5.2, and the characteristics of issue networks from tables 5.3 and 5.4. It uses a dissimilarity matrix of the Euclidian distances between pairs of issue areas for all variables in the four tables and three figures. The dissimilarity matrix is based on standardized versions of all of these variables.[31] Although the model is depicted in two dimensions, the results suggest no clean break in the number of dimensions. The measure of Stress_1, a fit statistic where lower numbers indicate a better fit, is .308 for a one-dimension solution, .145 for a two-dimension solution,

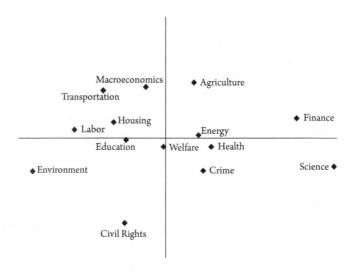

Figure 5.6 Nonmetric multidimensional scaling of dissimilarities among issue areas

The figure is a two-dimensional plot of nonmetric multidimensional scaling results of dissimilarities based on the reported factors in policy change since 1945 and the characteristics of their issue networks. The dissimilarities are based on standardized versions of the characteristics of issue areas reported in figures 5.1, 5.2, and 5.3 as well as tables 5.1, 5.2, 5.3, and 5.4.

.091 for a three-dimension solution, .055 for a four-dimension solution, and .037 for a five-dimension solution.

I also used k-means cluster analysis to divide the issue areas into subsets based on their dissimilarities. Different procedures for determining the appropriate number of clusters were inconclusive, with some producing improved fit statistics with 3 and 13 clusters and others producing improved fit statistics with 4 and 5 clusters. Beyond four clusters, however, the algorithm begins separating each issue area into a unique cluster. Rather than clear categories, distinctions among issue areas are best seen as continuous differences. The results suggest that there is no easy way to summarize the differences across the political processes surrounding each issue area and their associated issue networks. A two-by-two typology would have an especially poor fit with the data. We cannot be sure that two dimensions best account for issue area differences, that the issue areas divide cleanly along those dimensions, or that four clusters would be the most appropriate division.

I also analyze several reformulations of the data to ensure that the results were not a product of methodological decisions. First, I divide the data across time into subsets of 16-year periods and searched for an underlying structure. Second, I categorize the issue areas into a larger number of subtopics, each covering a smaller territory. Third, I analyze only the policy enactments considered significant by most authors in each area and limit the explanatory factors considered to only those with consensus across authors. Fourth, I construct distinct sets of dissimilarities based on network characteristics and based on the factors reportedly driving policy change. Issue area differences did not produce clear clustering on a few underlying dimensions in any of these analyses.

Making Sense of Issue Area Similarities and Differences

There are some seemingly universal features of the policy process, but there are also important differences in each issue area's politics. The 14 domestic policy areas differ in the frequency and ideological direction of policymaking, the common venues, the circumstantial factors enabling policy change, the actors responsible for enactments, and the structure of networks. On each dimension of issue area differences, most issue areas fall in the middle rather than at the extremes.

Issue typologies are unlikely to isolate the different features of policymaking in each issue area. Indeed, the available typologies are not predictive of the differences analyzed here. Theoretical distinctions made by Lowi and Wilson are not helpful in distinguishing among the types of politics present in each issue area.[32] Distinctions between iron triangles, issue networks, and policy communities are equally unhelpful. This is a sign that the theories that produce typologies should be subjected to more scrutiny. The project of creating minimalist models of the policy process based on ideal types may not be helpful. The iron triangle ideal type, for example, mixes three independently varying dimensions of network structure: a strong core, cross-institutional links, and bipartisan links. Each trait is important, but they do not go together.

Instead of assuming that issues will fall clearly into boxes, scholars should acknowledge that slight issue area differences are widespread but not very amenable to categorization. Table 5.5 lists descriptions of the features of each issue area that stand out when compared to the others, including the type of policymaking, the circumstances associated with policy enactments, and the composition and structure of the governing network. All policy areas stand out in some ways in comparison to the others. This comparative analysis should enable authors of case studies to check whether their findings are likely to apply only to a few issue areas or generalize to the policy process as a whole.

The issue area differences have important implications for the generalizability of research findings. Issue area case selection decisions make large differences in likely findings. For example, Kingdon's study of the policy process is based mostly on case studies of health and transportation.[33] If he had instead chosen to study education and labor, he might have shown more influence for public opinion and international factors. Likewise, because a great deal of scholarship

Table 5.5 **The Relative Features of Each Issue Area's Politics**

	Type of Policymaking	Relevant Circumstances	Network Composition	Network Structure
Agriculture	Regular, path dependent enactments	High executive branch and interest group influence	Small, mostly congressional network	Dense core-periphery network
Civil Rights and Liberties	Multi-branch, liberal, frequent, and path dependent	High judicial and state influence but low research influence	Large network with many interest groups	Core-periphery structure but low centralization
Criminal Justice	Disproportionately judicial enactments	High research influence but no international influence	Small network with central interest groups	Executive-congressional divide
Education	Path dependent liberal enactments by Congress	High executive and legislative branch influence	Large network dominated by members of Congress	Core with satellite clusters
Energy	Disproportionately administrative, event-driven	Low public opinion and high state/local influence	Small network, concentrated in Congress	Low centralization
Environment	Many enactments with congressional dominance	High media, state/local, and research influence	Disproportionately Democratic network	Dense core with high clustering
Finance and Commerce	Split conservative policy-making between Congress and courts	High judicial influence; low executive and research influence	Small, congressional and presidential network	Sparse decentralized network

	Type of Policymaking	Relevant Circumstances	Network Composition	Network Structure
Health	Many liberal enactments in Congress	No dominant influential factors	Large network, dominated by members of Congress	Sparse ties
Housing and Development	Path dependent liberal enactments in Congress	High state/local, low public opinion influence	Large diverse network	Centralized network with partisan divide
Labor and Immigration	Multi-branch enactments	High public opinion and group influence	Large, diverse network, centralized on AFL-CIO	Sparse network, with high clustering
Macroeconomics	Event-driven, ideologically-mixed legislative enactments	High public opinion and research influence; bipartisan coalitions	Congress-dominated network	Dense network with high inter-branch/bipartisan ties
Science and Technology	Disproportionately administrative enactments	Low public opinion but high international influence	Diverse, with many government organizations	Sparse, disconnected network with no core
Social Welfare	Infrequent, path dependent enactments	High media influence; no international influence	Congress-dominated network	Large divided network
Transportation	Regular congressional enactments	High interest group influence, no international influence	Large diverse network, with government organizations	Dense core-periphery network; high clustering

Note: The table reports descriptions of where each issue area stands out among the others, based on the analysis of policy area histories conducted here.

using advocacy coalitions focuses on environmental policy, scholars may be more likely to find influence by interest groups and research.[34]

The results may also show where each of the agenda setting theories could be productively applied. The research and coalition focus of the Advocacy Coalition Framework might be useful in studies of agriculture and housing. The focus on episodic determinants of policy change in Punctuated Equilibrium studies has been useful in studies of nuclear energy and budgets.[35] My comparative research shows that energy and macroeconomic policies more broadly are the most likely to be associated with episodic causes of policy change. Theories of path dependent policymaking may be most appropriate in agriculture, education, and housing.

There are also important similarities in policymaking that are reportedly common across issue areas, even though I rely on 14 distinct literatures on a broad spectrum of domestic policy. First, Congress is the most frequent maker of significant policy in nearly all issue areas and it is responsible for the bulk of policymaking in most areas. Second, all policy areas have some policy enactments where path dependent explanations are apt and others where event-related explanations are appropriate. Third, interest groups and research reportedly play a common role in policymaking in most issue areas whereas public opinion and media coverage play less frequent roles. Fourth, all issue areas are associated with networks of actors credited with policy change, including actors in the legislative and executive branch and interest groups.

These similarities suggest that policymaking is a mostly insular undertaking, regularly involving coalition and compromise among officials and activists no matter the topical concern. Across nearly all issue areas, the most common contributors to policy change involve internal leadership and negotiations in the branches of government and advocacy by interest groups. Policymakers in most areas also often incorporate previous policies and research in their decisions and respond to wars and economic downturns. In all issue areas, the artists of the possible include legislators, executive officials, and interest groups. Their alliances and negotiating patterns differ. Most actors have more ties to others within their institution and party even though bipartisan and cross-institutional links commonly help make policy change happen.

These findings also have implications for normative discussions of policymaking. Scholars who sought to divide policymaking into categories associated their typologies with judgments about the relationship between the policy process and democratic values.[36] If issue area politics cannot be easily predicted based on whether policies tend to benefit majorities or minorities, general claims about where policymaking is likely to be more or less democratic may not hold up to scrutiny. Politics in every issue area may be labeled "interest group politics" to some degree, even though groups are not the only important actors in any area.

Claims about iron triangles and issue networks were also meant to raise concerns that policymaking did not live up to America's founding principles. Iron triangles supposedly involved domination of policymaking by political insiders. Heclo also viewed issue networks with concern, arguing that they came with a "democratic deficit" because they empowered technocratic elites.[37] Disproportionate involvement by administrators and scientists is only one source of difficulty in matching our expectations of wide participation with the reality of the policy process. Disinterested citizens representative of the nation as a whole do not make up any issue network. Instead, each issue area is associated with distinct distributions of political elites.

Despite differences across issue areas, there are grounds for a general understanding of policymaking and an associated critique of the relationship between democracy in theory and practice. As issues like fuel efficiency standards and law enforcement tracking become objects of policymaker concern, observers should attend to both the usual differences associated with transportation and criminal justice policy as well as their shared likely course of resolution. Across the issue areas analyzed here, all issue areas involved multiple institutions, interest groups, and diverse policymakers. They incorporated several circumstantial factors and responded to both past policy development and current events. There are many factors in the policy process but some are much more frequently influential than others. Issue area differences are decipherable and should be emphasized, but the similarities in the relative importance of each component of policymaking across issue areas are just as important. The American national government has both a general policy process and some unique variants for each issue area.

CHAPTER 6

Explaining Policy Change

The first new law signed by President Obama was the Lilly Ledbetter Fair Pay Act, named in honor of a woman's pay discrimination lawsuit rejected by the Supreme Court. The law, which essentially reversed the Court's decision, was made possible by Democratic gains in Congress in 2008. Enacting the law was a legislative battle between all of the major civil rights organizations (in support) and major business associations (in opposition). The bill passed on largely party line votes, but with support from a few Republicans in each chamber.

The Jumpstart Our Business Startups (JOBS) Act was the last significant policy change of Obama's first term. Conservative Republican leader Eric Cantor was by Obama's side at the bill signing, having shepherded two versions of the bill through the House of Representatives. This change in financial regulation and securities law emerged out of a White House startup business initiative and a new lobbying organization of financial professionals in the "crowdfunding" industry. The bill passed with overwhelming bipartisan support, despite early opposition from the AARP, consumer groups, and unions.

Future historians of civil rights and financial regulation will likely cite both laws as important policy changes, calling attention to many of these circumstances. Although there may be some disagreement about the relative importance of congressional negotiations, interest group lobbying, and presidential support, all three factors will likely be seen as important in the enactment of both statutes. The stories of lawmaking in these two cases will likely diverge when it comes to the roles played by elections and partisanship and the actors responsible. Obama may be credited with both, but different business and advocacy groups, elected officials, and external activists were significant in each policymaking episode.

Dozens of circumstances and hundreds of actors can play a role in the policy process. But some matter a lot more often than others. With the goal of learning which circumstances and actors are most often influential, previous chapters analyzed hundreds of policy enactments from 1945 to 2004, including several that have causal stories similar to these two Obama administration initiatives. Different observers of the same events, however, may have different perceptions of the most important factors in policymaking. One future historian may credit more legislators with the fair pay legislation; another may credit more administration staffers with the JOBS Act. Comparing and aggregating multiple explanations provides a more complete picture.

This chapter moves the level of analysis to the individual explanation for a specific policy change by a particular author, reporting how often each circumstance and actor is credited with playing an important role and analyzing the inclusion of each type of factor in explanations for policy change. It compares the multifaceted explanations for policy enactments offered by policy historians with singularly focused *actor success* models. Despite differences across authors, methods, and circumstances, some factors are much more frequently referenced in historical accounts. Regardless of the storyteller, some factors also seem to work in tandem. Understanding policymaking requires attention to many aspects of politics, as well as the differences in perspective associated with different forms of investigation.

Analyzing Actor Success

Most scholarship on the determinants of policy change considers the influence of one set of actors at a time. These *actor success* models use the policy changes sought by one set of actors as the possibilities and count how many times they achieve their goals. Scholars do not ignore the rest of the policymaking process, but focus on how circumstances might influence the success of the particular actors whom they study. Other factors primarily condition the relationship between their actor's preferences and policy results. I consider five versions of these models, each with a different actor focus: presidents, congressional leaders, interest groups, scientists, and the American public.

Presidential studies analyze the success rates of each president, cataloging their legislative agenda and their success at winning congressional votes on each proposal. Paul Light argues that presidential success depends on timing within a presidential administration but, since the 1980s, has been inhibited by the shrinking scope of presidential initiatives.[1] Jon Bond and Richard Fleisher attribute presidential success to trends in partisanship and ideology in Congress, rather than presidential skills.[2] Brandice Canes-Wrone finds that presidents can help move policy toward majority public opinion if their position is closer to the public than the median opinion in Congress.[3] William Howell argues that presidents increasingly take policymaking into their own hands by issuing executive orders and using reviews of federal agency rulemaking.[4] The use of these tactics differs based on a president's likelihood of passing laws in Congress, but gives the president unilateral power in policymaking. These models tend to include items where the president takes a clear position, restricting the analysis to items on their agenda.

Because most policy is made in Congress, it may be more natural to assess the legislative agenda of congressional leaders. Using a measure of the congressional agenda based on *New York Times* editorials, Sarah Binder argues that divided government and polarization can lower congressional productivity.[5] Agendas expand during divided government, with each party proposing more policies, many of which never make it into law. Douglas Arnold argues that congressional leaders can occasionally build support for policy changes in the public interest, rather than those favored by interest groups, by taking advantage of potential support in public opinion.[6] In contrast to the presidency literature, studies of Congress see legislators as the primary coalition builders and assess policy outputs from their point of view.

Rather than starting with the agenda of policymakers, some research looks for the influence of external actors. One approach tests consistency between public opinion and policy outcomes. Martin Gilens finds that opinion among low-income earners does not typically help predict a policy's adoption but opinion among high-income earners usually does.[7] The extent to which there is a match depends on partisanship and the balance of active interest groups. The agenda of possible changes is taken from questions asked in public opinion polls, rather than only items that the public endorses; the content of poll questions nonetheless reflects anticipated public concerns.

Other studies assess whether policy follows the consensus of research or scientists. Ann Keller finds that scientists are most influential in agenda setting but face greater constraints during implementation.[8] She finds that the agendas of scientists, and the researchers that study their influence, are often concentrated in a few issue areas. Andrew Rich determines that researchers operating in think tanks have substantial influence on health care and tax policy.[9] This literature assesses whether policy follows scientific consensus, but often finds that scientific research produces uncertain or contradictory findings that can undergird the positions of opposing sides.[10]

Other researchers focus on whether and how policy reflects the relative mobilization of different interest groups. The view that interest group agendas guide policy was developed in pluralist accounts of competition between social and economic constituencies, but is even more prominent in the elitist theories of interest groups that challenged pluralist theory. Both agree that policy reflects group interests; the controversy between them is over the degree to which policy outcomes show the interests of the upper class, rather than several different interest groups.[11] Recent studies of interest groups start from the agenda of

Washington lobbyists, assessing whether policies are adopted on the basis of the resources mobilized by groups. The issues included are those that some part of the interest group community is paying a lobbyist to influence. Policy results are seen as following from the characteristics or activities of interest groups on each side, though most measures of their resources are unrelated to outcomes.[12]

Actor Success Models and Hedgehog Thinking

Starting with the agenda of any one set of actors is not likely to provide an impartial perspective on the factors governing policy change. Lobbyists, journalists, scientists, legislators, administrators, and individual citizens all make policy proposals, but consistency between their preferred option and the policy selected is not much evidence that they were responsible for a policy victory. Searching for the influence of one actor at a time is analogous to thinking like a hedgehog, interpreting evidence in light of one main idea, rather than like a fox, relying on no overarching narrative and assessing multiple possibilities.[13] Prediction experiments suggest that political scientists and economists that theorize like foxes are substantially more accurate than those whose thinking patterns resemble hedgehogs.[14]

Actor success models are attempting to limit the analysis to items that have some chance to be enacted (because they are on the agenda of a particular actor), comparing those that come to fruition to others that languish. As I demonstrated in chapter 3, starting from the agenda of policymakers offers only limited utility in assessing the issues, times, and places where significant policy change will occur. When scholars assume that policy change will come from the prior agenda of a mobilized actor, it also raises the same age-old criticisms leveled at pluralists: some actors may manipulate the process, preventing other constituencies from realizing their grievances or thwarting the development of actionable political issues.[15] Assessing the influence of all potential factors on policy development provides an alternative that considers issue advocacy and proposal negotiation without reifying any one stage of the policy process.

Actor success models are mostly driven by comparisons between the policy process and an ideal type of policymaking. No scholar expects policy to be universally consistent with public or policymaker preferences, the scientific community, or the majority of interest groups, but many explain deviations from dominance by a single actor or constituency. Other factors only enter the causal process when they disrupt the preferred relationship. Some of these ideal types are based in normative premises: the public opinion literature's objective is democratic accountability; the scientific influence literature seeks evidenced-based policy. The interest group literature is instead born of a dystopia, the idea that policy results are bought and sold. Assessments of these ideal types tend to become searches for confirming or disconfirming evidence for a single theory, rather than investigations of competing alternatives. *Actor success* models thus share two problems: (1) they bias the starting point, including only the agenda of potential proposals of concern to each set of actors, and (2) they look for deviations from agreement with the actor in question, assuming that agreement implies influence.

Analyzing Explanations

Policy historians look for influence from a variety of actors and circumstances, without privileging any one actor or starting from their agenda of policy goals. Compared with *actor success* models, policy history enables a search for influence by many factors that matter occasionally even if none matter in every case of policy change. Policy historians look at the process by which policy is developed, promoted, and adopted to assess the relative influence of many potentially important factors. Even though policy historians rarely formalize their assessment by looking for the presence or absence of each factor in successes and failures, they nonetheless are quite conscious of the prevalence of unsuccessful policymaking attempts. Having reviewed at least 10 years of policy history, they have selected the most important factors.

Their explanations do differ, however, and it is worth considering how and why. Do they investigate like hedgehogs, with different subsets of scholars focusing on different aspects of policymaking, or do their assessments converge on a shared ordering of the most significant factors in policy change? This chapter relies on the narratives of policy historians to assess whether interest groups, research, public opinion, presidents, congressional leaders, or any other actors or circumstances influence policy enactments. I analyze the factors considered relevant by each individual policy historian, rather than aggregating their views to build a composite history of each policy enactment. Each explanation is still attached to a particular policy change, but I include multiple authors assessing the same enactment as separate cases.

Because different observers may view the policy process differently, considering each of their explanations individually assesses whether aggregate results are dependent on particular characteristics of authors or their studies. I analyze the distribution of credited circumstances and actors across all explanations, acknowledging where factors may have entered the composite explanations for policy enactments only due to a few outlying authors or studies.

Table 6.1 **Most Cited Factors in Explanations for Significant Policy Enactments**

	% of Explanations
Supportive President	42.15
Pressure from Advocacy Organization	22.54
Extension of Previous Policy	21.56
Individual Member of Congress Led	16.93
Executive Agency Director Led	15.23
Focusing Event	12.40
Change in Power of the Two Parties	12.05
Congressional Committee Chair Led	11.89
Pressure from Corporations	11.48
Earlier Choice Made More Likely	11.01
Government Report Issued	10.91
House and Senate Reach Agreement	10.86
New Data Arises	10.40
Important Frame for Proponents	9.83
Congressional Lobbying	9.57
Affected by Economic Downturn	9.32
General Media Coverage	9.06
Court Ruling Stimulated Action	7.57
Key Congressional Floor Vote	7.31
Congressional/Party Leadership Led	7.05

Note: The table reports the percentage of explanations for policy change that cite each causal factor. $N = 1,943$.

Common Explanations for Policy Change

Policy historians mention over 60 different factors in their explanations for policy change, but some are much more consistently mentioned than others. Table 6.1 lists the most frequent factors cited in explanations for policy enactments. No factor is mentioned in a majority of explanations, but support from the president is mentioned in more than 42% of accounts. Next comes pressure from advocacy organizations, including public interest groups; this was cited in approximately one-out-of-four explanations. Policy historians also often see major policy change as an extension of previous policy, such as a reauthorization of a major bill. No other factor is mentioned in more than one-out-of-five explanations but ten additional factors were mentioned in at least one-in-ten explanations.

The list of commonly mentioned factors does not fall into any one category. There are several important factors in the legislative branch and two quite commonly mentioned executive branch factors. Interest groups are also a common component of top explanations for policy change. Factors related to path dependence, events, parties, research, ideas, media, and the judicial branch also make the list. The table only reports the top 20 factors; more than twice this many are components of less than 7% of explanations. There are a great variety of explanatory factors, but only some that appear regularly.

Few explanations for policy change involve only a single reported factor. Instead, policy historians typically explain policy change as a product of multiple factors working in tandem. They do not usually specify whether all of the factors were necessary or if any were sufficient. Some lists of factors from policy histories imply that interactions between multiple circumstances made a change more likely, though others simply observe several different potential independent routes to policy change. Either way, some explanatory factors are more commonly mentioned alongside other factors. Figure 6.1 shows the factors most often mentioned together, with arrows connecting those with high levels of association. I list factors where the bivariate relationship between the presence or absence of each explanatory factor was high, compared with the associations between all other pairs of factors.

The results suggest that there are many separable stories of policy change rather than a small number of major distinct themes. There is no evidence of a division between an "inside story" involving government and an "outside story" involving public mobilization. In fact, several pairs of commonly mentioned factors incorporate an agenda setting factor and an internal factor. Most factors are only commonly paired with a single other factor, and the interpretation is usually straightforward. An explanation that mentions the success of a proponent's argument often also mentions the lack of ideas from the opposition. Explanations mentioning economic downturns are also likely to mention government financial problems. Explanations involving state government action also tend to involve local government action.

A few other pairs of explanatory factors are more revealing. When an issue is raised in an election campaign, it is often by the president and is associated with support from him. A policy proposal often generates an influential media report when an advocacy organization issues research. When foundations are credited, the explanation often involves one side having more resources (possibly from the

Figure 6.1 Pairs of factors commonly cited together

The figure reports pairs of factors commonly cited together in explanations for policy change.

foundations). Media coverage tends to affect policy when constituents mobilize to call Congress. These patterns illustrate the interconnectedness of components of policymaking, but fail to delineate a few separable policymaking narratives.

Only two subsets of causal factors stand out in explanations for policy change. The first involves an interest group story, led by advocacy organizations. Whenever advocacy organizations are credited with policy change, it is often alongside unions, corporations, and other groups. Although these groups often work in formal coalitions, policy historians also mention multiple competing lobbying campaigns that policymakers reconcile. Take one description of the Violent Crime Control and Law Enforcement Act of 1994: "This behemoth of a law—many times bigger and more expensive than the Safe Streets Act—reflected the stunning variety of groups now seeking to be represented in crime legislation: women's groups, minority citizens living in urban poverty, the elderly, and law enforcement agencies."[16]

The second common conjunction of causes is a story relying on multiple factors within Congress. When historians credit individual backbench legislators with leadership roles in policymaking, they often point to important floor votes or also credit a committee chair. When committee chairs reportedly take a leadership role, it often entails a key committee vote. More surprisingly, committee chairs and party leaders do not appear to trade off in explanations for policy change but instead are often mentioned together. This is somewhat inconsistent

Table 6.2 **Categories of Factors Cited in Explanations for Significant Policy Enactments**

	% of Explanations
Congressional	41.17
Executive Branch	53.17
Judicial Branch	9.47
Interest Groups	36.13
Research	24.96
Public Opinion	17.04
Media	10.19
State/Local	6.74
International	5.35
Path Dependence	28.87
Events	26.04
Ideas	13.84

Note: The table reports the percentage of explanations for policy change that cite each category of causal factors. N = 1,943.

with a theme of the congressional literature, which posits that power in Congress has vacillated between committees and party caucuses.[17] The resolution is that, when major policy change passes, it is often because both committee and party leaderships are on board.

Both of these common agglomerations of causal factors are about institutional actors: legislators and interest groups. Figure 6.1 only includes pairs that are commonly cited together. Most other policy explanations still involve more than one factor, but not in a consistent formulation. To the extent that historians offer common stories of policy change, they involve internal negotiations in Congress or joint advocacy by multiple interest groups.

Rather than disaggregating explanations into their component parts, most of the book has focused on categories of explanatory factors in policy change. Table 6.2 assesses which of these categories are included most often in explanations. Congressional and administrative factors are most often cited, followed by interest group factors. A second tier of categories includes research, path dependence, and events. Policy historians mention factors related to public opinion, ideas, media, and the judiciary less commonly. Comparing this analysis of explanations from individual authors with chapter 3's analysis of composite explanations for policy enactments yields a few differences. If one author mentions legislative and executive factors, so do most of the other authors explaining that change. Yet factors related to path dependence, research, media coverage, and state and local government may enter a composite explanation based on only a single author's report. This suggests that consensus explanations revolve around internal negotiations within policymaking institutions.

The relative importance of these factors has changed slightly over time, but there are few consistent trends. Figure 6.2 illustrates these changes, using presidential administrations to mark time periods. The reported influence of factors related to Congress and interest groups was relatively constant and always high. Executive branch influence was consistently high but reached low points under Truman, Nixon, and Reagan. Judicial branch influence was reportedly low but reached a high point in the 1970s. The reported influence of public opinion is low but has been increasing since the 1970s, a finding that matches previous analysis of the relationship between opinion polls and policy results.[18] Research was usually more commonly influential than public opinion, with the exception of the last few administrations. Reports of path dependence or event-driven policymaking have fluctuated over time, but have not traded off with one another. Overall, the relative importance of these circumstances in policy change is not dependent on the time period in which authors focused or wrote their histories.

Some categories of factors tend to be cited together in explanations for policy change. Table 6.3 reports correlation coefficients among the number of factors cited within each category. Explanations involving interest groups tend to also involve congressional factors or research. Interest groups often lobby Congress and use information to do so. This points to the role of research in information exchange networks among legislators and interest groups. Explanations involving research are also more likely to involve administrative factors, perhaps because some administrative agencies are required to consult scientific evidence. Yet no two categories are always or ordinarily cited together.

The table also includes correlations between each category and the total number of factors cited in each explanation. When authors include a large number of factors in their explanation, they are more likely to credit Congress, the administration, the media, public opinion, interest groups, events, and research. The relative breadth of an author's explanation for policy change accounts for most of the differences in explanations across authors. Some authors produce idiographic explanations of their cases, accounting for all of the factors that may have played a role in policymaking. Others come closer to nomothetic explanations, including an explanatory factor only after ruling out other possibilities. When comparing individual explanations for the same events, the most likely difference in author perspective is the narrowness of their focus. When histories are aggregated, the differences do not have a major

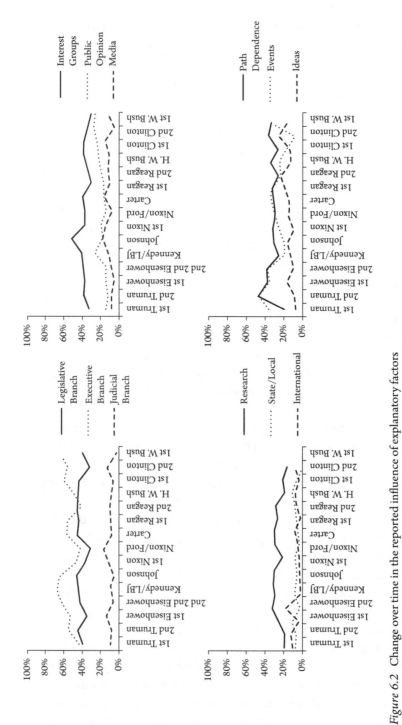

Figure 6.2 Change over time in the reported influence of explanatory factors

The figure reports the percentage of explanations for policy enactments that include a factor in each category during each presidential administration. N = 1,943

Table 6.3 **Correlation Coefficients among Explanatory Factors**

	Congress	Admin.	Judicial	State/Local	Media	Public Opinion	Interest Group	Inter-national	Events	Research	Path Depend.	Ideas
Administrative	0.26											
Judicial	-0.09	-0.10										
State / Local	-0.03	-0.04	0.14									
Media	0.21	0.13	0.01	0.07								
Public Opinion	0.20	0.16	0.03	0.02	0.28							
Interest Group	**0.34**	0.18	0.08	0.10	0.26	0.24						
International	-0.02	0.05	0.01	-0.03	0.05	0.05	0.05					
Events	0.03	0.05	0.00	0.04	0.08	0.03	0.04	0.14				
Research	0.16	**0.34**	0.04	0.15	0.26	0.17	**0.35**	0.08	0.10			
Path Dependence	0.08	0.03	-0.03	-0.01	0.01	-0.02	0.02	-0.02	0.08	0.05		
Ideas	0.08	-0.03	0.00	-0.01	-0.02	0.05	0.03	0.00	0.04	0.02	0.00	
No. of Factors Mentioned	**0.67**	**0.52**	0.11	0.18	**0.45**	**0.43**	**0.64**	0.16	**0.32**	**0.52**	0.27	0.06

Note: Table entries are correlation coefficients between each count of the number of circumstances of each type mentioned in each explanation for policy change.

N = 1,943

Table 6.4 **Categories of Specific Actors Credited with Policy Enactments**

Branch	% of Actors	Type of Actor	% of Actors	Party / Ideology	% of Actors
Legislative Branch	32.77	Interest Groups	22.89	Democratic Officials	21.21
Executive Branch	20.21	Presidents	1.15	Liberal Organizations	7.73
Judicial Branch	2.07	Members of Congress	26.11	Republican Officials	15.62
External	44.95	Government Organizations	15.39	Conservative Organizations	3.52
		Other	34.46	Other	51.91

Note: The table reports the percentage of actors credited with policy change that fall into each category, using three separate categorization schemes. N = 1,306.

effect on the relative frequency with which each factor is mentioned. My data shows some tendency to name more factors in explanations for larger policy changes, but this may be due to real differences in their causal process rather than author approach. Perhaps larger changes are harder to achieve and require more supportive circumstances.

The Diversity and Skew of the Actors Who Influence Policy

In addition to these categories of influential factors, policy historians often name specific actors that they hold responsible for policy change. If legislative alliances and lobbying coalitions are common explanations, they rely on particular people and organizations. What kinds of actors do policy historians credit for policy change? Although there is substantial diversity, a few patterns stand out. Table 6.4 reports three different distributions of the population of all actors credited with policy change since 1945. The first divides the actors by branch of government, but nearly half of the actors are not situated in government at all. Among those in government, a majority is in Congress. Judicial branch actors are rare. The second distribution categorizes the actors by type. Interest groups represent nearly a quarter of all actors; members of Congress are even more common. Many government organizations are mentioned, especially executive

Table 6.5 **Characteristics of Credited Actors and Their Connections**

	Median	Mean	Standard Deviation
Actor's Number of Enactments	1	2	3.7
Actor's Number of Connections	9.5	16.5	24.2
Connections to Members of Congress	3	4.9	7.5
Connections to Interest Groups	2	3.8	6.3

Note: The table reports descriptive data on the characteristics of actors credited with policy change, including the number of enactments with which they were partially credited and the actors that were credited alongside them. N = 1,306.

agencies. Most actors credited with policy change are therefore legislative and executive branch entities or interest groups.

I also report an ideological and partisan distribution. A majority of actors were not easily categorized as liberal or conservative; these included government organizations, individual activists, and nonpartisan interest groups. Democratic officials were more common than Republicans, consistent with their distribution within Congress over the period. More tellingly, liberal organizations were more than twice as common as conservative organizations. This likely reflects the liberal nature of most policy changes and the more common liberal ideological direction of policymaking since 1945.

Of course, not all actors in the policy process play an equal role. Chapter 3 listed and discussed the most frequently credited actors. Many actors were only credited in a single policy area and were only judged partially responsible for a single policy enactment. Table 6.5 reports characteristics of the uneven distributions of actor ties to policy enactments and other actors. More than half of the actors were credited with only a single enactment. Yet the mean is two and the standard deviation is higher; a few actors were responsible for substantially more changes. Table 6.5 reveals that most actors jointly enact policy with a small number of others, but a few have substantial policymaking ties. The average actor was jointly credited with 16.5 others, including 4.9 members of Congress and 3.8 interest groups. In each case, the median is lower than the mean and the standard deviation is higher. Even though the actors involved in policymaking are diverse, only a few actors amass a large number of policymaking partners.

Although many actors occasionally influence policy, only a few constitute institutionalized entrepreneurs with repeated influence. Because these actors influence policy with numerous allies and partners in compromise, they become central in governing networks. These well-connected actors tend to be presidents, long-serving legislators, and prominent interest groups. Even if the peripheral actors that join them in policymaking are diverse, explanations for policy change tend to repeatedly refer to the same subset of actors.

Explaining Differences in Policy Historian Judgment

Despite consensus among policy historians on the hierarchy of important factors in policy change, differences in judgment remain. Both author and enactment characteristics are likely to affect which factors policy historians cite in their explanations for policy change. Appendix B uses multivariate models to predict when different categories of factors are included in explanations. I assess the influence of author biographical characteristics and the methods used in studies as well as characteristics of the policy enactments. The most consistent finding is that an author's propensity to cite each individual factor is a function of the total number of factors that they cite. Breadth of explanation is the single most influential difference across the population of policy historians.

There are some genuine differences in perspective driven by author characteristics. Political scientists are less likely to cite judicial branch factors and path dependence in their explanations. History professors are more likely to cite media coverage and public opinion. Authors that served as government officials more often cite internal factors in Congress. Issue area specialists are the most likely to cite the influence of scientific research. Authors from any background that rely on interviews are more likely to cite media influence and less likely to cite executive branch factors. These differences are slight.

Most judgments of influence by policy historians are driven by factors related to the enactment itself, rather than historian background or methods. Reported executive branch influence is most likely on the largest enactments and least likely in court decisions. Interest group influence, in contrast, is most commonly reported in the smallest enactments and in the judiciary. Scientific influence is more common in administrative decisions. There are also some stable differences in explanations across issue areas; the largest issue area differences reported in chapter 5 are consistent with the evidence in multivariate models. There are no significant differences in the factors governing policymaking when comparing liberal and conservative enactments. Likewise, the same factors are reportedly involved in both enactments recognized as important at the time and those only seen as significant in retrospect. The same similarity was evident in the politics of enactments in both low- and high-profile issue areas.

The results generally confirm the findings from the first five chapters, even when accounting for differences in explanations across policy historians. There are some differences based on author background and the methods used to study policy history, but the most significant difference is simply that some authors point to more factors than others in driving policy change. This pattern of explanation diverges from those used in *actor success* models, where each set of authors concentrates on one set of influential factors; policy historians do not divide into camps focused on distinct policymaking narratives. The influence of each category of factors in the policymaking process is greater in certain circumstances, regardless of the type of author that reviews the evidence. Most importantly, the relative prevalence of each set of factors in explanations for enactments is not dependent on author or study characteristics. Internal factors in government institutions and interest group advocacy are most consistently influential. No actor is always decisive and no individual actor's agenda guides the policymaking system.

Appraising Actor Success Models

The reports from policy historians provide context for *actor success* models, though they do not invalidate any specific previous results. Chapter 3 demonstrated that policymaker agendas, the starting point for *actor success* models, are not reliable guides to significant policy change. Chapter 4 directly assessed the influence of the size of the congressional agenda on policy productivity (using Sarah Binder's measure), finding limited influence after accounting for the Long Great Society. The results from this chapter indicate that policy historians converge on a few major explanatory factors but perceive no individual actor as necessary for significant policy change. Policy historians do not seem to have opposing viewpoints on the actors that matter most; they see presidents, legislators, and interest groups as consistently influential, with path dependence and scientific research occasionally playing a role.

The global perspective on policy change provides somewhat distinct lessons from *actor success* models. In contrast to the presidential literature, policy histories show little evidence of declining executive branch influence or any consistent interaction between the roles of public opinion and presidential leadership. The results are more consistent with the emphasis on coalition building among legislators and interest groups in some studies of the congressional agenda. Policy histories also provide support for one claim from work on public opinion: overall influence is weak but appears to be rising. The results were less consistent with previous work on scientific influence: research appears more influential in the administration than in Congress and is tied to government reports and new data more often than think tanks. The findings are also curious given studies of interest group agendas: policy historians report regular influence from advocacy organizations, often in coalitions with corporations or unions, but do not often point to the relative resource mobilization of each side in policy debates.

The Limits of Aggregating Explanations for Policy Change

Policy history offers a worthwhile and independent perspective from that usually found in *actor success* models, but that does not mean its findings are definitive. Even if distinct author characteristics do not explain the book's findings, policy historians may collectively share biases that influence them. Although it is impossible to pinpoint where policy historians may differ from other types of investigators, chapter 2 explored several potential biases.

The aggregation contributes some additional limitations. I have assumed equality across policy changes of different scope and importance by reporting frequencies from the population of all significant policy enactments and all explanations. There is an inherent difficulty in comparing across policy changes from different issue areas and historical periods. In addition, many policy actions of concern to some individuals or groups fail to meet historians' threshold for reporting. The findings reported here apply only to significant domestic policy changes. Influence on adjustments to particular provisions of policy may not make the cut, even if they would constitute a victory from the perspective of the relevant proponents.

There are also some limitations involved in the content analysis. I compile explanations across authors with varying breadth of focus and different standards for adjudicating influence. Some authors cite more explanatory factors and credit more actors than others. Any differences in author approach may be amplified when I compile across authors and when more authors analyze some policy changes than others. Although these differences do not explain the results presented in earlier chapters, there remains unexplained variation in author judgments. Likewise, the network analyses reported here rely on credit given to specific actors for helping to bring about policy change. Because not all ties in the networks convey political collaboration and not all ties come from the same historian's explanation, the results are not directly comparable to previous studies of working relationships among policymakers or interest groups.

Another important limitation, as discussed in chapter 2, is that I only analyze cases of successful policy enactments. Although some authors do present in-depth studies of attempted policy changes that failed, most do not. Even when discussing failure to change policy, most authors refer to a general attempt solve a problem or advance a category of solutions, rather than pointing to a specific bill or regulation that was never enacted. When they do point to a specific proposal that failed, they choose the proposal that came the closest to enactment, making them less helpful comparison cases. Close analysis of policy change over long periods should provide some expertise in identifying causal factors. Nevertheless, the findings reported here only apply to reported influence on successful policy enactments.

Despite these limitations, policy history has several strengths that may help to correct for common problems in *actor success* models. First, policy history regularly compares the influence of each factor with that of all kinds of other factors. The lack of public opinion, media, or interest group influence may merely signal the greater importance of other factors, rather than the failure of the public, reporters, or groups. Second, it does not assume that the same set of tactics or the same level of resources deployed by each actor will be likely to have the same effect. It points to the history of working relationships among many disparate actors and central policymakers, emphasizing their interdependence. Third, policy history offers the perspective of reviewing policy development over an extended period to pick out the most significant events after policy decisions are taken. By investigating over a longer time horizon, the analysis provides a useful counterpoint to other approaches that focus on final votes.

Everything Matters, but Not in Equal Measure

Despite some differences in explanations for policy change, several conclusions are clear from the aggregate work of policy historians. The most important is that no actor or circumstance can be entirely excluded from explaining the policy process, but some matter much more consistently than others. The internal machinations of legislative and administrative institutions are paramount in the policy process. The role of interest groups is also substantial and tends to involve multiple groups allying with policymakers. Every other circumstance can affect these crucial factors in the policy process. The roles of path dependence, research, and events are particularly notable. Even when pushed along by these factors, coalitions or compromises among institutional actors are usually responsible for policy change. The kinds of actors that are equipped to repeatedly influence policy are somewhat limited, usually including the president, members of Congress, and major interest groups.

The *actor success* models that focus on the agendas of the president or congressional leaders will include many of the important policy changes enacted by government but also leave out some important changes (especially in administrative agencies and the courts). The universe of possible changes is not restricted to what those actors put on their agendas. The literatures that evaluate policy results by assessing their conformity with the concerns of external constituencies are also incomplete. Policy output is unlikely to reflect only public opinion, interest group mobilization, or the latest research. Assuming influence from these factors and attempting to explain divergent cases is ill advised. None of these three constituencies alone drive policymaking and we should not expect them to do so. Interest groups are reportedly the most influential, but their role arises from leadership by a few prominent groups, rather than from the overall balance of resources between the two sides of a policy debate. *Actor success* models, whether based on institutional agendas or concerns of external constituencies, are not likely to fully assess the national policymaking system. Policy historians provide a broader view, attentive to the relative influence of the many factors that drive policy change.

Returning to the examples that began this chapter can help illustrate. Both the Lilly Ledbetter Fair Pay Act and the JOBS Act were important achievements of the Obama administration, but they are best viewed as outcomes of multifaceted policymaking rather than as Obama successes. Court decisions and Democratic electoral gains were more important in the first case, whereas a Republican congressional leader was critical in the second. Both involved interest groups, but old advocacy groups won in the first case and a new business group won in the second case. When policy historians return to these topics years from now, they are likely to give credit to Obama and legislators, along with many of the same interest groups. Historians may disagree about the relative role of different circumstances outside of government, but the pivotal role of coalitions among policymakers and interest groups will likely be universally apparent.

In policymaking, everything matters, a little bit, sometimes—but the influence of different factors is not close to equivalent. Our view of policymaking should begin with the patterns of cooperation among institutional actors, but not the assumption that any one actor is critical for articulating potential changes and guiding them to enactment. The policy process does not conform to any individual's agenda or any single ideal type.

Conclusion

In March 2013, Barack Obama sought to heal frayed relationships with congressional Republicans in a much-heralded "charm offensive," including one-on-one meetings, a lavish dinner party, and public displays of contrition. The effort was a response to ramped up criticism of his leadership style, but Obama did not fully appreciate the efficacy of quality time with his adversaries: "Some folks still don't think I spend enough time with Congress. 'Why don't you get a drink with Mitch McConnell?' they ask. Really? Why don't you get a drink with Mitch McConnell?" he joked at the White House Correspondents' Dinner.[1]

As pundits repeatedly chided Obama for his lack of schmoozing and its perceived ties to a stalled agenda in Congress, political scientists saw the criticism as largely irrelevant and doubted the impact of any effort to shore up social ties with opposition party legislators. Obama's successes and failures, scholars say, are due to the fundamentals: he had the votes for his initiatives before losing them in the midterm elections in 2010.[2] Increasing ideological polarization and a recalcitrant Republican Party make it impossible to achieve many policy results, with or without social ties. As Matt Yglesias summarized in jest: "Political scientists are going to have a lot of egg on their faces when a single dinner party ends all this polarization."[3]

Undoubtedly, the fate of major legislation rarely hinges on a beer with one powerful senator. Parties of the political variety are far more important to policymaking than those that involve imbibing at the White House. Scholars may nevertheless be too quick to dismiss the importance of relationships among policymakers and shared efforts to find common ground, even if cooperation is not always built on social ties. The notion that dinner parties make Washington work is a caricature of a sentiment that is worthy of more consideration: policymaking requires cooperation among a small cadre of officials.

In harmony with this sentiment, this book has emphasized how political actors engage and compromise with one another, coalescing around proposals for policy change. It has supplied some empirical generalizations about policy history that can shed light on contemporary debates. As in the past, most proposals under consideration by Obama expand the scope of government even though their enactment will require Republican support. Today's Republican Party is a very different animal than the one that confronted Johnson or allied with Nixon; it is easy to see contemporary paralysis as an inevitable outcome of the steady outward ideological drift of the two parties. But policy outcomes are not inevitable consequences of the partisan or ideological climate. Just a decade ago, a Republican president and House were enacting massive expansions of federal intervention in education (No Child Left Behind) and health care (the prescription drug bill).

In considering the capacity for policy change, history suggests avoiding any single actor's perspective. Obama's agenda is hardly a list of probable enactments. Even in the wake of a shocking elementary school shooting, promoting gun control may not accomplish much. Even if election results motivate Republican movement on immigration, a federal overhaul still requires substantial coalition building. Following these efforts, a workable broad compromise may still be unattainable. Alternatively, some significant policy changes may arise without presidential intervention: as Obama focused on high-profile legislation, House and Senate committee chairs reached agreement on agriculture reform, courts ruled on gay rights, and the Department of Education used state waivers to require new policies on national standards and teacher accountability.[4]

None of this suggests that Obama's strategies are to blame for inaction on his priorities, but there is also reason to be skeptical of the competing claim that policy results follow steadfastly from the fundamentals. The most uncharitable recent comparisons, scolding Obama for lacking the skills of Johnson, point to the misleading baseline often used for considering current events. Johnson's established political ties mattered only in combination with the many enabling political trends of the Long Great Society—but that is not the same as saying they were irrelevant. Obama's recent record would look far better in comparison with either the unproductive 1950s (despite low polarization) or the late 1990s (with a Democratic president facing similar Republican opposition). Departures from the norm of inaction require sustained collaborations among many policymakers, alongside supportive circumstances.

This book has investigated which actors and circumstances matter most in the policy process, pointing to governing networks of institutionalized entrepreneurs. To conclude, I reconsider prior theories and highlight the implications of common patterns in policymaking. In light of the findings, I revise standards for evaluating American democracy. Policy history provides neither the foolproof strategy for executive leadership that Obama's pundit critics imagine nor the inevitable policy trends from political fundamentals that political scientists envisage. Although policymakers have autonomy, they lack individual control over policy outcomes: the sustained cooperation among the artists of the possible enables policy change.

Implications for Previous Views of American Policymaking

Four prior families of policy theory are inconsistent with the book's evidence. *Agenda setting* theories emphasize the stage of policy development where government prioritizes the problems facing the country, narrowing the issues that it will consider. I find that there is only a limited relationship between what policymakers discuss most often in any period and what policies they enact. There is little, if any, relationship between what the public cares most about or what the media discusses and what government directly addresses in significant new policy.

Policymaking is not productively viewed as a form of problem prioritization that limits the agenda of possible policy changes. The most important part of the policy process is agreement on policy proposals, which does not require or follow from a shared issue agenda. Although a proposal must formally make it on the legislative, administrative, or judicial docket to be enacted, neither the public nor the government agenda turn out to be a useful blueprint to understanding the time, institution, or issue area where policy change will take place.

Policy historians explain policy change by referencing internal factors in government institutions and bargaining among politicians and interest groups. Factors related to the machinations of the executive and legislative branches, as well as interest group advocacy, usually explain policy change. At a somewhat less frequent rate, policy historians point to both the event-driven policymaking emphasized by *agenda setting* models and the incremental policy development of historical institutionalism. When external factors like public opinion, election results, and media coverage reportedly influence policy change, they do so in tandem with internal factors in government institutions. Rarely is government as a whole swept along in response to social trends without substantial internal maneuvering. This process of elite cooperation and compromise is dominated by a small number of actors. Many different circumstances outside of government can help these institutionalized entrepreneurs, but their sustained relationships and compromises are the key components of policy development.

Macro politics models of policy output are also inconsistent with the findings of policy historians. I find that trends in ideology, partisanship, and public opinion make surprisingly little difference in understanding the flow of policy output. They matter, but only in conjunction with institutional and behavioral changes. Policymaking was more active and liberal for a prolonged period in the Long Great Society. This is not only a demonstration that one historical era is unaccounted for by existing theory but also a sign that the factors influencing policy may differ over time. Neither the amount nor the ideological direction of policymaking follows consistently from the same political inputs.

The policymaking system does not respond like a pendulum, moving left and right in response to public opinion and election results. Policy output is not a simple function of the partisanship or ideology of legislators, presidents, or judges. The conservative or liberal nature of policy advancement is not well predicted by the parties in control of government, the median ideology of policymakers, or liberal or conservative trends in the American public. Likewise, the total amount of significant policy produced by government is not especially responsive to ideological polarization, divided party government, or the rise of new presidents or new parties. Models of policy output and ideological direction based on these variables do not fit the historical data since 1945, even accounting for inertia from one year to the next.

The classification of the Long Great Society as a unique period alone explains the productivity and ideological direction of all three branches of government better than traditional *macro politics* models. This is not to say that putting the remaining years in an "other" box is a successful model, only that a realistic assessment of the causes of policy change requires more than simple and constant relationships between political inputs and policy output.

This book's evidence is also inconsistent with *issue typologies* that suggest dividing policy areas into clear categories, each with a different form of policymaking. Issue area differences do not amount to distinct policymaking types; instead, I find a series of issue-specific exceptions to the general policy process. Policymaking is broadly similar across issue areas; the differences are multidimensional and continuous, rather than the abrupt categories that traditional typologies envision. Issue area politics cannot be summarized with a two-by-two table.

Although differences cannot be ignored, typologies are not likely to bear fruit. Issue area differences encompass both institutional characteristics of policymaking, such as how often and in what venues policy change occurs, and the circumstantial characteristics responsible for policymaking, such as the relative role of research and media coverage. All issue areas are somewhat episodic and somewhat path dependent, but there are differences in degree. The pattern of subtle variation also applies to the actors responsible for policy change in each domain and the structure of their relationships. Ideal types like iron triangles (tight alliances among actors from three different institutions) and issue networks (discussion groups of like-minded experts) are unhelpful in distinguishing policymaking in different issue areas. The findings also suggest that prior studies disproportionately focus on one or two features of policymaking when they use case studies of issue areas where those factors are most important.

The similarities across issue areas correspond to the general findings from policy history: no matter the issue concern, institutionalized entrepreneurs coalescing and compromising within government institutions are key components of policymaking. I find no issue areas where policy outcomes are primarily a product of public opinion, media coverage, or research trends. Insular policymaking via cooperation among political officials and interest groups is not merely a type of political conflict; it is the typical form of policymaking across the issue spectrum. Occasional issue area divergence from this pattern is a matter of degree, rather than type.

Another family of theories explores differences across actors, rather than issue areas. *Actor success* models focus on one category of actors and assess their influence on policy, explaining whether and how actors achieve their goals. I reviewed five sets of these models, finding consistency in form despite disagreements about the most important actors in policymaking. These areas of scholarship each find that their preferred actors have conditional influence due to their character and context: some presidents, legislators, interest groups, scientists, and public subgroups are more successful than others.

My critique of these theories began with a difference in perspective. Presidential and congressional success rates are not necessarily indicative of the influence of either actor; finding policy consistent with public opinion or scientific evidence likewise does not demonstrate influence. A policy change may have support from all or none of these quarters. Since no actor's agenda is a definitive guide to potential policy changes, there is little reason to assume that the policies enacted from each actor's list are indicative of their success.

The approach of the *actor success* models is at odds with the historical evidence of the many different factors that influence public policy. No single policymaker or type of advocate appears in a majority of explanations for policy change, much less reportedly plays a definitive role in all enactments. Across evidence from different methods and types of scholars, policy history is most consistent with a strong role for negotiations inside political institutions. Even though each policy historian may focus on different components of the policy process, they still come to agreement in aggregate on the most important factors in policymaking. Aided by a wide variety of stimulating circumstances, rotating subsets of the policy community build coalitions and forge compromises that enable wide acquiescence. Some historians cast a wider net in their explanations for policy change, but not with a consistent difference in emphasis. No actor determines policy, but presidents, legislators, and interest groups are more commonly influential.

Implications of the Most Common Patterns in Policy History

Despite inconsistency with previous theory, policy history provides grounds for a systematic view of American policymaking. The findings from my aggregation of the judgments of policy historians suggest empirical regularities to guide future scholarship. American policy history since 1945 is not amenable to modeling with a few exogenous variables, but it is hardly a random series of events. Even though policymaking is complicated, there are clear lessons from policy history concerning both the nature of most policy changes and their causes.

IDEOLOGICAL ASYMMETRY

The first generalization concerns the ideological nature of most significant policy changes: they expand the scope of government responsibility. Comparatively few contract government's scope.[5] Path dependence and inertia in policymaking are not ideologically neutral. Status quo bias makes it most difficult to unmake previous government programs, rather than prevent government incursion into new areas of concern. Most mechanisms for self-reinforcing policy feedback involve support and expansion: policies create constituencies of interest groups, bureaucrats, and legislators that support extension or at least maintenance of the policy. Contractions of government are thus more difficult. This pattern is not merely applicable to incremental adjustments or bureaucratic policymaking: I find a long-running and cross-branch pattern of liberal policy change being more common.

Some issue areas are almost entirely stories of liberal expansion, like civil rights. Even in issue areas like housing, where most policymaking occurred outside of the Long Great Society, liberal policy still predominates. It is hard to find issue areas where enactments have mostly contracted government over an extended period, though there are some—especially macroeconomics—with a more even mix of expansion and contraction. In some historical periods, conservatives thought government expansion was inevitable and made compromises in order to shape that expansion. In others, liberals built a reform coalition with conservatives that expanded government in many areas while contracting it in a few. The most conservative periods of policymaking since 1945 were both short-lived: the first biennium following Reagan's election in the executive branch and the 1995-1996 congress following the Republican takeover. Far more common were time periods where little new policy moved forward; through policy drift and lack of remedial action, this inaction may have produced conservative results.

Scholars studying policy productivity and its ideological direction are largely analyzing the same time series. Trends toward relative conservatism are often trends toward lower productivity, even though previous models predicted them with different sets of variables. Because there is a fundamental asymmetry in policy, predicting liberalism with Democratic control of government while predicting productivity with partisan division is inappropriate. Higher productivity and a more liberal direction must, in part, be associated with the same precursors. The advancement of liberalism may be dependent as much on cooperation among governing officials and interest groups as on an increasingly liberal composition of Congress.

The ideological asymmetry of policy change may explain why observers often view contemporary Republicans as intransigent.[6] Given that most potential policy changes expand the scope of government, it is understandable that conservatives are not typically proactive partners in the process of policy change. Nevertheless, polarized ideological patterns in the legislature, or between Congress and the President, have sometimes coincided with bipartisan coalitions behind significant policy changes—as the second Reagan and first George W. Bush administrations illustrate. Polarized congressional voting in macroeconomics and health consistently co-existed with relatively bipartisan coalitions behind enacted policy changes. Consensus-oriented policymaking designed to expand federal government responsibility is surprisingly common. Patterns of cooperation among institutionalized entrepreneurs are only partially explained by their ideology and partisanship—and ideological homogeneity is no guarantor of productivity. Some historical periods, such as the 1940s and 1950s, were associated with low levels of significant policymaking despite low polarization.

Concern over the upward trend in congressional polarization may obscure two important types of enacting coalitions: (1) Republicans have sometimes voted in unison behind expansions of government responsibility, such as the Medicare prescription drug bill and (2) a few conservative actors like Nixon and the National Association of Manufacturers have worked with mostly liberal coalitions to enact expansionary policies. The breakdown of twenty-first-century Washington policymaking may not be an inevitable consequence of decades of polarization, but a product of the particular actors currently in power and their failures of cooperation. The contemporary Republican move to the right likely inhibits both significant policy change and liberal advancement, but the mechanisms may not be straightforward. Conservative participation in policymaking coalitions may be more forthcoming under Republican presidents. The lack of a few willing conservative partners geared toward having their names attached to significant policy changes may dampen policy productivity more than aggregate moves in congressional opinion.

The more fundamental implication is that policymaking by conservative and liberal governments will not be mirror images. Republicans may enact a less extensive and more ideologically mixed set of policies, perhaps by seeking market-oriented expansions of government responsibility alongside a few major contractionary policies. Dysfunctions in coalition building and governance will tend to encumber liberals more than conservatives; polarization may dampen liberal victories even as conservative activists complain that their leaders are compromising too much. The baseline expectation should be for low levels of policymaking and government expansion, with few periods of overwhelming liberal advancement but even fewer of across-the-board contraction.

THE MOST IMPORTANT FACTORS IN POLICY CHANGE

The aggregate view from policy history delineates the most and least important factors in American policymaking. A few causal factors predominate in explanations for significant policy change, even though occasional causes are diverse. The factors that matter most often are those within national political institutions. Lots of external circumstances can push action along, but coalition and compromise among policymakers is nearly always critical. Explanations for policy change emphasize leadership by particular individuals and organizations, especially presidents, legislators, and interest groups. Government enacts many policies without much external pressure, but few without internal negotiations and coalition building.

There do not seem to be major changes in the relative importance of different factors across time. There is a consistent top tier of causal factors in major policymaking: internal negotiations in the legislative and executive branch alongside interest group advocacy. There is also a relatively consistent middle tier of factors responsible for policy change: path dependence from previous policies, scientific research and reports, and external real-world events. Although factors related to public opinion and elections are of increasing importance, they usually fall in a third tier of important factors in American policymaking alongside media coverage, ideas, judicial decisions, and international and sub-national actions. There is a clear pecking order of which types of factors are most important: those interested in federal policymaking should look first at congressional maneuvering, executive branch leadership, and interest group advocacy. Beyond that, dozens of other factors are worth considering, but none are consistently important.

INSULAR POLICYMAKING

The findings undercut the common notion that US policymaking derives from the preferences of the American public. The liberalism of public opinion is not predictive of the liberalism of policy because policymakers can ignore public backlashes; the most significant divergence was in the latter part of the Long Great Society. Public opinion tends to move in the opposite ideological direction following policy change, but policy does not move back consistently in response. Policymaking in all three branches of government lacks a consistent responsive pattern.

There are other signs of insularity from public pressure. There is little relationship between the issue areas of concern to the public and those that policymakers address. To the extent that government responds to the public's concerns, it seems to do so in less important bills and executive statements. Despite quite a few idiosyncratic differences in policymaking across issue areas, there was no policy domain where public pressure was the most important factor driving policy change.

There is a long road from election results to policy outcomes. To play a role in policy, elections may need to produce consistent and overwhelming results that are either heeded directly by policymakers or lead to a new breed of elected officials willing to pursue different policies. Even this mechanism is restricted to legislative policymaking, where ideological trends often develop slowly with low levels of replacement. One historical period, the first Clinton administration, did entail Democratic victories and two years of liberal policy followed quickly by Republican victories and conservative policy, but this pattern is far from the norm.

Presidents, congressional leaders, and interest groups play the most important role in major policy outcomes. Although these actors all have superficial connections to public constituencies, voters cannot easily predict their behavior. Certainly, Nixon voters in 1968 did not expect a continuation of the Great Society and Clinton voters in 1996 did not expect the most conservative second term since 1945. The most heavily involved interest groups also make claims of public representation, but there is little reason to believe that they are merely passing through public views to policymakers.[7]

The lack of a consistent role for public opinion also challenges common periodizations of American politics. Scholars pointing to activist eras claim that public opinion is the main input to a historical period, even though opinion is often moving against the trend in policy (as in the Reagan years). When historians describe the mood of an era, they may be focusing on an elite consensus rather than measured public opinion. Policymakers may reach agreement on a particular direction or decide that it is inevitable, even absent substantial change in public input.

INSTITUTIONALIZED ENTREPRENEURS

One reason that the public may be unable to direct policy is that a small subset of policymakers and activists lead the development of policy proposals, the coalition-building process, and the negotiations that lead to compromises. Equilibrium-based theories of voting in institutions based on pivotal voters or formal powers will not predict policy development, which draws more from entrepreneurs pushing proposals and building working coalitions than on

satisfying members with stable and known ideological preferences. Allied entrepreneurs are often based in separate institutions and not tied to a single policy
area subsystem. Building separate models of each American national institution
or analyzing separate policymaking communities based on issue areas is unlikely
to successfully explain how a small group of institutionalized entrepreneurs succeed in driving policy change across contexts.

Observers of American policymaking must pay attention to these entrepreneurs, especially serial workhorse policymakers. The next Moynihan, Kennedy,
Dole, or Javits could emerge to tackle a variety of problems, finding workable
solutions and selling them to multiple constituencies. Actors that seek to make
contributions in many policy areas and are willing to make compromises nearly
always play a role in policymaking. Institutionalized entrepreneurs tend to think
in terms of "what can be achieved that I support" rather than "how can I move
policy to my ideal point in the areas of my chief concerns." Following the Reagan
and George W. Bush elections, Ted Kennedy selected issue areas on which he
could find common ground with both (despite his role as liberal icon). These
actors also block policy, but tend to favor action.

Two traits seem to distinguish institutionalized entrepreneurs from other
policymakers. First, they desire change for its own sake; they want something to
show for their work. They may like to have their name attached to legislation or
seek a legacy. Alternatively, they may have more faith that the governing process
reconciles competing concerns and that compromises will move policy in a productive direction. This attitude likely makes them more devoted to working on
policy proposal development, long before they know what the eventual compromise will entail. Presidents may be especially likely to favor action, even when
they assume that their policy goals will be diluted, because they feel obliged to
accumulate achievements. Even presidential policy-oriented behavior, however,
is not easily predicted: Nixon acted like a Democrat in many areas of domestic
policy, Johnson surprisingly embraced Kennedy's agenda, and Reagan reversed
his ideological course midway in several issue areas.

A second shared trait is the willingness to see the perfect as enemy of the
good. Institutionalized entrepreneurs often possess a monomaniacal obsession
with resolving disputes so that some policy can be enacted. They are willing to
trade favors, give in on secondary concerns, and avoid hot button issues that
engender criticism. They find ways to respond to critics' concerns. They cajole
usual allies to avoid pushing pet concerns that might curtail a proposal's chance
of success. In 2013, this process was evident in the concessions made by the
"Gang of Eight" senators pushing immigration reform. They sought a broad
group of supporters to project consensus, neutralized key interest group and
Senate opponents with side deals, and convinced allies to withhold amendments that they supported but thought would derail their bill.[8] Not all of these

efforts succeed, but the profusion of Senate "gangs" around various issue areas signals that coalitions among bipartisan workhorses continue to help drive policy change. The repeated inclusion of the same senators in these groups illustrates how these entrepreneurs distinguish themselves from other policymakers through their repeated involvement.

GOVERNING NETWORKS

Institutionalized entrepreneurs do not operate as lonesome heroes, but as cogs in broader patterns of cooperation in American governance. I have conceptualized the relationships among actors responsible for policy change as governing networks. The idea is that the behavior of policymakers and activists is interdependent, such that no individual leadership and no specific deal should be viewed in isolation. The aggregate patterns of advocacy, coalition, and compromise among actors in a time period or issue area illustrate the productive cooperation that makes policy change possible. The centrality of actors in these networks provides a measure of the most critical institutionalized entrepreneurs. The structure of relationships among all actors provides clues about what distinguishes each policy community and what enables activist eras.

The most important feature of the governing network of the Long Great Society was the sustained cross-issue and cross-branch relationships that it featured, with a core of central actors responsible for policymaking in all three branches in many domains over sixteen years. This implies that the traditional concept of issue networks is too limiting. A network of actors may surround an issue area, but its most important members may be those that transcend the issue, such as presidents or congressional leaders. A network may not be a replacement for a subsystem, but a means of connecting actors across institutional and policy contexts.

Nevertheless, networks that enable activist eras are rare. A governing network evolves over time as actors are replaced and make new connections. Scholars tend to see abrupt regime changes even when slow transitions and long-term trends may be operating. Stories involving the collapse of a subsystem, the balkanization of an issue network, or the capture of government agencies by interest groups may be simplifications of slow changes in network composition and structure. One network hardly ever replaces another entirely. Even when a new president from a new party comes to Washington, they do not always bring a transformation of participation or alliances. They rely on existing working relationships and build connections with the most involved actors. Slow trends such as interest group expansion and ideological polarization also may be influencing network structure and composition, even as new presidents or congressional leaders arise.

Governing networks are diverse in their composition across issue areas; some have more legislators, others more interest groups, and others more administrative agencies. They are also diverse in structure; some are centralized around a single dominant actor, some have a core–periphery structure, and some have dense connections throughout the whole network. The content of policy output reflects the composition of governing networks more than the general ideology of Congress, but there is still a gap between the ideological composition of the network and the direction of policymaking. Polarized voting in Congress does not always produce a polarized governing network; a few polarized issue networks are still associated with extensive and bipartisan policy change. Because network differences are multidimensional, scholars should not expect to repeatedly see specific network types with the same combination of characteristics.

The promise of network analysis is that it focuses on the interdependence of actors. Classic statistical models assume that each observation is independent, but that is unlikely in a phenomenon like congressional voting. Networks enable assessments of how the structure of ties among actors changes both individual behavior and aggregate outcomes. Nevertheless, network researchers should be cautious in attempting to discover standard structures that describe policy communities. I emphasize that network composition may be just as important as structure. Most network studies define a population within a particular venue or issue area and study their pattern of interaction—but determining who is active in an area may be half the investigation. There is a substantial skew to policymaking participation in most networks. Some actors have many more connections than most; others have bridging connections across the political system. Network roles are hardly equal, even in institutions like Congress where every vote counts the same.

If policymaker behavior is interdependent and driven by system-wide patterns of cooperation in different historical periods and issue areas, it will not be easy to distinguish the relative role played by each actor. The network approach assumes that each actor's singular role cannot be independently observed. When actors jointly enact policy change, it is not readily apparent whether each actor was necessary or sufficient for the change to occur. Visualizing the patterns of cooperation over an extended period, however, can demonstrate what kinds of actors and ties tend to be regularly associated with policy change. Policy history suggests that most actors have minimal roles compared to a few central institutionalized entrepreneurs; their ties across branches, parties, and issue areas are consistently important.

The Long Great Society as an Exceptional Period

American policymaking has been extensive in only one era since 1945: during the Long Great Society from 1961 to 1976. This era saw a tremendous expansion in the scope of government in nearly every policy area and across all branches of government. Rather than wait for issues to rise on the agenda, institutionalized entrepreneurs allied on a broad liberal program. This empowered four successive experienced presidents, dozens of long-serving members of Congress, and several well-known interest groups to enact numerous policy changes across the issue spectrum. The confluence of many political trends in the 1960s and 1970s helped create a separable era of policymaking. The repeated coalitions and compromises of major political actors enabled policies to build on themselves even after facing headwinds from conservative shifts in public opinion and Republican victories.

This one extended instance does not mean that all eras of productive or liberal policymaking will take the same shape. The New Deal and Progressive eras may have also involved a confluence of supportive circumstances and successful entrepreneurs, but not all liberal eras may draw from the same underlying conditions. Since extensive policymaking is far from the norm, the process leading to productive eras is likely to involve many factors that interact to change the system-level features of American policymaking. Scholars cannot reduce each institution to a system operating on its own. Trends in each branch of government and in the external factors that influence them can interact to create a historical period that overcomes normally endemic status quo bias.

The Long Great Society entailed both liberal and productive policymaking, consistent with underlying mechanisms that make liberal policy change more likely than conservative change. The era featured four presidents with congressional experience; as a result, each had ties to many of the same interest groups and legislators. All three branches of government moved together toward more liberal policy. Action by the courts and administrative agencies drew from pressure by the same interest groups as well as influence from Congress and the president. System-level transformations that affect all branches and issue areas, though infrequent, may be the most important changes in policymaking.

The Long Great Society sometimes serves as an unwarranted comparison for what policymaking is supposed to entail. Concerns about polarization or gridlock often take the 1960s and 1970s as the normal baseline even though the period is a substantial outlier. Rather than equal bipartisanship, the period was dominated by the centrality of liberal policymakers accompanied by a few willing Republicans. Nixon and Ford were directly tied to the liberal governing network, including an external apparatus of interest groups and activists. In addition to bipartisan compromises, the period also featured liberal initiatives where conservatives remained mostly on the sidelines.

This height of liberalism was not taken as a triumph for liberals at the time. Johnson and Nixon, the chief antagonists of the era's street protestors, led government expansion. Since the Vietnam War was the public focus of attention, liberal activists did not recognize the exceptional nature of the latter part of the period for major domestic policy innovation. The conservative opposition later regrouped, but not before the American state had dramatically expanded. The lack of an early conservative counter-mobilization and interest group infrastructure may have frustrated efforts to create a competing coalition. Perhaps a sustained liberal governing coalition is less foreseeable in today's era with conservative Republicans accompanied by external conservative interest groups.

Many different trends converged to create the Long Great Society, including Democratic majorities, an expanded issue agenda, more interest groups, social movements, an expansion of the presidential branch and individual Senate staff, and changes in the rules of evidence and standing in the courts. Each trend may individually be associated with increased potential for government action, but scholars should watch for periods in which multiple trends point in the same direction. Trends enabling government expansion should be especially promising for enabling a productive era, whereas a system-wide era of government retraction would be more unprecedented. Although contemporary policymaking is far from that seen in the Long Great Society, no individual trend is the culprit. Limited policy change is the historical norm.

The Lessons for Democratic Accountability

Most overviews of American government begin with the public: it elects the politicians and provides its consent for their behavior. Since drawing from public preferences is the essence of democracy, the lack of connection between public opinion and policy outcomes in my findings should be jarring. There is certainly reason to hope that the American public plays some permanent and important role in policymaking, but that does not imply that it does.

Previous theories that emphasize public input highlight its importance for democratic accountability. If the public were able to focus policymaker attention by deciding what problems government should address, agenda setting would be another route to democratic governance.[9] If this avenue of influence is weak, the role of the public in guiding elite concerns is less apparent. Policymakers will act more often in some issues and time periods, regardless of the public's concerns. Elite response to top public concerns may entail symbolic actions at best.

Models of policy change based on trends in ideology, partisanship, and public mood also claim a democratic vision of American governance. The public provides its consent through broad changes in ideology, mandate elections, or backlashes against policymakers that move too far to the left or right. If public opinion trends and policymaker ideology do not lead to foreseeable policy outcomes, this vision of democratic influence is less attractive. The public may occasionally attempt to send a message regarding policy direction, but that does not mean that policymakers will listen. The aggregate results of interactions among elected officials may not resemble the sentiments in public opinion that helped bring them to power.

The view that only some issues are ripe for public influence, whereas others are best seen as driven by interest groups, generated no more support. The hope for public input into decision-making cannot rest on the claim that it is merely restricted to some issue areas. Neither participation nor policy outcomes are predictable based on whether the potential benefits and costs of action or narrow or wide. No issue area seems properly conceived as public-dominated. Likewise, no issue network is representative of the broader public. Participants in governing networks have their own interests, ideas, and habits that help to shape policy outcomes.

To the extent that the public matters in policymaking, the influence is usually indirect: the public elects particular officials; public subgroups help to form interest groups. Elected officials and interest groups are not simply delegates; they are guided by personal views and tendencies. The institutionalized entrepreneurs that guide policymaking see themselves as trustees; they often ignore public opinion to pursue their own view of the public interest. Even if elites respond to public concerns, coalition and compromise among interest groups and policymakers is not guided primarily by their representative roles.

Because a small subset of the policy community is responsible for the bulk of policy change, traditional notions of public representation may not offer much hope for public influence on policy results. Members of Congress may be more likely to vote on the side of their constituents' opinions or economic interests, but that will matter only if the final vote is more than a foregone conclusion in a long process of policy development. Interest groups may represent a wide variety of public interests, but broad mobilization will be less germane if only a few groups make an enduring mark on policy history. The compromises that are forged by policymakers and activists tend to satisfy the most pressing concerns among the most active participants, rather than those of the public. Even when policymaking is less insular, public opinion is only one among many sources of external influence; policy is also guided by research, events, and past policies that may have little input from the public.

This explains why both liberals and conservatives in the American public can be unsatisfied, with both sides viewing government as unresponsive. Liberals see problems that must be solved and solutions that are widely acceptable— and yet no action is taken. They think politics gets in the way of problem solving and cannot understand how conservatives keep blocking necessary change. Conservatives, meanwhile, see a government that regularly expands its responsibilities with little opportunity to reassess its previous actions. The leaders they elect seem to lose touch when in office, compromising with liberals to expand government. Each ideological view can be seen as a perspective on the same underlying policy process; there is substantial status quo bias but comparatively few contractions of government responsibility.

As critics on both sides allege, policy is mostly a result of actions "inside the beltway." Across policy areas, the public lacks substantial input into the concerns that government addresses and the direction that its solutions take. Policymakers and interest group leaders are far removed from public pressure and presume to govern on the public's behalf. Within the range of policy options that the national government usually considers, the public plays at best a peripheral role—despite their mechanisms for theoretically controlling the actions of elected officials. Elites chastise the public for re-electing the same leaders while distrusting their institutions, but disenchantment is reasonable given the loose connections between the public's electoral tools and the aggregate policy results of government.

None of this is meant to suggest that the United States fails the test of democracy. Accountability may operate by keeping politicians within a range of acceptable outcomes (including most of those up for debate in national institutions). The fear of a public backlash may limit the scope of the actions that government takes, helping to entrench the status quo. One could certainly imagine a counterfactual where sustained public opposition to a party's agenda led to a new government with new policies, even if overwhelming and impactful public shifts are rare. Because the public chooses not to endorse one governing ideology with full-throated support, policy development is usually limited and slow.

There may thus be a way to reconcile policy history with a more democratic view of American government. Nonetheless, the findings undercut several attempts to reconcile the contemporary practice of policymaking with foundational views in democratic theory. The public may be the ultimate source of politicians and some interest groups; it may theoretically be able to respond to policy change by holding political leaders accountable. In practice, these public roles seem quite circumscribed, at least in helping to determine the content, direction, and amount of policy change. National policymaking is substantially more insular and elite-directed than defenders of the Americans system want to believe.

The Practice of American Policymaking and Its Future

Since this book has been a compendium of the past, readers cannot be sure whether its findings will help predict the next direction of American policy. What can the collective wisdom of policy historians tell us about where government is likely to move in the future? Traditionally, pundits and scholars look at elections and ideological trends. Obama was elected to a second term on the basis of demographic change, an unpopular Republican party, and an economy in recovery: perhaps liberals are in ascendance. The parties, however, continue to polarize ideologically and a divided Congress seems incapable of substantial policymaking. Surprisingly, policy history suggests that future policy change may follow from neither of these trends.

To understand today's potential for policy change, Americans should look at the relationships among central policymakers and large interest groups. Harry Reid, John Boehner, Obama, and the major business and advocacy groups are best positioned to influence policy development. A focus on the headlines nonetheless has costs; it is easy to become distracted by atmospherics and political posturing where no policy is likely to change. Observers should also follow the many different components of policymaking that might occasionally play a role in policy innovation. No one event, media report, or public survey should be taken too seriously as an omen of policy to come, but neither can they be ignored.

Institutionalized entrepreneurs will do the hard work, channeling promising trends, compromising on actionable proposals, and building coalitions to gain wide acquiescence. Individuals and their relationships matter for policy success. Observers should watch participants in Senate "gangs" and veterans of previous compromises for a glimpse of potential serial policymakers. Perhaps Chuck Schumer and John McCain or Mitch McConnell and Joe Biden are the institutionalized entrepreneurs of today. It also pays to look at issues seemingly off the agenda, recognizing the slow development of consensus as well as ongoing conflicts. Perhaps innovations in federal technology or education policy may come without much notice.

The best bet in Washington politics is always on the status quo. "Not much" is still the best answer for what might happen over the next decade. Obama's first administration was marked by coalitions of legislators and interest groups on each side of the political spectrum but little evidence of effective compromises between the parties or productive communication across the ideological divide. No doubt pundits will continue to lodge complaints about Obama's lack of social ties with legislators; political scientists will continue to emphasize how policymaker decisions are governed by the fundamentals. Policy history suggests that Americans should expect a gradual expansion of the scope of government, with a few major policy changes each year. Lots of trends would have to converge to create a new golden age of policymaking, but a few fortuitous factors could lead to new policy development in some issue areas.

Most Americans will be spectators in the policymaking process. Individual activists and public constituencies can influence policy, but long-established policymakers and interest groups are likely to have much more central roles. Since no policy response is inevitable and influence can come from many quarters, pursuing policies through all available channels may still be the best course for activists seeking change. Established policymakers must cooperate to shape policy, but a new proposal or an idea for compromise can come from anywhere. Even though extensive and direction-changing policymaking is rare, the decentralized American system is open to many different possibilities. Politics is the art of the possible, even if few ideas from any individual are likely to become the law of the land. As its authors contemplate their next moves, the future of American policy is not yet written.

Appendix A

POLICY HISTORY SOURCES AND CONTENT ANALYSIS QUESTIONS

Policy History Sources by Area

AGRICULTURE—14 BOOKS, 3 ARTICLES

Bowers, Douglas, Wayne D. Rasmussen, and Gladys L. Baker. "History of Agricultural Price-Support and Adjustment Programs, 1933–84." *Agriculture Information Bulletin* 485, no. 1 (1984): 1–58.

Cochrane, Willard W. *American Farm Policy, 1948–1973*. Minneapolis: University of Minnesota Press, 1976.

Coleman, William D., Grace D. Skogstad, and Michael M. Atkinson. "Paradigm Shifts and Policy Networks: Cumulative Change in Agriculture." *Journal of Public Policy* 16 (1996): 273–301.

Conkin, Paul K. *A Revolution Down on the Farm: The Transformation of American Agriculture since 1929*. Lexington: University Press of Kentucky, 2008.

Gardner, Bruce L. *American Agriculture in the Twentieth Century: How it Flourished and What it Cost*. Cambridge, MA: Harvard University Press, 2002.

Lehrer, Nadine. *U.S. Farm Bills and Policy Reforms: Ideological Conflicts over World Trade, Renewable Energy, and Sustainable Agriculture*. Amherst, NY: Cambria Press, 2010.

Moyer, H. Wayne, and Timothy Edward Josling. *Agricultural Policy Reform: Politics and Process in the EU and US in the 1990s*. London: Ashgate Publishing, 2002.

Opie, John. *The Law of the Land: Two Hundred Years of American Farmland Policy*. Lincoln: University of Nebraska Press, 1994.

Orden, David, Robert Paarlberg, and Terry Roe. *Policy Reform in American Agriculture: Analysis and Prognosis*. Chicago: University of Chicago Press, 1999.

Pasour, E. C., Jr., Randall R. Rucker, and Bruce L. Gardner. *Plowshares and Pork Barrels: The Political Economy of Agriculture*. Washington, DC: Independent Institute, 2005.

Patashnik, Eric M. *Reforms at Risk: What Happens After Major Policy Changes are Enacted*. Princeton: Princeton University Press, 2008.

Rapp, David. *How the U.S. Got into Agriculture and Why it Can't Get Out*. Washington, DC: CQ Press, 1988.

Schnidman, Frank. "The Evolving Federal Role in Agricultural Land Preservation." *Urban Law* 18, no. 1 (1986): 423.

Sheingate, Adam D. *The Rise of the Agricultural Welfare State: Institutions and Interest Group Power in the United States, France, and Japan.* Princeton: Princeton University Press, 2003.

Ulrich, Hugh. *Losing Ground: Agricultural Policy and the Decline of the American Farm.* Chicago: Chicago Review Press, 1989.

United States Department of Agriculture. *History of Agriculture Price-Support and Adjustment Programs, 1933–84.* Washington, DC: United States Department of Agriculture, 1985.

Winders, Bill, and James C. Scott. *The Politics of Food Supply: U.S. Agricultural Policy in the World Economy.* New Haven: Yale University Press, 2012.

CIVIL RIGHTS AND LIBERTIES—24 BOOKS, 4 ARTICLES

Alley, Robert S. *School Prayer: The Court, the Congress and the First Amendment.* Amherst, NY: Prometheus Books, 1994.

Ashmore, Harry S. *Civil Rights and Wrongs.* New York: Pantheon, 1994.

Bok, Marcia. *Civil Rights and the Social Programs of the 1960's.* Westport, CT: Praeger Publishers, 1992.

Browne-Marshall, Gloria J. *Race, Law and American Society.* New York: Routledge, 2007.

Burstein, Paul. *Discrimination, Jobs, and Politics: The Struggle for Equal Employment Opportunity in the United States since the New Deal.* Chicago: University of Chicago Press, 1985.

Conway, M. Margaret, David W. Ahern, and Gertrude A. Steuernagel. *Women and Public Policy.* Washington: CQ Press, 1999.

D'Emilio, John, William B. Turner, and Urvashi Vaid. *Creating Change: Sexuality, Public Policy, and Civil Rights.* New York: St. Martin's, 2000.

Edelman, Marian Wright. "Southern School Desegregation. 1954–1973: A Judicial-Political Overview." *The ANNALS of the American Academy of Political and Social Science* 407, no. 1 (1973): 32–42.

Foerstel, Herbert N. *Freedom of Information and the Right to Know.* Santa Barbara, CA: Greenwood Publishing Group, 1999.

Graham, Hugh Davis. *The Civil Rights Era: Origins and Development of National Policy, 1960-1972.* Oxford: Oxford University Press, 1990.

——. "The Origins of Affirmative Action: Civil Rights and the Regulatory State." *The ANNALS of the American Academy of Political and Social Science* 523, no. 1 (1992): 50–62.

Harrison, Cynthia. *On Account of Sex.* Berkeley: University of California Press, 1988.

Jenness, Valerie, and Ryken Grattet. *Making Hate A Crime: From Social Movement to Law Enforcement.* New York: Russell Sage Foundation, 2001.

Koltlowski, Dean. "With All Deliberate Delay: Kennedy, Johnson, and School Desegregation." *Journal of Policy History* 17, no. 2 (2005): 155–192.

Landsberg, Brian K. *Enforcing Civil Rights: Race Discrimination and the Department of Justice.* Lawrence: University Press of Kansas, 1997.

Laughlin, Kathleen A. *Women's Work and Public Policy: A History of the Women's Bureau, U.S. Department of Labor, 1945–1970.* Boston: Northeastern University Press, 2000.

Lawson, Steven F. *Black Ballots: Voting and Rights in the South 1944-1969.* New York: Columbia University Press, 1976.

——. *Running for Freedom: Civil Rights and Black Politics in America since 1941.* New York: McGraw-Hill, 1997.

Layton, Azza Salama. *International Politics and Civil Rights Policies in the United States, 1941-1960.* Cambridge: Cambridge University Press, 2000.

Lichtman, Allan. "The Federal Assault Against Voting Discrimination in the Deep South, 1957-1967." *Journal of Negro History* 54, no. 4 (1969): 346–367.

Riddlesperger, James, Jr., and Donald Jackson. *Presidential Leadership and Civil Rights Policy.* Westport, CT: Greenwood, 1995.

Rimmerman, Craig A., Kenneth D. Wald, and Clyde Wilcox, eds. *The Politics of Gay Rights.* Chicago: University of Chicago Press, 2000.

Schrecker, Ellen. *The Age of McCarthyism.* New York: St. Martin's Press, 2002.

Shull, Steven A. *American Civil Rights Policy from Truman to Clinton: The Role of Presidential Leadership.* Armonk, NY: M. E. Sharpe, 1999.

Skrentny, John D. *The Minority Rights Revolution.* Cambridge, MA: Belknap Press of Harvard University Press, 2002.

Solinger, Rickle. *Abortion Wars: A Half Century of Struggle, 1950–2000.* Berkeley: University of California Press, 1998.

Stetson, Dorothy McBride. *Women's Rights in the USA.* New York: Garland Publishing, 1997.

Switzer, Jaqueline Vaugh. *Disabled Rights: American Disability Policy and the Fight for Equality.* Washington, DC: Georgetown University Press, 2003.

CRIMINAL JUSTICE—15 BOOKS

Feeley, Malcom M., and Austin D. Sarat. *The Policy Dilemma: Federal Crime Policy and the Law Enforcement Assistance Administration, 1968-1978.* Minneapolis: University of Minnesota Press, 1981.

Jenness, Valerie, and Ryken Grattet. *Making Hate a Crime: From Social Movement to Law Enforcement.* New York: Russell Sage Foundation, 2001.

Marion, Nancy. *Criminal Justice in America: The Politics behind the System.* Durham, NC: Carolina Academic Press, 2002.

——. *A History of Federal Crime Control Initiatives, 1960-1993.* Westport, CT: Praeger Publishers, 1994.

——. *A Primer in the Politics of Criminal Justice,* 2nd ed. Monsey, NY: Criminal Justice Press, 2007.

Miller, Lisa L. *The Perils of Federalism: Race, Poverty, and the Politics of Crime Control.* New York: Oxford University Press, 2008.

O'Brien, John T., and Marvin Marcus, eds. *Crime and Justice in America: Critical Issues for the Future.* Oxford: Pergamon Press, 1980.

Olvier, Willard, Nancy Marion, and Barbara Ann Stolz. *The Making of Criminal Justice Policy in the United States: Essays on the Role of the President, the Congress, and the Public.* Lewiston, NY: Edwin Mellen Press, 2008.

Scheingold, Stuart. *The Politics of Street Crime: Criminal Process and Cultural Obsession.* Philadelphia, PA: Temple University Press, 1992.

Shelden, Randall G. *Controlling the Dangerous Classes: A Critical Introduction to the History of Criminal Justice.* Boston, MA: Allyn and Bacon, 2001.

Simon, Jonathan K. *Governing through Crime: How the War on Crime Transformed American Democracy and Created a Culture of Fear.* New York: Oxford University Press, 2007.

Spitzer, Robert J. *The Politics of Gun Control,* 4th ed. Washington, DC: CQ Press, 2007.

Stolz, Barbara. *Criminal Justice Policy Making: Federal Roles and Processes.* Westport, CT: Praeger Publishers, 2001.

Walker, Samuel. *Popular Justice: A History of American Criminal Justice.* Oxford: Oxford University Press, 1980.

Wilson, Harry L. *Guns, Gun Control, and Elections.* Lanham, MD: Rowman & Littlefield Publishers, 2006.

EDUCATION—12 BOOKS, 4 ARTICLES

Anderson, Lee W. *Congress and the Classroom: From the Cold War to 'No Child Left Behind.'* University Park: Pennsylvania State University Press, 2007.

Brademas, John. *The Politics of Education: Conflict and Consensus on Capitol Hill.* Norman: University of Oklahoma Press, 1987.

Cross, Christopher T. *Political Education: National Policy Comes of Age.* New York: Teachers College Press, 2003.

Davies, Gareth. *See Government Grow: Education Politics from Johnson to Reagan.* Lawrence: University Press of Kansas, 2007.

DeBray, Elizabeth H. *Politics, Ideology, and Education: Federal Policy during the Clinton and Bush Administrations.* New York: Teacher's College Press, 2006.

Fraser, James W. *Between Church and State: Religion and Public Education in a Multicultural America.* New York: St. Martin's Press, 1999.

Hill, Paul. "The Federal Role in Education." In *Brookings Papers on Education Policy*, ed. Diane Ravitch. Washington, DC: Brookings Institution, 2000.

Jeynes, William H. *American Educational History: School, Society, and the Common Good.* New York: Russell Sage Foundation, 2007.

Moran, Rachel. "The Politics of Discretion: Federal Intervention in Bilingual Education." *California Law Review* 76 (1988): 1249–1250.

Osgood, Robert L. *The History of Special Education: A Struggle for Equality in American Public Schools.* Santa Barbara, CA: Greenwood Publishing Group, 2008.

Ravitch, Diane. *The Troubled Crusade: American Education 1945-1980.* New York: Basic Books, 1985.

Rudy, Willis. *Building America's Schools and Colleges: The Federal Contribution.* Cranbury, NJ: Cornwall Books, 2003.

Spring, Joel. *Conflict of Interests: The Politics of American Education.* New York: Longman, 1993.

Strach, Patricia. "Making Higher Education Affordable: Policy Design in Postwar America." *Journal of Policy History* 21, no. 1 (2009): 61–88.

Thomas, Janet, and Kevin Brady. "The Elementary and Secondary Education Act at 40: Equity, Accountability, and the Evolving Federal Role in Public Education." *Review of Research in Education* 29, no. 1 (2005): 51–67.

Vinovskis, Maria A. *The Birth of Head Start: Preschool Education Policies in the Kennedy and Johnson Administrations.* Chicago: University of Chicago Press, 2005.

ENERGY—13 BOOKS, 1 ARTICLE

Beaubouef, Bruce Andre. *The Strategic Petroleum Reserve: U.S. Energy Security and Oil Politics, 1975-2005.* College Station: Texas A&M University Press, 2007.

Campbell, John L. *Collapse of an Industry: Nuclear Power and the Contradictions of Policy.* Ithaca, NY: Cornell University Press, 1988.

Chick, Martin. *Electricity and Energy Policy in Britain, France and the United States since 1945.* Northampton, MA: Edward Elgar Publishers, 2007.

Duffy, Robert J. *Nuclear Politics in America: A History and Theory of Government Regulation.* Lawrence: University of Kansas Press, 1997.

Goodwin, Craufurd D. W. *Energy Policy in Perspective: Today's Problems, Yesterday's Solutions.* Washington, DC: Brookings, 1981.

Jasper, James M. *Nuclear Politics: Energy and the State in the United States, Sweden, and France.* Princeton: Princeton University Press, 1990.

Kash, Don E., and Robert Rycroft. *U.S. Energy Policy: Crisis and Complacency.* Norman: University of Oklahoma Press, 1984.

Laird, Frank N. *Solar Energy, Technology Policy, and Institutional Values.* Cambridge: Cambridge University Press, 2001.

Miller, Allan S. "Energy Policy from Nixon to Clinton: From Grand Provider to Market Facilitator." *Environmental Law* 25, no. 17 (1985): 715.

Randall, Stephen J. *United States Foreign Oil Policy Since World War I*, 2nd ed. Montreal: McGill-Queen's University Press, 2005.

Rutledge, Ian. *Addicted to Oil: America's Relentless Drive for Energy Security.* London: I. B. Tauris, 2006.

Sanders, M. Elizabeth. *The Regulation of Natural Gas: Policy and Politics, 1938-1978.* Philadelphia, PA: Temple University Press, 1981.

Tugwell, Franklin. *The Energy Crisis and the American Political Economy: Politics and Markets in the Management of Natural Resources.* Stanford, CA: Stanford University Press, 1988.

Vietor, Richard H. K. *Energy Policy in America since 1945: A Study of Business-Government Relations.* Cambridge: Cambridge University Press, 2008.

ENVIRONMENT—18 BOOKS, 3 ARTICLES

Andrews, Richard N. L. *Managing the Environment, Managing Ourselves: A History of American Environmental Policy*, 2nd ed. New Haven: Yale University Press, 2006.

Czech, Brian, and Paul R. Krausman. *The Endangered Species Act: History, Conservation Biology and Public Policy*. Baltimore: Johns Hopkins University Press, 2001.

Davis, Charles E. *The Politics of Hazardous Waste*. New York: Prentice Hall, 1992.

Fiorino, Daniel J. *Making Environmental Policy*. Berkeley: University of California Press, 1995.

Fretwell, Holly Lippke. *Who Is Minding the Federal Estate?: Political Management of America's Public Lands*. Lanham, MD: Lexington Books, 2009.

Graham, Otis L., Jr., ed. *Environmental Politics and Policy, 1960s-1990s*. University Park: Pennsylvania State University Press, 2000.

Greve, Michael S., and Fred L. Smith. *Environmental Politics: Public Costs, Private Rewards*. Westport, CT: Praeger Publishers, 1992.

Hahn, Robert W. "United States Environmental Law: Past, Present, and Future." *Natural Resources Journal* 34, no. 2 (1994): 305–348.

Hays, Samuel P. *A History of Environmental Politics since 1945*. Pittsburgh: University of Pittsburgh Press, 2000.

Hays, Samuel P., and Barbara D. Hays. *Beauty, Health, and Permanence: Environmental Politics in the United States, 1955-1985*. Cambridge: Cambridge University Press, 1989.

Howlett, Michael. "Beyond Legalism? Policy Ideas, Implementation Styles and Emulation-Based Convergence in Canadian and U.S. Environmental Policy." *Journal of Public Policy* 20, no. 3 (2000): 305–329.

Klyza, Christopher McGrory, and David J. Sousa. *American Environmental Policy, 1990-2006: Beyond Gridlock*. Cambridge, MA: MIT Press, 2008.

Layzer, Judith A. *The Environmental Case: Translating Values into Policy*, 3rd ed. Washington, DC: CQ Press, 2011.

Milazzo, Paul Charles. *Unlikely Environmentalists: Congress and Clean Water, 1945-1972*. Lawrence: University Press of Kansas, 2006.

Portney, Paul R., and Robert N. Stavins, eds. *Public Policies for Environmental Protection*. Washington, DC: Resources for the Future, 2000.

Smith, Zachary A. *Environmental Policy Paradox*, 5th ed. Upper Saddle River, NJ: Prentice Hall, 2008.

Sussman, Glenn, Byron Daynes, and Jonathan P. West. *American Politics and the Environment*. New York: Longman, 2001.

Tzoumis, Kelly. *Environmental Policymaking in Congress: The Role of Issue Definitions in Wetlands, Great Lakes and Wildlife Policies*. New York: Routledge, 2009.

VanNijnatten, Debora L. "Participation and Environmental Policy in Canada and the United States: Trends Over Time." *Policy Studies Journal* 27, no. 2 (1999): 267–287.

Vietor, Richard H. K. *Environmental Politics and the Coal Coalition*. College Station: Texas A&M University Press, 1980

Vig, Norman J., and Michael E. Kraft, eds. *Environmental Policy: New Directions*. Washington, DC: Congressional Quarterly Press, 2000.

Weber, Edward P. *Pluralism by the Rules: Conflict and Cooperation in Environmental Regulation*. Washington, DC: Georgetown University Press, 1998.

FINANCE AND COMMERCE—16 BOOKS, 3 ARTICLES

Bak, Thomas, John Golmant, and James Woods. "A Comparison of the Effects of the 1978 and 2005 Bankruptcy Reform Legislation on Bankruptcy Filing Rates." *Bankruptcy Developments Journal* 25, no. 1 (2008): 11–38.

Bean, Jonathan. *Big Government and Affirmative Action: The Scandalous History of the Small Business Administration*. Lexington: University Press of Kentucky, 2001.

——. *Beyond the Broker State: Federal Policies toward Small Business, 1936-1961*. Chapel Hill: University of North Carolina Press, 1996.

Birkland, Thomas A. *Lessons of Disaster: Policy Change after Catastrophic Events.* Washington, DC: Georgetown University Press, 2006.

Eisner, Marc Allen. *The American Political Economy: Institutional Evolution of Market and State.* New York: Taylor & Francis, 2011.

Eisner, Marc Allen. *Antitrust and the Triumph of Economics: Institutions, Expertise, and Policy Change.* Chapel Hill: University of North Carolina Press, 1991.

Frey, James H. "Federal Involvement in U.S Gaming Regulation." *The ANNALS of the American Academy of Political and Social Science* 556, no. 1 (1998): 138–152.

Freyer, Tony. *Regulating Big Business: Antitrust in Great Britain and America, 1880-1990.* Cambridge: Cambridge University Press, 1992.

Friedman, Jeffrey, and Wladimir Kraus, eds. *Engineering the Financial Crisis: Systemic Risk and the Failure of Regulation.* Philadelphia: University of Pennsylvania Press, 2011.

Hendrickson, Jill M. *Regulation and Instability in U.S. Commercial Banking: A History of Crises.* New York: Palgrave Macmillan, 2011.

High, Jack C., ed. *Regulation: Economic Theory and History.* Ann Arbor: University of Michigan Press, 1992.

High, Jack C., and Wayne E. Gable, eds. *A Century of the Sherman Act: American Economic Opinion, 1890-1990.* Fairfax, VA: George Mason University Press, 1992.

Holland, David S. *When Regulation Was Too Successful—The Sixth Decade of Deposit Insurance: A History of the Troubles of the U.S. Banking Industry in the 1980's and Early 1990's.* Westport, CT: Praeger Publishers, 1998.

McGowan, Richard. *Government Regulation of the Alcohol Industry: The Search for Revenue and the Common Good.* Westport, CT: Greenwood Publishing Group, 1997.

Nadel, Mark V. *The Politics of Consumer Protection.* New York: MacMillan Publishing Company, 1971.

Phillips-Fein, Kim, and Julian E. Zelizer. *What's Good for Business: Business and American Politics since World War II.* New York: Oxford University Press, 2012.

Pottage, Alain, and Brad Sherman. *Figures of Invention: A History of Modern Patent Law.* New York: Oxford University Press, 2010.

Skeel, David A. *Debt's Dominion: A History of Bankruptcy Law in America.* Princeton: Princeton University Press, 2003.

Tabb, Charles Jordan. "The History of Bankruptcy Laws in the United States." *American Bankruptcy Institute Law Review* 3, no. 5 (1995): 5–51.

HEALTH—22 BOOKS, 2 ARTICLES

Aaron, Henry. *The Problem That Won't Go Away: Reforming U.S. Health Care Financing.* Washington, DC: Brookings Institution Press, 1995.

Brown, Lawrence, ed. *Health Policy in Transition: A Decade of Health Politics, Policy, and Law.* Durham, NC: Duke University Press, 1987.

Field, Robert I. *Health Care Regulation in America: Complexity, Confrontation, and Compromise.* New York: Oxford University Press, 2006.

Fox, Daniel M. "Health Policy and the Politics of Research in the United States." *Journal of Health Politics, Policy, and Law* 15, no. 3 (1990): 481–499. Frank, Richard G., and Sherry A. Glied. *Better But Not Well: Mental Health Policy in the United States since 1950.* Baltimore: Johns Hopkins University Press, 2006.

Funigiello, Philip J. *Chronic Politics: Health Care Security from FDR to George W. Bush.* Lawrence: University Press of Kansas, 2005.

Kunitz, S. J. "The History and Politics of US Health Care Policy for American Indians and Alaskan Natives." *American Journal of Public Health* 86, no. 10 (1996): 1464–1473.

Kronenfeld, Jennie Jacobs. *The Changing Federal Role in U.S. Health Care Policy.* Westport, CT: Praeger Publishers, 1997.

Longest, Beaufort. *Health Policymaking in the United States,* 5th ed. Chicago: Health Administration Press, 2010.

Marcus, Alan. *Health Care Policy in Contemporary America*. University Park: Pennsylvania State University Press, 1993.

Marmour, Theodor. *The Politics of Medicare*. New Brunswick, NJ: Aldine Transaction, 2000.

Mechanic, David. *From Advocacy to Allocation: Evolving American Health Care System*. New York: Free Press, 1986.

Morone, James A., Theodor J. Litman, and Leonard S. Robins. *Health Politics and Policy*, 4th ed. Florence, KY: Delmar Cengage Learning, 2008.

Mueller, Keith. *Health Care Policy in the United States*. Lincoln: University of Nebraska Press, 1993.

Oberlander, Jonathan. *The Political Life of Medicare*. Chicago: University of Chicago Press, 2003.

Olson, Laura Katz. *The Politics of Medicaid*. New York: Columbia University Press, 2010.

Patel, Kant, and Mark Rushefsky. *Health Care Politics and Policy in America*. Armonk, NY: M. E. Sharpe, 2006.

Quadagno, Jill. *One Nation, Uninsured: Why the U.S. has No National Health Insurance*. Oxford: Oxford University Press, 2005.

Smith, David G. *Entitlement Politics: Medicare and Medicaid, 1995-2001*. New Brunswick, NJ: Aldine Transaction, 2002.

Smith, David G., and Judith D. Moore. *Medicaid Politics and Policy: 1965-2007*. New Brunswick, NJ: Transaction Publishers, 2008.

Stevens, Rosemary. *The Public-Private Health Care State*. New Brunswick, NJ: Transaction Publishers, 2007.

Strickland, Stephen P. *Politics, Science, and Dread Disease: A Short History of United States Medical Research Policy*. Cambridge, MA: Harvard University Press, 1972.

Studlar, Donley T. *Tobacco Control: Comparative Politics in the United States and Canada*. Toronto: University of Toronto Press, 2002.

Weissert, Carol, and William Weissert. *Governing Health: The Politics of Health Policy*. Baltimore: Johns Hopkins University Press, 2006.

HOUSING AND COMMUNITY DEVELOPMENT—11 BOOKS, 8 ARTICLES

Caves, Roger W. "An Historical Analysis of Federal Housing Policy from the Presidential Perspective: An Intergovernmental Focus." *Urban Studies* 26, no. 1 (1989): 59–76.

Cooper, Clarence A., and Frank R. Cooper. "Where the Rubber Meets the Road: CRA's Impact on Distressed Communities." In *Public Policies for Distressed Communities Revisited*, ed. F. Stevens Redburn and Terry F. Buss. Lexington, MA: Lexington Books, 2002.

Dreussi, Amy Shriver, and Peter Leahy. "Urban Development Action Grants Revisited." *Review of Policy Research* 17, no. 2 (2002): 120–137.

Ferguson, Ronald F., and William T. Dickens. *Urban Problems and Community Development*. Washington, DC: Brookings Institutions Press, 1999.

Gelfand, Mark I. *A Nation of Cities: The Federal Government and Urban America, 1933-1965*. Oxford: Oxford University Press, 1975.

Goering, John M. *Housing Desegregation and Federal Policy*. Chapel Hill: University of North Carolina Press, 1986.

Graham, Hugh Davis. "The Surprising Career of Federal Fair Housing Law." *Journal of Policy History* 12, no. 2 (2000): 215–232.

Gunther, John J. *Federal-City Relations in the United States: The Role of the Mayors in Federal Aid to Cities*. Newark: University of Delaware Press, 1990.

Hays, R. Allen. *The Federal Government and Urban Housing: Ideology and Change in Public Policy*. Albany: State University of New York Press, 1995.

Hunt, D. Bradford. "How Did Public Housing Survive the 1950s." *Journal of Policy History* 17, no. 2 (2005): 193–216.

James, Franklin J., and Ron Kirk. "Can Urban Policies Be Responsive to Changing Urban Needs?" In *Public Policies for Distressed Communities Revisited*, ed. F. Stevens Redburn and Terry F. Buss. Lexington, MA: Lexington Books, 2002.

Keith, Nathaniel S. *Politics and the Housing Crisis since 1930.* New York: Universe Books, 1974.

Martin, Curtis H., and Robert A. Leone. *Local Economic Development: The Federal Connection.* Lexington, MA: Lexington Books, 1977.

Mitchell, Paul. *Federal Housing Policy and Programs: Past and Present.* Piscataway, NJ: Rutgers University Press, 1985.

Peters, Alan H., and Peter S. Fisher. *State Enterprise Zone Programs: Have They Worked?* Kalamazoo, MI: W. E. Upjohn Institute, 2002.

Schwartz, Alex F. *Housing Policy in the United States: An Introduction.* London: Routledge, 2006.

Sidney, Mara S. *Unfair Housing: How National Policy Shapes Community Action.* Lawrence: University of Kansas Press, 2003.

Snow, Douglas R. "Strategic Planning and Enterprise Zones." *Review of Policy Research* 17, no. 2 (2002): 13–28.

Teaford, Jon C. *The Twentieth-Century American City: Problem, Promise, and Reality.* Baltimore: Johns Hopkins University Press, 1993.

LABOR AND IMMIGRATION—19 BOOKS, 1 ARTICLE

Baumer, Donald C. *The Politics of Unemployment.* Washington: CQ Press, 1985.

Chen, Anthony S. *The Fifth Freedom: Jobs, Politics, and Civil Rights in the United States, 1941-1972.* Princeton: Princeton University Press, 2009.

Gimpel, James, and James Edwards. *The Congressional Politics of Immigration Reform.* New York: Longman, 1998.

Gross, James A. "Conflicting Statutory Purposes: Another Look at Fifty Years of NLRB Law Making." *Industrial and Labor Relations Review* 39, no. 1 (1985): 7–18.

LeMay, Michael C. *Anatomy of a Public Policy: The Reform of Contemporary American Immigration Law.* Westport, CT: Praeger Publishers, 1994.

Lichtenstein, Nelson. *State of the Union: A Century of American Labor.* Princeton: Princeton University Press, 2003.

Moreno, Paul D. *From Direct Action to Affirmative Action: Fair Employment Law and Policy in America.* Baton Rouge: Louisiana State University Press, 1999.

Morgan, Kimberly. *Working Mothers and the Welfare State: Religion and the Politics of Work-Family Policies in Western Europe and the United States.* Stanford, CA: Stanford University Press, 2006.

Newton, Lina. *Illegal, Alien, or Immigrant: The Politics of Immigration Reform.* New York: New York University Press, 2008.

Nordlund, Willis. *The Quest for a Living Wage.* Santa Barbara, CA: Greenwood Press, 1997.

Ong Hing, Bill. *Defining America through Immigration Policy.* Philadelphia: Temple University Press, 2003.

Rockoff, Hugh. *Drastic Measures: A History of Wage & Price Controls in the United States.* Cambridge: Cambridge University Press, 1984.

Shanks, Cheryl. *Immigration and the Politics of American Sovereignty, 1890-1990.* Ann Arbor: University of Michigan Press, 2001.

Togman, Jeffrey M. *The Ramparts of Nations.* Santa Barbara, CA: Greenwood Press, 2001.

Waltman, Jerold. *The Politics of the Minimum Wage.* Champaign: University of Illinois Press, 2000.

Weir, Margaret. *Politics and Jobs: The Boundaries of Employment Policy in the United States.* Princeton: Princeton University Press, 1993

Whittaker, William G. *Child labor in America: History, Policy, and Legislative Issues.* Hauppauge, NY: Nova Publishers, 2003.

Wisensale, Steven K. *Family Leave Policy: The Political Economy of Work and Family in America.* Armonk, NY: M. E. Sharpe, 2001.

Wong, Carolyn. *Lobbying for Inclusion: Rights Politics and the Making of Immigration Policy.* Palo Alto, CA: Stanford University Press, 2006.

Zieger, Robert H. *American Workers, American Unions.* Baltimore: Johns Hopkins University Press, 2002.

MACROECONOMICS—21 BOOKS, 1 ARTICLE

Axilrod, Stephen H. *Inside the Fed: Monetary Policy and its Management, Martin through Greenspan to Bernanke.* Cambridge, MA: MIT Press, 2011.

Berkman, Michael B. *The State Roots of National Politics: Congress and the Tax Agenda, 1978–1986.* Pittsburgh: University of Pittsburgh Press, 1993.

Bingham, Richard D. *Industrial Policy American Style: From Hamilton to HDTV.* Armonk, NY: M. E. Sharpe, 1998.

Brownlee, W. Elliot. *Federal Taxation in America: A Short History.* Cambridge: Cambridge University Press, 2004.

——. *Funding the Modern American State, 1941-1995: The Rise and Fall of the Era of Easy Finance.* Cambridge: Cambridge University Press, 2003.

Chessman, Tyler L. *Understanding the United States Debt.* Seattle, WA: Createspace, 2011.

Makin, John, and Norman Ornstein. *Debt and Taxes: How America Got into its Budget Mess and What to Do about It.* New York: Crown Publishing Group, 1994.

Meltzer, Allan H. *A History of the Federal Reserve. Vol. 2, Books 1-2, 1951–1986.* Chicago: University of Chicago Press, 2010.

Nester, William R. *A Short History of American Industrial Policies.* New York: Macmillan Press, 1998.

Orfield, Gary. *Congressional Power: Congress and Social Change.* Boston, MA: Houghton Mifflin Harcourt Press, 1975.

Peritz, Rudolph J. R. *Competition Policy in America: History, Rhetoric, Law.* Oxford: Oxford University Press, 2001.

Pollack, Sheldon. *The Failure of U.S. Tax Policy: Revenue and Politics.* University Park: Pennsylvania State University Press, 1998.

Pollack, Sheldon. *Refinancing America: The Republican Antitax Agenda.* Albany: State University of New York Press, 2003.

Schick, Allen. *The Federal Budget: Politics, Policy, Process.* Washington, DC: Brookings Institution Press, 2000.

Stabile, Donald, and Jeffrey A. Cantor. *The Public Debt of the United States: An Historical Perspective, 1775-1990.* Westport, CT: Praeger Publishers, 1991.

Stein, Herbert. *Presidential Economics: The Making of Economic Policy from Roosevelt to Clinton.* Washington, DC: AEI Press, 1994.

Steinmo, Sven. "The Evolution of Policy Ideas: Tax Policy in the 20th Century." *British Journal of Politics & International Relations* 5, no. 2 (2003): 206–236.

Steuerle, C. Eugene. *Contemporary U.S. Tax Policy.* Washington, DC: Urban Institute Press, 2004.

Sundquist, James L. *Politics and Policy: The Eisenhower, Kennedy, and Johnson Years.* Washington, DC: Brookings Institution Press, 1968.

Timberlake, Richard H. *Monetary Policy in the United States: An Intellectual and Institutional History.* Chicago: University of Chicago Press, 1993.

Witte, John F. *The Politics and Development of the Federal Income Tax.* Madison: University of Wisconsin Press, 1986.

Zelizer, Julian E. *Taxing America: Wilbur D. Mills, Congress, and the State, 1945–1975.* Cambridge: Cambridge University Press, 2000.

SCIENCE AND TECHNOLOGY—15 BOOKS, 5 ARTICLES

Bryner, Gary C., ed. *Science, Technology, and Politics: Policy Analysis in Congress.* Boulder, CO: Westview Press, 1992.

DiFilippo, Anthony. *From Industry to Arms: The Political Economy of High Technology.* Santa Barbara, CA: Greenwood Publishing Group, 1990.

Eisenmann, Thomas R. "The U.S. Cable Television Industry, 1948-1995: Managerial Capitalism in Eclipse." *Business History Review* 74, no. 1 (2000): 1–40.

Guston, David. *Between Politics and Science: Assuring the Integrity and Productivity of Research*. Cambridge: Cambridge University Press, 2007.

Guston, David H., and Daniel Sarewitz, eds. *Shaping Science and Technology Policy: The Next Generation of Research*. Madison: University of Wisconsin Press, 2006.

Jaffe, Adam B. "The U.S. Patent System in Transition: Policy Innovation and the Innovation Process." *Research Policy* 29, no. 4 (2000): 531–557.

Jasanoff, Sheila. *The Fifth Branch: Science Advisors as Policymakers*. Cambridge, MA: Harvard University Press, 1990.

Johnson, Ann. "The End of Pure Science: Science Policy from Bayh-Dole to the NNI." In *Discovering the Nanoscale*, ed. D. Baird, A. Nordmann and J. Schummer. Amsterdam: IOS Press, 2004.

Kraemer, Sylvia. *Science and Technology Policy in United States: Open Systems in Action*. Piscataway, NJ: Rutgers University Press, 2006.

Lane, Neal. "US Science and Technology: An Uncoordinated System that Seems to Work." *Technology in Society* 30, no. 3-4 (2008): 248–263.

Launius, Roger D., and Howard E McCurdy. *Spaceflight and the Myth of Presidential Leadership*. Champaign: University of Illinois Press, 1997.

Marcus, Alan I., and Amy Sue Bix. *The Future is Now: Science & Technology Policy in America since 1950*. Amherst, NY: Prometheus Books, 2007.

Marks, Harry. *The Progress of Experiment: Science and Therapeutic Reform in the United States, 1900–1990*. Cambridge: Cambridge University Press, 2000.

McDougall, Walter A. *The Heavens and the Earth: A Political History of the Space Age*. Baltimore: Johns Hopkins University Press, 2008.

Moore, Kelly. *Disrupting Science: Social Movements, American Scientists, and the Politics of the Military, 1945–1975*. Princeton: Princeton University Press, 2008.

Savage, James D. *Funding Science in America: Congress, Universities, and the Politics of the Academic Pork Barrel*. Cambridge: Cambridge University Press, 1999.

Sheingate, Adam D. "Promotion vs. Precaution: The Evolution of Biotechnology Policy in the United States." *British Journal of Political Science* 36, no. 2 (2006): 243–268.

Smith, Bruce L. R. *American Science Policy since World War II*. Washington, DC: Brookings Institution Press, 1990.

Sterling, Christopher H., Phyllis W. Bernt, and Martin B. H. Weiss. *Shaping American Telecommunications: A History of Technology, Policy, and Economics*. Mahwah, NJ: Lawrence Erlbaum Associates, 2006.

Wang, Zuoyue. *In Sputnik's Shadow: The President's Science Advisory Committee and Cold War America*. New Brunswick, NJ: Rutgers University Press, 2008.

SOCIAL WELFARE—19 BOOKS, 1 ARTICLE

Axxin, June J., and Mark J. Stern. *Social Welfare: A History of the American Response to Need*. Boston, MA: Allyn & Bacon, 2007.

Beland, Daniel. *Social Security: History & Politics from the New Deal to the Privatization Debate*. Lawrence: University of Kansas Press, 2007.

Berkowitz, Edward D. *America's Welfare State: From Roosevelt to Reagan*. Baltimore: Johns Hopkins University Press, 1991.

Blank, Rebecca, and Ron Haskins, eds. *The New World of Welfare*. Washington, DC: Brookings Institution Press, 2001.

Davies, Gareth. *From Opportunity to Entitlement: The Transformation and Decline of Great Society Liberalism*. Lawrence: University Press of Kansas, 1999.

Friedman, Sheldon, and David Jacobs, eds. *The Future of the Safety Net: Social Insurance and Employee Benefits*. Ithaca, NY: Cornell University Press, 2001.

Goldberg, Gertrude Schaffer, and Sheila D. Collins. *Washington's New Poor Law: Welfare Reform and the Roads Not Taken, 1935 to the Present*. New York: Apex Press, 2001.

Hacker, Jacob. *The Divided Welfare State: The Battle over Public and Private Social Benefits in the United States*. Cambridge: Cambridge University Press, 2002.

Howard, Christopher. *The Hidden Welfare State: Tax Expenditures and Social Policy in the United States*. Princeton: Princeton University Press, 1999.

——. *The Welfare State Nobody Knows: Debunking Myths about U.S. Social Policy.* Princeton: Princeton University Press, 2006.

Katz, Michael B. *The Price of Citizenship: Redefining the American Welfare State.* Philadelphia: University of Pennsylvania Press, 2008.

Mink, Gwendolyn, and Rickie Solinger, eds. *Welfare: A Documentary History of U.S. Policy and Politics.* New York: New York University Press, 2003.

O'Connor, Brendon. *A Political History of the American Welfare System: When Ideas Have Consequences.* Lanham, MD: Rowman & Littlefield Publishers, 2003.

Patterson, James T. *America's Struggle Against Poverty in the Twentieth Century.* Cambridge, MA: Harvard University Press, 2000.

Roof, Tracy. *American Labor, Congress, and the Welfare State, 1935-2010.* Baltimore: Johns Hopkins University Press, 2011.

Rosenfeld, Sam. "Fed by Reform: Congressional Politics, Partisan Change, and the Food Stamp Program, 1961-1981." *Journal of Policy History* 22, no. 4 (2010): 474–507.

Schieber, Sylvester J., and John B. Shoven. *The Real Deal: The History and Future of Social Security.* New Haven: Yale University Press, 1999.

Skocpol, Theda, ed. *Social Policy in the United States: Future Possibilities in Historical Perspective.* Princeton: Princeton University Press, 1995.

Teles, Steven M. *Whose Welfare? AFDC and Elite Politics.* Lawrence: University Press of Kansas, 1996.

Trattner, Walter I. *From Poor Law to Welfare State: A History of Social Welfare in America.* New York: Free Press, 1998.

TRANSPORTATION—12 BOOKS, 1 ARTICLE

Brown, Anthony E. *The Politics of Airline Deregulation.* Knoxville: University of Tennessee Press, 1987.

Derthick, Martha, and Paul J. Quirk. *The Politics of Deregulation.* Washington, DC: Brookings Institution Press, 1985.

Dilger, Robert Jay. *American Transportation Policy.* Santa Barbara, CA: Greenwood Publishing Group, 2003.

Gertz, Carsten. "Lessons from a Landmark U.S. Policy for Transportation, Land Use and Air Quality, and Implications for Policy Changes in Other Countries." *International Social Science Journal* 55, no. 176 (2003): 307–317.

Jones, David W. *Mass Motorization and Mass Transit: An American History and Policy Analysis.* Bloomington: Indiana University Press, 2008.

Lewis, Tom. *Divided Highways: Building the Interstate Highways, Transforming American Life.* New York; Penguin, 1999.

Robyn, Dorothy. *Braking the Special Interests: Trucking Deregulation and the Politics of Policy Reform.* Chicago: University of Chicago Press, 1987.

Rose, Mark H., Bruce E. Seely, and Paul F. Barrett. *The Best Transportation System in the World: Railroads, Trucks, Airlines, and American Public Policy in the Twentieth Century.* Columbus: Ohio State University Press, 2006.

Rothenberg, Lawrence S. *Regulation, Organizations, and Politics.* Ann Arbor: University of Michigan Press, 1994.

Stone, Richard D. *The Interstate Commerce Commission and the Railroad Industry: A History of Regulatory Policy.* Westport, CT: Praeger Publishers, 1991.

Taebel, Delbert A., and James V. Cornehls. *The Political Economy of Urban Transportation.* Port Washington, NY: Kennikat Press, 1977.

Weiner, Edward. *Urban Transportation Planning in the United States: History, Policy, and Practice.* New York: Springer, 2008.

Whitnah, Donald Robert. *U.S. Department of Transportation: A Reference History.* Santa Barbara, CA: Greenwood Press, 1998.

Codes and Categories

These are the relevant passages from the instructions given to coders.

What you are looking for:

Specific US federal government policy enactments mentioned by the author, including legislation that passed Congress, executive orders issued by the president, administrative agency or department rulings, and court decisions. You do not need to analyze policy that is mentioned in passing or mentioned in describing another event. You only need to include policy changes that the author of each book considers significant.

Every time you find a specific policy change:

1. Provide a short name/description of the policy change
2. Report the date of the policy change
3. Classify it as legislative (change in law, new legislation passed by Congress), administrative (change in regulation or by administrative agency or department), presidential (change initiated by President, executive order), or judicial (court decision).
4. List all named proponents of the policy change, including individuals, government organizations, or interest groups.
5. Report whether both political parties were involved, only the Democrats, or only the Republicans. If neither party is mentioned, report that. If both parties were involved, but one party led, report that.
6. List each and every factor from the list (provided on the following page) that is mentioned by the author in their explanation for the public policy change.
7. Include the Policy Agendas Project category code most appropriate for the policy change.
8. Report whether the policy change was small, medium, or large.
9. Report whether the policy change was recognized as important at the time.
10. Report whether the policy change was liberal, conservative, or neither.
11. Include any concerns or questions you have about the coding. Report any additional factor mentioned by the author but not included in my list of potential factors.
12. Provide an illustrative quote from the book that provides the causal explanation for the policy change given by the author. In other words, why does the author say the policy change occurred? If there is no quote, paraphrase the explanation in your own words.

After reading the book, report the author's organizational affiliation and educational discipline. Also specify whether they used any of the following methods: first-hand interviews, quantitative data, or government archives.

These are the relevant factors given in a list to coders (with examples that are omitted):

Congressional:
> A Congressional Committee Chair played a key role
> The Congressional Leadership (e.g. Speaker or Majority Leader) played a key role
> An individual Member of Congress played a key role
> The House and Senate Reached Agreement (e.g. a conference report is mentioned)
> A Key Congressional Floor Vote is Mentioned
> A Key Congressional Committee Vote is Mentioned

Executive:
> The President is Supportive
> A Cabinet Secretary is Supportive
> An Agency or Department Head is Supportive

Judicial:
> A Court Ruling Required Action
> The Fear of Courts Played a Role
> There were Threats to Sue over Current Policy

Events:
> An event highlighted a problem
> The policy was affected by a war
> The policy was affected by economic downturn
> The policy was affected by government financial problems
> An event highlighted an unsuccessful previous policy

Path Dependence:
> The policy was an extension or revision of an earlier policy
> An earlier choice made the policy more likely
> An earlier choice eliminated a potential alternative policy

Media Coverage:
> There was media coverage
> There was a specific media report
> Public Opinion:
> There was supportive public opinion or a change in public opinion
> The issue was raised in an election campaign

Constituents raised concerns with policymakers
There was a public protest that stimulated action

Interest Groups:

There was pressure from non-governmental organizations or
advocacy groups
There was pressure from corporations or business interests
There was professional association involvement
There was union involvement
An interest group changed their mind on an issue
A new interest group mobilized
There was congressional lobbying

International:

There was a foreign example
There was international pressure
There was an international government agreement

State or Local:

State action preceded federal action
Local action preceded federal action
A report was issued by state officials
The federal policy was modeled on a state plan

Research:

A government report was issued
New data arose on a problem or policy
A private (non-governmental) report was issued
There was involvement by a think tank
There was involvement by professors or researchers
Parties (in addition to general party codes):
An increase or decrease in the power of one political party

Ideas (added after the first several dozen readings):

An Important Argument or Frame Was Developed by the Proponents
The Opponents of the Policy Lacked a Compelling Argument or Frame
No One Was Willing to Come Out Against the Policy

Appendix B

MODELS OF EXPLANATIONS FOR POLICY CHANGE

This appendix uses multivariate models to predict whether each category of factors is included in an explanation for policy change. The units of analysis are explanations for enactments, with each author's explanation for each change analyzed separately. For each factor, I use several independent variables to predict whether influence is reported.

Congressional Attention measures the total number of hearings Congress held on the subtopic of the enactment over the entire time period, using data from the Policy Agendas Project.[1] This assesses the common expectation that there is a distinct policymaking process for policy choices at the top of the government agenda, compared with those that are conducted under the public's radar. *Years since 1945* is a variable to assess the possibility of a simple linear time trend. Are some factors becoming more or less important in the policymaking process? The models also include *Venue* variables to account for the branch of government where the enactment took place. Because this is a categorical distinction, I use dummy variables for administrative and judicial enactments, where the legislative branch is the excluded category. That means that the results indicate whether explanations are more likely to include each factor if an enactment occurs in the administrative or judicial branch than if it occurs in Congress. I use *Party* dummy variables to account for whether a policy historian reports that a policy change was pushed more by one of the two parties. Nonpartisan or bipartisan enactments are the excluded category, so the models assess whether Republican- or Democratic-led initiatives feature different reported causal patterns. Most enactments were coded as bipartisan or nonpartisan, the excluded category, but some authors specifically mentioned that one party was responsible.

The models also include several variables (described in chapter 2) to differentiate types of enactments. I use the three-category *Size of Enactment* variable that distinguishes large and small enactments from those that are somewhere in the middle.[2] Enactments that make very large changes to current policy may involve different factors than those that are mostly incremental, even if significant in the eyes of historians. I also use the three-category *Liberal or Conservative* ideological variable that measures whether an enactment expanded or contracted the scope of government or neither.[3] Perhaps liberal enactments have distinct determinants, compared with conservative ones. I also include a dummy variable for *Original Importance*, tracking whether an enactment was considered important at the time or only became accepted as significant after the later history of policy development. This accounts for the possibility, voiced by some critics of Mayhew's analysis of policy histories, that the determinants of enactments recognized to be important at the time would be different than those that became important only in the eyes of those making later retrospective judgments.[4] These variables are associated with each author's independent assessment, rather than measured at the enactment-level.

The models also introduce several variables to assess characteristics of each author and historical study that may influence their assessments about the influence of various factors on policy enactments. The *Author* dummy variables assess whether each type of policy historian is more likely to include a factor in their explanation. The variables compare political scientists, policy academics, historians (those trained in history), and government officials with all other author types. Most of the unlisted types are specialists in a particular issue domain, such as health or the environment. I also include three variables to assess the influence of the *Method* used by each policy historian. *Interviews* and *Quantitative Data* are dummy variables indicating whether or not the author used significant evidence from first-hand interviews or quantitative data. These assess the possibility that quantitative or qualitative methods may lead to different conclusions. Yet some authors used both or neither of these methods. *No. of Pages* measures the length of the policy history to account for the possibility that some factors are mentioned only when the policy historian provides a more in-depth account.

Total No. of Factors Cited, the final variable listed in each model, measures the total number of factors cited by each author. Although this variable is endogenous because it includes the factor assessed in each model, it is still necessary to account for the possibility (shown in table 6.5) that each factor in the policymaking process is more likely to be mentioned by authors who provide more thorough explanations for a policy change. All of the variables in these models are based on coding of the author's account of each policy enactment. The results do not change substantially if *Total No. of Factors Cited* is removed.

The models also incorporate dummy variables for each issue area, with enactments in any other area as the excluded type. For the sake of brevity, these coefficients are not reported in the tables. I point out all significant differences in the text below. These differences are largely consistent with the stable issue area differences in the policy process found in chapter 5.

Cross-Branch Influence on Policy

The first models, reported in table B.1, assess the reported influence of factors in each branch of government. Yet the vast majority of enactments in each branch are associated with some circumstances in that branch. New laws often involve congressional factors; executive branch enactments likewise involve administrative influence and judicial decisions involve judicial factors. Instead of confirming these obvious relationships, table 6.6 looks at cross-branch influence: when do factors related to one branch of government influence policymaking in another branch? I predict whether or not an explanation for a policy enactment incorporates any factors related to another branch of government other than the one that directly enacted it. Each model thus includes only cases of enactments in other branches of government; this decision accounts for the much smaller population of explanations included in the congressional model. In all three models, the number of total factors mentioned in an explanation is unsurprisingly associated with whether branch factors are reported. This replicates the bivariate analysis in table 6.5; some policy historians simply credit more factors than others, including all types of cross-branch influence.

The *Administrative* model includes explanations for new laws and court decisions since 1945, assessing whether they include any factor related to the executive branch (the most popular of which were support from the president or an administrative agency official). The venue variable for this model reports the difference between administrative influence in the judicial and legislative branches. Policy historians are more likely to include administrative branch factors in explanations for new laws in comparison with court decisions. Explanations for enactments in education, transportation, and crime are significantly more likely to include administrative branch factors, though I do not report issue area differences in the table. Larger changes in public policy are associated with more reported influence from the administration, largely because the president is more involved in larger policy initiatives. There is only one major difference based on author and method: policy historians using interviews are less likely to note influence from the administration, perhaps due to their lack of access to the White House.

The *Congressional* model includes only 519 explanations for court cases and administrative actions. There are no significant differences based on issue area.

Table B.1 **Logit Models Predicting Reported Influence on Policymaking in Other Branches**

		Administrative	Congressional	Judicial
Congressional Attention		.01	.09	−.06
		(.02)	(.05)	(.04)
Years since 1945		−.00	.00	.01
		(.00)	(.00)	(.01)
Venue	Administrative	—	—	0.38
				(0.34)
	Judicial	−2.98***	−.56	—
		(.35)	(.41)	
Party	Democratic	−.12	1.63***	−.70
		(.21)	(.49)	(.49)
	Republican	.30	1.68**	−.83
		(.29)	(.54)	(.76)
Enactment	Size of Enactment	.20*	−.10	−.03
		(.09)	(.22)	(.19)
	Liberal	.08	−.41	−.18
		(.10)	(.23)	(.21)
	Original	−.11	.46	.24
	Importance	(.20)	(.40)	(.45)
Author	Political Scientist	.14	.17	−.96**
		(.15)	(.39)	(.35)
	Policy School	.21	.56	−.46
		(.23)	(.57)	(.44)
	Historian	−.04	.21	−.17
		(.18)	(.44)	(.34)
	Government	−.00	2.66***	−.92
	Official	(.37)	(.63)	(1.06)
Method	Interviews	−.46*	−.36	.14
		(.16)	(.41)	(.33)
	Quantitative Data	−.15	.13	−.21
		(.14)	(.33)	(.29)
	No. of Pages	.09	.17	−.03
		(.04)	(.12)	(.09)

(Continued)

Table B.1 **Continued**

	Administrative	Congressional	Judicial
Total No. of Factors Cited	.44***	.49***	.21***
	(.03)	(.07)	(.03)
Constant	−1.83	−4.57	−2.78
Pseudo R²	.26	.33	.16
N	1,664	519	1,685

Note: Table entries are logit coefficients, with standard errors in parentheses. The models predict whether or not an explanation for an enactment incorporates factors related to each branch of government, excluding enactments in its own branch. The excluded venue category is legislative enactments (or judicial enactments for the congressional model). The excluded party variable is nonpartisan or bipartisan enactments. The excluded author type is unlisted disciplines. The models incorporate dummy variables for each issue area but these coefficients are not reported. *$p < .05$ (two-tailed).

The model demonstrates that policy initiatives led by members of either political party are more likely to involve congressional factors than nonpartisan or bipartisan initiatives. The only difference based on author characteristics is that government officials are more likely to mention congressional influence on other branches, perhaps because some of these officials worked in administration agencies and saw it first hand.

The *Judicial* model includes explanations for new laws, executive orders, and agency rules, assessing whether they include any factor related to the judicial branch, such as a court ruling that required action. The venue variable reports the difference between administrative and legislative enactments, but shows no difference. Explanations for health, agriculture, and social welfare policy changes are significantly less likely to include judicial branch factors than those in other issue areas, though these coefficients are excluded from the table. The models do show one effect for author characteristics: political scientists are less likely to include judicial factors in their explanations for policy change compared with the excluded category, which is mostly made up of issue area specialists. Overall, the model does not account for much variation across authors in whether their explanations involve judicial influence.

External Influence on Policy

I next assess the reported influence of four different types of factors outside of government in explanations for policy change. These models incorporate

Table B.2 **Logit Models Predicting Reported External Influential Factors**

		Interest Groups	Research	Public Opinion	Media
Congressional Attention		−.04	.00	−.05	.00
		(.02)	(.00)	(.03)	(.00)
Years since 1945		.00	.00	.01*	.01
		(.00)	(.00)	(.01)	(.01)
Venue	Administrative	−.10	.42*	.16	.41
		(.18)	(.18)	(.21)	(.27)
	Judicial	.50*	−.51	−.39	.12
		(.22)	(.27)	(.30)	(.37)
Party	Democratic	.17	−.57*	.38	.19
		(.20)	(.22)	(.21)	(.29)
	Republican	−.25	−.23	.56	−.91
		(.28)	(.29)	(.29)	(.52)
Enactment	Size of Enactment	−.23**	−.03	−.03	.21
		(.09)	(.09)	(.11)	(.14)
	Liberal	.19	.18	.04	−.18
		(.10)	(.10)	(.11)	(.15)
	Original Importance	.08	−.09	.26	.13
		(.19)	(.20)	(.25)	(.35)
Author	Political Scientist	−.06	−.49**	.14	−.08
		(.15)	(.16)	(.18)	(.24)
	Policy School	−.29	−.75***	−.41	.09
		(.22)	(.24)	(.30)	(.34)
	Historian	−.02	−.57**	.61**	.66*
		(.17)	(.18)	(.20)	(.26)
	Government Official	−.69	.17	−.81	.08
		(.40)	(.35)	(.51)	(.54)
Method	Interviews	−.14	.12	.24	.52*
		(.15)	(.15)	(.18)	(.21)
	Quantitative Data	−.06	−.09	−.21	.20
		(.13)	(.14)	(.16)	(.21)
	No. of Pages	−.01	−.03	−.05	.04
		(.04)	(.05)	(.06)	(.07)

(Continued)

Table B.2 **Continued**

	Interest Groups	Research	Public Opinion	Media
Total No. of Factors Cited	.55***	.42***	.35***	.45***
	(.03)	(.03)	(.03)	(.03)
Constant	−2.26	−2.45	−2.94	−6.39
Pseudo R²	.27	.21	.23	.31
N	1,927	1,927	1,927	1,927

Note: Table entries are logit coefficients, with standard errors in parentheses. The models predict whether or not an explanation for a policy enactment incorporates interest groups, research, public opinion, or media coverage. The excluded venue category is legislative enactments. The excluded party variable is nonpartisan or bipartisan enactments. The excluded author type is unlisted disciplines. The models incorporate dummy variables for each issue area but these coefficients are not reported. *p <.05 (two-tailed).

enactments in all three branches of government. Table B.2 reports models predicting whether or not an explanation for a policy enactment incorporates any factors related to interest groups, research, public opinion, or media coverage. I use the same independent variables in these models. Although the table does not report coefficients for issue area differences, I do find that they are consistent with the findings from chapter 5. Interest groups are significantly more likely to be credited in explanations for policy changes in civil rights, the environment, and transportation. Research, media coverage, and public opinion are all credited more often in criminal justice policymaking. Public opinion is reportedly less influential in energy, transportation, housing, finance, and science policymaking than in other areas.

The results show two differences based on policymaking venue: executive branch enactments are more likely to involve influence from research, probably due to administrative agencies' requirements to assess scientific literature, and significant judicial decisions are more likely to involve interest groups because groups like the American Civil Liberties Union often act as litigants. There is one time trend apparent in these data. Consistent with figure 6.2, the reported influence of public opinion is increasing (although the effect is small). The only important difference in explanations due to partisanship is that nonpartisan initiatives are more likely to include research than Democratic initiatives. The only difference based on enactment type is that policy historians are more likely to credit interest groups with smaller changes in public policy. This is consistent with previous theory: interest groups are most influential when it comes

Table B.3 **Logit Models Predicting Other Reported Influential Factors**

		State and Local	International	Path Dependence	Events
Congressional Attention		.00	.00	.00	.00
		(.00)	(.04)	(.00)	(.01)
Years since 1945		.00	.00	.00	.00
		(.01)	(.00)	(.00)	(.00)
Venue	Administrative	−.27	.89***	−.30	.08
		(.35)	(.27)	(.17)	(.17)
	Judicial	1.46***	.07	−.73**	−.02
		(.28)	(.48)	(.25)	(.23)
Party	Democratic	−.55	−.69	.10	−.47*
		(.36)	(.42)	(.19)	(.22)
	Republican	−1.35	−.78	−.33	.19
		(.75)	(.57)	(.27)	(.26)
Enactment	Size of Enactment	.20	.13	−.09	.01
		(.15)	(.16)	(.08)	(.08)
	Liberal	−.14	−.14	.03	.12
		(.17)	(.19)	(.09)	(.09)
	Original Importance	−.25	.48	−.09	.00
		(.29)	(.37)	(.17)	(.18)
Author	Political Scientist	.35	−.03	−.39**	−.04
		(.24)	(.28)	(.14)	(.14)
	Policy School	.48	−2.48*	.22	−.31
		(.36)	(1.03)	(.19)	(.21)
	Historian	.09	.49	.13	−.11
		(.29)	(.29)	(.16)	(.17)
	Government Official	.70	−.53	.07	.10
		(.48)	(1.04)	(.35)	(.38)
Method	Interviews	−.42	.32	−.02	−.13
		(.28)	(.27)	(.15)	(.15)
	Quantitative Data	.01	.60*	−.22	−.01
		(.21)	(.27)	(.13)	(.13)
	No. of Pages	.02	.02	−.14***	.03
		(.07)	(.08)	(.04)	(.04)

(*Continued*)

Table B.3 **Continued**

	State and Local	International	Path Dependence	Events
Total No. of Factors Cited	.21***	.20***	.20***	.27***
	(.03)	(.03)	(.02)	(.02)
Constant	−3.74	−4.06	−1.03	−2.06
Pseudo R^2	.15	.15	.12	.15
N	1,927	1,593	1,927	1,927

Note: Table entries are logit coefficients, with standard errors in parentheses. The models predict whether or not an explanation for a policy enactment incorporates interest groups, research, public opinion, or media coverage. The excluded venue category is legislative enactments. The excluded party variable is nonpartisan or bipartisan enactments. The excluded author type is unlisted disciplines. The models incorporate dummy variables for each issue area but these coefficients are not reported. *$p < .05$ (two-tailed).

to narrower concerns.[5] Unlike some suggest, public opinion does not appear to take over when interest groups are absent.

The results also indicate some differences across authors. Political scientists, policy school professors, and historians are all less likely to mention research in explanations for policy enactments, compared with others. Perhaps these authors are less sanguine about policymakers attending to evidence. The excluded category, however, includes lots of researchers within specific fields like health and the environment; these authors may report on influential research within their fields more often in accounting for policy change. Authors trained in the discipline of history are more likely to include references to public opinion and media coverage. They may be more attentive to broader trends in society, rather than particular factors within political institutions. Authors using interviews in their policy histories are also more likely to include media coverage in their explanations, perhaps because insiders report media influence. Once again, the most consistent finding is that the number of total factors mentioned in an explanation is associated with whether each external factor is reportedly influential.

Other Factors in Policymaking

In the final analyses, I assess the reported influence of state and local government, international factors, path dependence, and events in explanations for policy change, including explanations for policy change in all three branches of government. Table B.3 reports models predicting whether or not an explanation incorporates each of these factors, including the same variables I used before. I again find issue area differences that are consistent with those in chapter 5. Macroeconomic and finance policy enactments are significantly less likely to include state and local influence. International factors are not at all included in explanations for social welfare, housing, crime, and transportation policy changes; as a result, the model predicting international influence excludes these enactments. Agriculture, energy, and finance policy changes are significantly more likely to rely on explanations involving path dependence. Many new laws in these areas, like the regular farm bills, are extensions of the last version of the same law. There are also substantial issue area differences in the extent to which focusing events are credited with policy change. Consistent with the focus of the literature using Punctuated Equilibrium theory, macroeconomic and energy policy changes are the most likely to be associated with events (usually recessions, wars, or catastrophes).

All four models in table B.3 explain less variation than the previous models. The influence of these four categories of factors may not be as systematically predictable. Again, the total number of factors cited is the most strong and consistent predictor; these factors may be mentioned only if policy historians exhaust other possibilities for potential influence. The models do show substantial differences in influence based on policymaking venue. State and local factors are more prevalent in explanations for judicial decisions, often because governments are litigants in the cases or because the decisions overturn state court rulings. Policy historians are more likely to mention international factors in explanations for administrative changes, mostly executive orders during the Cold War. Strangely, judicial decisions are less often associated with path dependence even though they rely on precedent. This is likely because judicial decisions mostly consistent with precedent are not considered significant policy changes. There is also one unexplained difference based on party leadership: Democratic initiatives are less often associated with events, perhaps because Democrats do not wait for events to try to expand government whereas Republicans do so more in the wake of renewed focus on a problem.

There are also differences based on author characteristics. Political scientists are less likely to rely on path dependence in their explanations, especially compared with authors in policy schools and historians. Perhaps our discipline is less likely to notice long-term trends in policy development. Policy school professors, on the other hand, are less likely to see international forces at work in domestic policy change, especially compared with historians. Perhaps these scholars are more singularly focused on a single nation's politics. There are two differences based on method: policy historians using quantitative data are less likely to point to international factors, perhaps because comparable cross-national data is absent, and those writing shorter histories are more likely to use path dependence in their explanations, perhaps because they collapse history into a single narrative of policy development.

NOTES

Introduction

1. Frank R. Baumgartner and Bryan D. Jones, *Agendas and Instability in American Politics* (Chicago: University of Chicago Press, 1993); John W. Kingdon, *Agendas, Alternatives and Public Policies*, 2nd ed. (New York: Addison-Wesley, 2010); Paul A. Sabatier and Hank C. Jenkins-Smith, *Policy Change and Learning: An Advocacy Coalition Approach* (Boulder, CO: Westview Press, 1993).

2. Robert S. Erikson, Michael B. Mackuen, and James A. Stimson, *The Macro Polity* (Cambridge: Cambridge University Press, 2002).

3. Nolan McCarty, "The Policy Effects of Political Polarization," in *The Transformation of American Politics: Activist Government and the Rise of Conservatism*, ed. Paul Pierson and Theda Skocpol (Princeton: Princeton University Press, 2007), 239–271; David R. Mayhew, *Divided We Govern: Party Control, Lawmaking, and Investigations, 1946–2002* (New Haven: Yale University Press, 2005).

4. Policy histories discuss many policy changes that have no clear or consistent ideological direction, as well as conservative changes that contract the scope of government responsibility. I analyze the explanations for all of these enactments. Yet I find that liberal enactments substantially outnumber conservative enactments and that conservative enactments are typically accompanied by liberal enactments in other areas. In chapter 1, I argue that this ideological asymmetry is not a function of partisanship or ideology. The coalitions that make policy change possible and the compromises that they require are inherently easier to build for those that want to expand government (although coalitions opposing any change face the least difficulty).

5. e.g., Theodore Lowi, "American Business, Public Policy, Case-Studies, and Political Theory," *World Politics* 16, no. 4 (1964): 677–715; James Q. Wilson, "The Politics of Regulation," in *The Politics of Regulation*, ed. James Q. Wilson (New York: Basic Books, 1980), 357–394.

6. I limit the analysis to domestic policymaking. As a matter of intellectual division of labor, scholars of international relations usually study foreign policy and tend to focus on the national level of analysis. They are often concerned with relationships among nations, the development of international institutions, and changes in the balance of power between nations. This division in research is somewhat theoretically justified because the causes of foreign policy changes are commonly external to the US government and the foreign policymaking process differs substantially from the equivalent in domestic policy. Because this book's analysis relies on secondary sources of policy history, it must reflect the divisions in scholarship that scholars themselves have drawn. This analysis remains open, however, to foreign determinants of domestic policy and tracks the reported influence of these factors over time in the United States.

7. Some scholars of policy are hesitant to declare that policy has changed unless the goals or assumptions of policymakers or the way that policy is implemented on the ground have been altered. Neither policy historians nor this book use this higher standard.

8. James MacGregor Burns, *The Deadlock of Democracy: Four-Party Politics in America* (Upper Saddle River, NJ: Prentice Hall, 1963); Thomas H. Hammond and Gary J. Miller, "The Core of the Constitution," *American Political Science Review* 81, no. 4 (1987): 1155–1174; Keith Krehbiel, *Pivotal Politics: A Theory of U.S. Lawmaking* (Chicago: University of Chicago Press, 1998); George Tsebelis, *Veto Players: How Political Institutions Work* (Princeton: Princeton University Press, 2002).

9. The relationships among those who are willing to pursue policy change are more important to policy development than the coalitions that seek to oppose policy change. The opposing coalitions do not typically need much help to prevent action; most potential changes fail to move forward despite a lack of any organized opposition. Patterns of association among those who disagree on aspects of policy but cooperate to achieve change, however, are quite important.

10. e.g., Adam D. Sheingate, "Political Entrepreneurship, Institutional Change, and American Political Development," *Studies in American Political Development* 17, no. 3 (2003): 185–203.

11. Chapter 1 further defines "governing networks" and chapter 2 explains my method of measuring and reconstructing them. I also analyze several alternative conceptualizations of policymaker networks and the impact of different measurement techniques on the results.

12. Several mechanisms for cooperation among institutional actors are affected by ideological agreement and party control of Congress and the presidency. Yet no one factor drives these arrangements. Every other factor that influences the policy process also affects the cooperation patterns, including interest group lobbying, media coverage, and research findings. Compromises are also sometimes the product of the accumulation of idiosyncratic characteristics of individual actors, such as Richard Nixon's willingness to expand government or Ted Kennedy's proactive attempts to build relationships across the aisle.

13. All three quotations are attributed to Otto von Bismarck, though with somewhat different reports of the language he used. Ralph Keyes, *The Quote Verifier: Who Said What, Where, and When* (New York: St. Martin's Griffin, 2006), 170.

14. The Policy Agendas Project divides policymaking into 19 categories. Three categories cover foreign policy and two categories do not have an associated separable policy history literature (government operations and public lands). Jones and Baumgartner also eliminate government operations and public lands from their analyses, because they find that most policymaking in these areas is housekeeping in nature. I include major public lands enactments in the environmental category. See Bryan D. Jones and Frank R. Baumgartner, *The Politics of Attention: How Government Prioritizes Problems* (Chicago: University of Chicago Press, 2005).

15. See Mayhew, *Divided We Govern*. To locate the 268 sources used here, I reviewed more than 800 books and articles. Most of the 800 sources did not identify the most important enactments or review the political process surrounding them, even though their titles or descriptions suggested that they might. Appendix A lists all of the sources used in the analysis and chapter 2 reviews the implications of several alternative criteria for inclusion in the population of studies.

16. I coded notable policy enactments into three categories corresponding to different levels of significance: small, medium, and large. A majority of notable enactments were new laws, but there were enactments at all three levels of significance in Congress, the administration, and the courts. Chapter 2 addresses the implications of using several different potential standards for the significance of policy enactments.

17. I also recorded every actor that opposed a significant enactment. Chapter 6 investigates differences across authors in the relative mentions of each actor as well as total actor mentions in explanations for policy change.

18. Chapter 2 explains the construction of these networks and reviews alternative versions.

19. All are based on the same coding of issue area topics and are made available at http://www. policyagendas.org. The data used here were originally collected by Frank R. Baumgartner and Bryan D. Jones, with the support of National Science Foundation grant numbers SBR 9320922 and 0111611, and were distributed through the Department of Government at the University of Texas at Austin. Neither NSF nor the original collectors of the data bear any responsibility for the analysis reported here.

20. For measures of landmark laws per year, see Mayhew, *Divided We Govern*; Joshua D. Clinton and John S. Lapinski, "Measuring Legislative Accomplishment, 1877-1994," *American Journal of Political Science* 50, no. 1 (2006): 232–249; William Howell, Scott Adler, Charles Cameron, and Charles Riemann, "Divided Government and the Legislative Productivity of Congress, 1945-94," *Legislative Studies Quarterly* 25, no. 2 (2000): 285–312; for the measure of ideological orientation, see Erikson, Mackuen, and Stimson, *The Macro Polity*; for the measures of polarization, see Nolan McCarty, Keith T. Poole, and Howard Rosenthal, *Polarized America: The Dance of Ideology and Unequal Riches* (Cambridge, MA: MIT Press, 2006).

21. The quote is from Abraham Lincoln in the Gettysburg address. The text is available at: http://showcase.netins.net/web/creative/lincoln/speeches/gettysburg.htm.

Chapter 1

1. Mayhew, *Divided We Govern*; Krehbiel, *Pivotal Politics*; Baumgartner and Jones, *Agendas and Instability in American Politics*.
2. Federalist 10. http://thomas.loc.gov/home/histdox/fedpapers.html.
3. Hammond and Miller, "The Core of the Constitution."
4. Krehbiel, *Pivotal Politics*.
5. George Tsebelis, *Veto Players: How Political Institutions Work* (Princeton: Princeton University Press, 2002).
6. Paul Pierson, *Politics in Time: History, Institutions, and Social Analysis* (Princeton: Princeton University Press, 2004).
7. Andrea Louise Campbell, *How Policies Make Citizens: Senior Political Activism and the American Welfare State* (Princeton: Princeton University Press, 2005).
8. Jacob S. Hacker, *The Divided Welfare State: The Battle over Public and Private Social Benefits in the United States* (Cambridge: Cambridge University Press, 2002).
9. Pierson, *Politics in Time*.
10. Herbert Simon, "Bounded Rationality and Organizational Learning," *Organization Science* 2, no. 1 (1991): 125–134.
11. Charles Lindblom, *The Intelligence of Democracy: Decision Making through Mutual Adjustment* (New York: Free Press, 1965).
12. Paul A. Sabatier, *Theories of the Policy Process*, 2nd ed. (Boulder, CO: Westview Press, 2007).
13. Baumgartner and Jones, *Agendas and Instability in American Politics*.
14. Ibid.; Kingdon, *Agendas, Alternatives and Public Policies*; Sabatier and Jenkins-Smith, *Policy Change and Learning*.
15. Jones and Baumgartner, *The Politics of Attention*.
16. Kingdon, *Agendas, Alternatives and Public Policies*.
17. Sabatier and Jenkins-Smith, *Policy Change and Learning*.
18. Erikson, Mackuen, and Stimson, *The Macro Polity*.
19. McCarty, Poole, and Rosenthal, *Polarized America*.
20. Andrew D. Martin and Kevin M. Quinn, "Dynamic Ideal Point Estimation via Markov Chain Monte Carlo for the U.S. Supreme Court, 1953-1999," *Political Analysis* 10, no. 2 (2002): 134–153; B. Dan Wood and Richard W. Waterman, "The Dynamics of Political-Bureaucratic Adaptation," *American Journal of Political Science* 37, no. 2 (1993): 497–528.
21. Jeffrey A. Segal, "Separation-of-Powers Games in the Positive Theory of Congress and Courts," *American Political Science Review* 91, no. 1 (1997): 28–44.

22. Emmette S. Redford, *Democracy in the Administrative State* (New York: Oxford University Press, 1969), 107.

23. Philip Converse, "The Nature of Belief Systems in Mass Publics," *Ideology and Discontent*, ed. David E. Apter (New York: Free Press, 1964), 106–261.

24. John Zaller, *The Nature and Origins of Mass Opinion* (Cambridge: Cambridge University Press, 1992).

25. Michael X. Delli Carpini and Scott Keeter, *What Americans Know about Politics and Why It Matters* (New Haven: Yale University Press, 1997).

26. Michael S. Lewis-Beck, Helmut Norpoth, William G. Jacoby, and Herbert F. Weisberg, *The American Voter Revisited* (Ann Arbor: University of Michigan Press, 2008).

27. Chris Wlezien, "The Public as Thermostat: Dynamics of Preferences for Spending," *American Journal of Political Science* 39, no. 4 (1995): 981–1000.

28. Lawrence R. Jacobs and Robert Y. Shapiro, *Politicians Don't Pander: Political Manipulation and the Loss of Democratic Responsiveness* (Chicago: University of Chicago Press, 2000).

29. e.g. Theodore Lowi, "American Business, Public Policy, Case-Studies, and Political Theory," *World Politics* 16, no. 4 (1964): 677–715; James Q. Wilson, "The Politics of Regulation," in *The Politics of Regulation*, ed. James Q. Wilson (New York: Basic Books, 1980), 357–394.

30. Lowi, "American Business, Public Policy, Case-Studies, and Political Theory."

31. Wilson, "The Politics of Regulation."

32. Paul Light, *The President's Agenda: Domestic Policy Choice from Kennedy to Clinton*, 3rd ed. (Baltimore: Johns Hopkins University Press, 1998).

33. Jon R. Bond and Richard Fleisher, *The President in the Legislative Arena* (Chicago: University of Chicago Press, 1992).

34. Brandice Canes-Wrone, *Who Leads Whom?: Presidents, Policy, and the Public* (Chicago: University of Chicago Press, 2005).

35. Sarah A. Binder, *Stalemate: Causes and Consequences of Legislative Gridlock* (Washington, DC: Brookings Institution Press, 2003).

36. R. Douglas Arnold, *The Logic of Congressional Action* (New Haven: Yale University Press, 1992).

37. Erikson, Mackuen, and Stimson, *The Macro Polity*; Martin Gilens, *Affluence & Influence: Economic Inequality and Political Power in America* (Princeton: Princeton University Press, 2012).

38. Gilens, *Affluence & Influence*. Policymakers may share the opinions of the socioeconomically advantaged because they are rich themselves, because they listen to similarly predisposed interest groups, or because they respond to parties that draw disproportionately from the well off.

39. Paul R. Portney and Robert N. Stavins, eds., *Public Policies for Environmental Protection* (Washington, DC: Resources for the Future, 2000); Otis L. Graham, Jr., ed., *Environmental Politics and Policy, 1960s–1990s* (University Park: Pennsylvania State University Press, 2000).

40. Ann Campbell Keller, *Science in Environmental Policy* (Cambridge, MA: MIT Press, 2009).

41. Reiner Grundmann, "Climate Change and Knowledge Politics," *Environmental Politics* 16, no. 3 (2007): 414–432; Zdravka Tzankovaa, "The Science and Politics of Ecological Risk: Bioinvasions Policies in the US and Australia," *Environmental Politics* 18, no. 3 (2009): 333–350.

42. Jeffrey R. Henig, *Spin Cycle: How Research is Used in Policy Debates: The Case of Charter Schools* (New York: Russell Sage Foundation, 2008).

43. David B. Truman, *The Governmental Process: Political Interests and Public Opinion* (New York: Knopf, 1951).

44. Elmer E. Schattschneider, *The Semisovereign People: A Realist's View of Democracy in America* (New York: Holt, Rinehart and Winston, 1960).

45. Frank R. Baumgartner, Jeffrey M. Berry, Marie Hojnacki, David C. Kimball, and Beth L. Leech, *Lobbying and Policy Change: Who Wins, Who Loses, and Why* (Chicago: University of Chicago Press, 2009).

46. The distinction between foxes and hedgehogs is credited to Archilochus ("the fox knows many things, but the hedgehog knows one big thing") but made famous by Isaiah Berlin.

47. Political and economic theorists categorized as foxes are substantially better at prediction than those categorized as hedgehogs. See Philip E. Tetlock, *Expert Political Judgment: How Good Is It? How Can We Know?* (Princeton: Princeton University Press, 2006).

48. Hammond and Miller, "The Core of the Constitution."

49. Ibid.

50. Krehbiel, *Pivotal Politics.*

51. Ibid.

52. Pierson, *Politics in Time.*

53. Ibid.

54. Stephen Skowronek, *Building a New American State: The Expansion of National Administrative Capacities, 1877–1920* (Cambridge: Cambridge University Press, 1982).

55. Eric M. Patashnik, *Reforms at Risk: What Happens after Major Policy Changes are Enacted* (Princeton: Princeton University Press, 2008).

56. Daniel Carpenter, *The Forging of Bureaucratic Autonomy: Reputations, Networks, and Policy Innovation in Executive Agencies, 1862-1928* (Princeton: Princeton University Press, 2001).

57. Patashnik, *Reforms at Risk*; Campbell, *How Policies Make Citizens.*

58. Karen Orren and Stephen Skowronek, *The Search for American Political Development* (Cambridge: Cambridge University Press, 2004).

59. Pierson, *Politics in Time.*

60. Ibid.

61. Arthur M. Schlesinger, Jr., *The Cycles of American History* (Boston: Houghton Mifflin, 1986).

62. Huntington, *American Politics.*

63. Kingdon, *Agendas, Alternatives and Public Policies.*

64. Michael Mintrom, *Policy Entrepreneurs and School Choice* (Washington, DC: Georgetown University Press, 2000).

65. Ibid.

66. Ibid.

67. Dimitrios C. Christopoulos, "Relational Attributes of Political Entrepreneurs: A Network Perspective," *Journal of European Public Policy* 13, no. 5 (2006): 757–778.

68. Kingdon, *Agendas, Alternatives and Public Policies.*

69. Mintrom and Norman, "Policy Entrepreneurship and Policy Change."

70. Carpenter, *The Forging of Bureaucratic Autonomy.*

71. Frances S. Berry, Ralph S. Brower, Sang Ok Choi, Wendy Xinfang Goa, Heesoun Jang, Myungjung Kwon, and Jessica Word, "Three Traditions of Network Research: What the Public Management Research Agenda can Learn from Other Research Communities," *Public Administration Review* 64, no. 5 (2004): 539–553.

72. Hugh Heclo, "Issue Networks and the Executive Establishment," in *The New American Political System*, ed. Anthony King (Washington, DC: American Enterprise Institute, 1978).

73. Ibid.

74. Paul M. Hallacher, *Why Polity Issue Networks Matter: The Advanced Technology Program and the Manufacturing Extension Partnership* (Lanham, MD: Rowman & Littlefield Publishers, 2005).

75. To be fair, ACF authors have described the intended domain of their framework as circumscribed, applying only to some issue areas and contexts. See Paul Sabatier and Christopher Weible, "The Advocacy Coalition Framework: Innovation and Clarification," in *Theories of the Policy Process*, ed. Paul A. Sabatier (Boulder, CO: Westview Press, 2007).

76. Sabatier and Jenkins-Smith, *Policy Change and Learning.*

77. The "great man theory" was popularized by Thomas Carlyle and critiqued by Herbert Spencer. See Sidney Hook, *The Hero in History* (New York: Humanities Press, 1950), 67.

78. Robert A. Caro, *The Passage of Power: The Years of Lyndon Johnson* (New York: Knopf, 2012).

79. Rick Perlstein, *Nixonland: The Rise of a President and the Fracturing of America* (New York: Scribner, 2008).

80. Samuel Kernell, *Going Public: New Strategies of Presidential Leadership* (Washington, DC: CQ Press, 2006); George C. Edwards, *On Deaf Ears: The Limits of the Bully Pulpit* (New Haven: Yale University Press, 2006). Kernell tracks the increase in public-oriented activity. Edwards shows that these activities have limited influence on the public or Congress.

81. Richard E. Neustadt, *Presidential Power and the Modern Presidents: The Politics of Leadership from Roosevelt to Reagan*, Revised Edition (New York: Free Press, 1991).

82. Giliberto Capano and Michael Howlett, "Introduction: The Determinants of Policy Change: Advancing the Debate," *Journal of Comparative Policy Analysis: Research and Practice* 11, no. 1 (2009): 1–5.

83. Ibid.

84. This is the definition preferred by Erikson, Mackuen, and Stimson, *The Macro Polity*.

85. These statistics are based on my own calculations, comparing the table of laws in Erikson, Mackuen, and Stimson, *The Macro Polity* with the table in Mayhew, *Divided We Govern*.

86. Steven Kent Vogel, *Freer Markets, More Rules: Regulatory Reform in Advanced Industrial Countries* (Ithaca, NY: Cornell University Press, 1996).

87. Jacob S. Hacker, and Paul Pierson, *Winner-Take-All Politics: How Washington Made the Rich Richer—and Turned Its Back on the Middle Class* (New York: Simon & Schuster, 2010).

88. David W. Brady and Craig Volden, *Revolving Gridlock: Politics and Policy from Jimmy Carter to George W. Bush* (Boulder, CO: Westview Press, 2005).

89. Lindblom, *The Intelligence of Democracy*.

90. Richard Fenno, *Congressmen in Committees* (Boston: Little Brown and Company, 1973).

91. James L. Payne, "Show Horses & Work Horses in the United States House of Representatives," *Polity* 12, no. 3 (1980): 428–456.

92. David R. Mayhew, *America's Congress: Actions in the Public Sphere, James Madison through Newt Gingrich* (New Haven: Yale University Press, 2002).

93. Mayhew, *America's Congress*.

94. Baumgartner and Jones, *Agendas and Instability in American Politics*.

95. Matt Grossmann, *The Not-So-Special Interests: Interest Groups, Public Representation, and American Governance* (Stanford, CA: Stanford University Press, 2012).

Chapter 2

1. Quoted in Sarah Wheaton, "Clinton's Civil Right's Lesson," *nytimes.com*. Available at: http://thecaucus.blogs.nytimes.com/2008/01/07/civilrights/.

2. Mayhew, *Divided We Govern*, 245–252.

3. The PAP has 19 categories; three cover foreign policy and two do not have an associated literature.

4. Studying political institutions over an extended period is the only method of insuring that analysts are attentive to multiple big and slow causes for a single effect as well as patterns of effects related to single causes. See Pierson, *Politics in Time*. Long-term historical studies are also required to investigate how policy entrepreneurs develop and combine proposals, waiting for the right time to move forward. See Mintrom, *Policy Entrepreneurs and School Choice*.

5. The problem is not generic to policy research; many of the sources I use have an associated theory but all attempt to chronicle the events surrounding policy change independent of their theory testing goals. The exclusion is necessary to avoid studies that only assess the role of one set of variables, without assessing the presence or absence of other factors. At least 80 policy studies using the ACF and at least 35 policy studies undertaken to study Punctuated Equilibrium theory (listed at http://www.policyagendas.org) are excluded. For a list of ACF studies, see Christopher M. Weible, Paul Sabatier, and Kelly McQueen, "Themes and Variations: Taking Stock of the Advocacy Coalition Framework," *Policy Studies Journal* 37, no. 1 (2009): 121–140. Policy historians also share biases, but their collective

judgment serves as a useful comparison to theoretically driven research. For a comparison of the advantages of each, see Matt Grossmann, "Interest Group Influence on US Policy Change: An Assessment Based on Policy History," *Interest Groups & Advocacy* 1, no. 2 (2012): 1–22.

6. I obtained a larger number of resources for some areas than others. Analyzing additional volumes covering the same policy area, however, reached a point of diminishing returns. The first five resources covered most of the significant policy enactments in most areas.

7. I exclude policy changes mentioned by authors if we later found that they were never enacted or if we could find no other confirmation that they were significant events.

8. For the list of policy enactments, an assistant reassessed codes for policymaking venue and issue area and, where available, compared our codes to those in the PAP database. The Krippendorff's Alpha reliability score was .903 for the venue analysis and .848 for the issue area analysis.

9. Erikson, Mackuen, and Stimson, *The Macro Polity.* Where the ideological direction was ambiguous, where there were ideological trade-offs among different parts of the enactment, or where there was any question or disagreement about the direction of a bill, we coded it as neither liberal nor conservative. The Krippendorff's Alpha for an inter-coder reliability analysis of two coders of three volumes for this variable was .64.

10. The other measures are from Clinton and Lapinski, "Measuring Legislative Accomplishment" and Howell, Adler, Cameron, and Riemann, "Divided Government and the Legislative Productivity of Congress."

11. Krehbiel, *Pivotal Politics.*

12. Erikson, Mackuen, and Stimson, *The Macro Polity.*

13. Tracy Roof, *American Labor, Congress, and the Welfare State, 1935-2010* (Baltimore: Johns Hopkins University Press, 2011).

14. Percent agreement is the only acceptable inter-coder reliability measure for many different coders analyzing a single case; other measures are undefined due to lack of variation across cases. If many coders analyzed many cases, I would expect less agreement in traditional measures of inter-coder reliability because percent agreement tends to overstate reliability when many factors are considered.

15. The results for the role of arguments and ideas in policy history are not as reliable as the other indicators. Coders began coding for ideas after reading the first several dozen sources; the numbers for ideas are therefore (slightly) artificially low and not fully comparable to the others.

16. I use this standard because some policy histories did not credit specific actors with enactments. Analysis using different standards (such as majority rule across authors) revealed similar results.

17. Percent agreement is the only inter-coder reliability measure appropriate for compilation of lists from an undefined universe where there is little similarity across cases.

18. Actors that could not be easily categorized by type of organization or ideological viewpoint were put in separate unidentified categories.

19. The networks are not made up of all of the participants in policy communities. Instead, they include people credited with policy enactments in each issue area. All of the issue areas analyzed here therefore have some network of actors jointly credited with influencing policy. The ties in the networks do not necessarily imply active political collaboration.

20. If an individual and an organization of which they were a part were both credited, they are treated as separate actors in the network. These instances accounted for a small minority of all connections and do not account for the overall structure of relationships.

21. For example, see Frances Fox Piven and Richard A. Cloward, *Poor People's Movements: Why They Succeed, How They Fail* (New York: Vintage Books, 1977); and Doug McAdam, *Political Process and the Development of Black Insurgency, 1930-1970* (Chicago: University of Chicago Press, 1982).

22. John D. Skrentny, *The Minority Rights Revolution* (Cambridge, MA: Belknap Press of Harvard University Press, 2002).

23. Howell, Adler, Cameron, and Riemann, "Divided Government and the Legislative Productivity of Congress"; Clinton and Lapinski, "Measuring Legislative Accomplishment."
24. Mayhew, *Divided We Govern*.

Chapter 3

1. A transcript is available at: http://www.whitehouse.gov/photos-and-video/video/making-higher-education-more-affordable#transcript and was accessed on January 16, 2012.
2. In this book, I use "agenda setting" research to identify the scholarly project to understand how government decides which policy issues to address, including the focus on the problems and concerns of the public, media, and government officials. Some view "agenda setting" research as a wider project including investigation of how issues are framed and how interest groups and the public are motivated to get involved in policy disputes. This book does not assess this wider literature. For example, it does not seek to challenge ideas about issue containment or expansion.
3. Roger Cobb and Charles Elder, *Participation in American Politics: The Dynamics of Agenda Building*, 2nd ed. (Baltimore: Johns Hopkins University Press, 1983), xi.
4. Ibid., 12.
5. Baumgartner and Jones, *Agendas and Instability in American Politics*.
6. Ibid., 10.
7. Jones and Baumgartner, *The Politics of Attention*, 18.
8. Ibid., 255.
9. Ibid., 262.
10. Bryan D. Jones, Heather Larsen-Price, and John Wilkerson, "Representation and American Governing Institutions," *Journal of Politics* 71, no. 1 (2009): 277–290.
11. Kingdon, *Agendas, Alternatives and Public Policies*, 17.
12. Ibid., 164.
13. Ibid., 205.
14. Sabatier and Weible, "The Advocacy Coalition Framework," 193.
15. Ibid., 199.
16. Edella Schlager, "A Comparative Analysis of Policy Theories," in *Theories of the Policy Process*, ed. Paul A. Sabatier (Boulder, CO: Westview Press, 2007), 310.
17. For example, see chapter 2 of Jones and Baumgartner, *The Politics of Attention* and chapter 1 of Sabatier, *Theories of the Policy Process*.
18. Jones and Baumgartner, *The Politics of Attention*.
19. Jones, Larsen-Price, and Wilkerson, "Representation and American Governing Institutions."
20. Chapter 5 analyzes differences across issue areas. I find that enactments in some issue areas are more episodic whereas enactments in other areas are more path dependent.
21. Christopher F. Baum, *An Introduction to Modern Econometrics Using Stata* (College Station, TX: Stata Press, 2006).
22. The results are substantially similar to the results for random effects and fixed effects panel regressions, although some significant results in the first model in each set are not significant in the models based on panel data. Although panel regressions are more appropriate, they present more difficult tests. Given that the theory proposed here expects largely null results, I report the models with lower standards. This also allows readers to see where previous investigations may have confused issue-specific patterns with more general associations.
23. Another possible set of tests for differences across issues in the underlying associations would be to use seemingly unrelated regression on the covariates for each issue area. This specification shows no consistency in the predictors of lawmaking (or policymaking in other branches) across issues for these covariates. Baum, *An Introduction to Modern Econometrics Using Stata*.
24. Jones and Baumgartner, *The Politics of Attention*.
25. Jones, Larsen-Price, and Wilkerson, "Representation and American Governing Institutions."

26. Jones, Larsen-Price, and Wilkerson (2009) use a version of the CQ articles measure to assess important congressional enactments, but the measure is correlated with total laws at .9. See Jones, Larsen-Price, and Wilkerson, "Representation and American Governing Institutions." Even for this measure, the average correlation between public opinion and output across issue areas was .06. Other measures of significant policy enactments from Mayhew, Clinton and Lapinski, and Howell et al. are not as closely tied to total law-making and are more closely correlated with the measures that I derive from policy histories. Mayhew, *Divided We Govern*; Clinton and Lapinski, "Measuring Legislative Accomplishment"; Howell, Adler, Cameron, and Riemann, "Divided Government and the Legislative Productivity of Congress."

27. Colleen McCain Nelson, "Tough Slog for Obama's Gun Orders," *Wall Street Journal*, April 29, 2013, A4.

28. Gilens, *Affluence and Influence*.

29. Using a more limited standard that requires a majority of policy historians studying each policy change to include the factor in their explanations, all of the factors are less common but their relative frequency is similar. Requiring unanimity among policy historians substantially reduces the number of explanatory factors associated with each enactment, but again does not meaningfully change the relative frequency of the factors reported.

30. Elizabeth H. DeBray, *Politics, Ideology, and Education: Federal Policy during the Clinton and Bush Administrations* (New York: Teacher's College Press, 2006), 126.

31. John Brademas, *The Politics of Education: Conflict and Consensus on Capitol Hill* (Norman: University of Oklahoma Press, 1987).

32. Christopher T. Cross, *Political Education: National Policy Comes of Age* (New York: Teachers College Press, 2003).

33. Jerold Waltman, *The Politics of the Minimum Wage* (Champaign: University of Illinois Press, 2000).

34. Sylvester J. Schieber and John B. Shoven, *The Real Deal: The History and Future of Social Security* (New Haven: Yale University Press, 1999).

35. Christopher Howard, *The Welfare State Nobody Knows: Debunking Myths about U.S. Social Policy* (Princeton: Princeton University Press, 2006), 80.

36. Otis L. Graham, Jr., ed., *Environmental Politics and Policy, 1960s-1990s* (University Park: Pennsylvania State University Press, 2000).

37. Sam Rosenfeld, "Fed by Reform: Congressional Politics, Partisan Change, and the Food Stamp Program, 1961–1981," *Journal of Policy History* 22, no. 4 (2010): 479.

38. Howard, *The Welfare State Nobody Knows*.

39. Paul Mitchell, *Federal Housing Policy and Programs: Past and Present* (Piscataway, NJ: Rutgers University Press, 1985).

40. Stephen P. Strickland, *Politics, Science, and Dread Disease: A Short History of United States Medical Research Policy* (Cambridge, MA: Harvard University Press, 1972), 46.

41. Steven K. Wisensale, *Family Leave Policy: The Political Economy of Work and Family in America* (Armonk, NY: M. E. Sharpe, 2001), 150.

42. Craig A. Rimmerman, Kenneth D. Wald, and Clyde Wilcox, eds., *The Politics of Gay Rights* (Chicago: University of Chicago Press, 2000).

43. Sven Steinmo, "The Evolution of Policy Ideas: Tax Policy in the 20th Century," *British Journal of Politics & International Relations* 5, no. 2 (2003): 218.

44. Gareth Davies, *See Government Grow: Education Politics from Johnson to Reagan* (Lawrence: University Press of Kansas, 2007).

45. Don E. Kash and Robert Rycroft, *U.S. Energy Policy: Crisis and Complacency* (Norman: University of Oklahoma Press, 1984).

46. Harry L. Wilson, *Guns, Gun Control, and Elections* (Lanham, MD: Rowman & Littlefield Publishers, 2006).

47. Richard G. Frank and Sherry A. Glied, *Better but Not Well: Mental Health Policy in the United States since 1950* (Baltimore: Johns Hopkins University Press, 2006).

48. Donley T. Studlar, *Tobacco Control: Comparative Politics in the United States and Canada* (Toronto: University of Toronto Press, 2002).

49. W. Elliot Brownlee, *Funding the Modern American State, 1941–1995: The Rise and Fall of the Era of Easy Finance* (Cambridge: Cambridge University Press, 2003), 182.

50. Grossmann, *The Not-So-Special Interests.*

51. Paul Charles Milazzo, *Unlikely Environmentalists: Congress and Clean Water, 1945-1972* (Lawrence: University Press of Kansas, 2006).

52. Christopher McGrory Klyza and David J. Sousa, *American Environmental Policy, 1990-2006: Beyond Gridlock* (Cambridge, MA: MIT Press, 2008): 50.

53. Jeffrey Togman, *The Ramparts of Nations* (Santa Barbara, CA: Greenwood Press, 2001), 70.

54. C. Eugene Steuerle, *Contemporary U.S. Tax Policy* (Washington, DC: Urban Institute Press, 2004), 180–181.

55. Ibid., 210.

56. Mark H. Rose, Bruce E. Seely, and Paul F. Barrett, *The Best Transportation System in the World: Railroads, Trucks, Airlines, and American Public Policy in the Twentieth Century* (Columbus: Ohio State University Press, 2006).

57. Mark V. Nadel, *The Politics of Consumer Protection* (New York: MacMillan Publishing Company, 1971).

58. Suzanne Mettler, "Reconstituting the Submerged State: The Challenges of Social Policy Reform in the Obama Era," *Perspectives on Politics* 8, no. 3 (2010): 803–824.

Chapter 4

1.   The 1996 Republican Party Platform is available at: http://www.presidency.ucsb.edu/ws/index.php?pid=25848.

2.   Erikson, Mackuen, and Stimson, *The Macro Polity.*

3.   Nathan J. Kelly, "Political Choice, Public Policy, and Distributional Outcomes," *American Journal of Political Science* 49, no. 4 (2005): 865–880; Bartels, *Unequal Democracy.*

4.   McCarty, Poole, and Rosenthal, *Polarized America.*

5.   For some counterexamples, see Lawrence J. Grossback, David A. M. Peterson, and James A. Stimson, *Mandate Politics* (Cambridge: Cambridge University Press, 2007).

6.   Theodore Lowi, *The End of Liberalism: The Second Republic of the United States* (New York: W. W. Norton, 1979); Marshall Kaplan and Peggy L. Cuciti, eds., *The Great Society and Its Legacy: Twenty Years of U.S. Social Policy* (Durham, NC: Duke University Press, 1986); Hacker and Pierson, *Winner-Take-All Politics.*

7.   Mayhew, *Divided We Govern.*

8.   Howell, Adler, Cameron, and Riemann, "Divided Government and the Legislative Productivity of Congress."

9.   Clinton and Lapinski, "Measuring Legislative Accomplishment."

10. McCarty, "The Policy Effects of Political Polarization."

11. Ibid.; Howell, Adler, Cameron, and Riemann, "Divided Government and the Legislative Productivity of Congress." Several scholars have noted the bulge in lawmaking from 1961-1976 but have not found a way to explain it based on any macro-political conditions. See Krehbiel, *Pivotal Politics*; Andrew J. Taylor, "Explaining Government Productivity," *American Politics Research* 26, no. 4 (1998): 439–458; David R. Mayhew, *Parties and Policies: How the American Government Works* (New Haven: Yale University Press, 2008).

12. Erikson, Mackuen, and Stimson, *The Macro Polity.*

13. Arthur M. Schlesinger, Jr., *The Cycles of American History* (Boston: Houghton Mifflin, 1986), 32.

14. Ibid., 33.

15. Huntington, *American Politics*, 167.

16. Ibid., 172.

17. Sidney Milkis, "Lyndon Johnson, the Great Society, and the 'Twilight' of the Modern Presidency," in *The Great Society and the High Tide of Liberalism*, ed. Sidney M Milkis and Jerome M. Mileur (Amherst: University of Massachusetts Press, 2005), xix.

18. Barry B. Bosworth, "The Evolution of Economic Policy," in *The Great Society and Its Legacy: Twenty Years of U.S. Social Policy*, ed. Marshall Kaplan and Peggy L. Cuciti (Durham, NC: Duke University Press, 1986).

19. Kimberly J. Morgan, *Working Mothers and the Welfare State: Religion and the Politics of Work—Family Policies in Western Europe and the United States* (Stanford, CA: Stanford University Press, 2006), 98.

20. Milkis, "Lyndon Johnson, the Great Society, and the 'Twilight' of the Modern Presidency."

21. Kaplan and Cuciti, *The Great Society and Its Legacy*.

22. Erikson, Mackuen, and Stimson, *The Macro Polity*.

23. Sarah A. Binder, *Stalemate: Causes and Consequences of Legislative Gridlock* (Washington, DC: Brookings Institution Press, 2003).

24. Jack L. Walker, *Mobilizing Interest Groups in America: Patrons, Professions, and Social Movements* (Ann Arbor: University of Michigan Press, 1991); Theda Skocpol, *Diminished Democracy: From Membership to Management in American Civic Life* (Norman: University of Oklahoma Press, 2003).

25. Milkis, "Lyndon Johnson, the Great Society, and the 'Twilight' of the Modern Presidency"; Paul Frymer, "Acting When Elected Officials Won't: Federal Courts and Civil Rights Enforcement in U.S. Labor Unions, 1935–85," *American Political Science Review* 97, no. 3 (2003): 483–499.

26. Adam Sheingate, "The Terrain of the Political Entrepreneur," in *Formative Acts: American Politics in the Making*, ed. Stephen Skowronek and Matthew Glassman (Philadelphia: University of Pennsylvania Press, 2007); John Hart, *The Presidential Branch: From Washington to Clinton* (London: Chatham House, 1995).

27. Barbara Sinclair, *The Transformation of the U.S. Senate* (Baltimore: Johns Hopkins University Press, 1989).

28. Sarah Staszak, "Institutions, Rulemaking, and the Politics of Judicial Retrenchment," *Studies in American Political Development* 24, no. 2 (2010): 168–189; Frymer, "Acting When Elected Officials Won't."

29. Sheingate, "The Terrain of the Political Entrepreneur."

30. R. Shep Melnick, "From Tax and Spend to Mandate and Sue," in *The Great Society and the High Tide of Liberalism*, ed. Sidney M Milkis and Jerome M. Mileur (Amherst: University of Massachusetts Press, 2005).

31. Ibid., 394.

32. Hacker and Pierson, *Winner-Take-All Politics*.

33. Lowi, *The End of Liberalism*.

34. Heclo, "Issue Networks and the Executive Establishment."

35. Davies, *See Government Grow*, 37.

36. R. Allen Hays, *The Federal Government and Urban Housing: Ideology and Change in Public Policy* (Albany, NY: State University of New York Press, 1995), x.

37. Schieber and Shoven, *The Real Deal*, 156–157.

38. Willis Rudy, *Building America's Schools and Colleges: The Federal Contribution* (Cranbury, NJ: Cornwall Books, 2003).

39. Charles R. Epp, *The Rights Revolution: Lawyers, Activists, and Supreme Courts in Comparative Perspective* (Chicago: University of Chicago Press, 1998).

40. Milazzo, *Unlikely Environmentalists*, 118.

41. Johnson's efforts even included transportation: "Johnson sought to make transportation firms and federal transportation agencies part of his Great Society and part of a presidential nation." Rose, Seely, and Barrett, *The Best Transportation System in the World*, 137.

42. It is possible that policy historians overemphasize the role of the president in policymaking. I assess how the collective assessments of these historians change over time; they were far more likely to credit presidents with policy enactments during the Long Great Society.

43. See Polsby, *Consequences of Party Reform*. In addition, the institutional resources available to presidents for executive branch management and congressional relations expanded prior to this era and continued during the Long Great Society. See Hart, *The Presidential Branch*.

44. President Obama entered office with more legislative experience than most recent presidents, but he spent most of his four years in the Senate preparing to run for president or campaigning.

45. Sheingate, "Political Entrepreneurship, Institutional Change, and American Political Development."

46. Sheldon Friedman and David C. Jacobs, eds., *The Future of the Safety Net: Social Insurance and Employee Benefits* (Ithaca, NY: ILR Press, 2001).

47. Joan Hoff, *Nixon Reconsidered* (New York: Basic Books, 1995); Dean J. Kotlowski, *Nixon's Civil Rights: Politics, Principle, and Policy* (Cambridge, MA: Harvard University Press, 2002).

48. The measure of unified government is from Mayhew, *Divided We Govern*; the measure of polarization is from McCarty, Poole, and Rosenthal, *Polarized America*.

49. Tests for dispersion confirmed that negative binomial models were more appropriate than poisson models. McCarty also includes a linear time trend, but this is not theoretically justified. Including this year term increases the effect of polarization but does not change other results. See McCarty, "The Policy Effects of Political Polarization."

50. The polarization measure is from Tom S. Clark, "Measuring Ideological Polarization on the United States Supreme Court," *Political Research Quarterly* 62, no. 1 (2009): 146–157. I constructed an alternative measure of unified government for party unity between the president and the majority of Supreme Court justices (based on the party of their appointing president). This variable does not help explain Court policymaking or change the effect of other variables.

51. For the models with a lag term, the period effect increases enactments by 1.4 times in the legislative branch, 1.6 times in the executive branch, and 2.2 times in the judicial branch. A cross-sectional time-series model to predict enactments per issue-congress also finds a significant period effect after controlling for issue-level fixed effects.

52. Supreme Court polarization is unexpectedly positively associated with judicial policy enactments in the base model, suggesting that Court polarization may grow when Court decisions make policy.

53. I used the original data from Mayhew, *Divided We Govern*. The measure of most important landmarks is from Howell, Adler, Cameron, and Riemann, "Divided Government and the Legislative Productivity of Congress." The aggregated measure is from Clinton and Lapinski, "Measuring Legislative Accomplishment."

54. Binder, *Stalemate*.

55. Krehbiel, *Pivotal Politics*. Krehbiel's measure is based on change in election results for the House and Senate and is used to predict changes in the number of laws passed. I also predicted changes in legislative productivity and liberalism (from the previous Congress) but found no significant relationship with the gridlock interval.

56. The Erikson, Mackuen, and Stimson measure, which is based only on contemporary judgments from Mayhew's sweep one, coded only 3.6% of significant laws as conservative (and 51.8% of the laws as liberal). See Erikson, Mackuen, and Stimson, *The Macro Polity*.

57. Wood and Waterman, "The Dynamics of Political-Bureaucratic Adaptation."

58. Nixon lost important cases before the federal courts and opposed many liberal decisions, but the judiciary was making liberal policy on civil rights and criminal justice at the same time that he was helping to expand government in other issue areas up to the mid-1970s.

59. Using a two-year lag for public opinion instead does not change the results. Including public opinion in these models eliminates the first four bienniums; removing public opinion, ideology becomes a significant predictor of legislative liberalism but no other results change.

60. Martin and Quinn, "Dynamic Ideal Point Estimation via Markov Chain Monte Carlo for the U.S. Supreme Court."

61. I constructed an alternative measure of partisanship of the judiciary using the number of Supreme Court justices appointed by Democratic presidents. Including this variable does not help explain the ideological direction of Court policymaking or change the effect of other variables.

62. David Krackhardt, "Predicting with Networks: Nonparametric Multiple Regression Analysis of Dyadic Data," *Social Networks* 10 (1988): 359–381.

63. The dependent variable is the pairwise correlations between all administration networks. The independent variables are each differences or similarities between the administrations. The standard errors reported in the regression are not directly interpretable and do not represent the source of the non-parametric significance tests used in QAP regression.

64. Judges were not credited with judicial policy changes as often as interest groups that brought cases to the courts; these groups were connected to the broader liberal network of the era. See Epp, *The Rights Revolution*.

65. I also tracked networks of actors that opposed policy enactments from 1945 to 2004. The results did not show a substantial change in opposition during the Long Great Society. Opponents of one policy change were often proponents of other changes and are already included in the network.

66. For the interest group increase, see Walker, *Mobilizing Interest Groups in America*. For the increase in government units, see Heclo, "Issue Networks and the Executive Establishment."

67. John P. Heinz, Edward O. Laumann, Robert L. Nelson, and Robert H. Salisbury, *The Hollow Core: Private Interests in National Policy Making* (Cambridge, MA: Harvard University Press, 1993).

68. Sheingate, "Political Entrepreneurship, Institutional Change, and American Political Development."

69. David W. Rohde, *Parties and Leaders in the Postreform House* (Chicago: University of Chicago Press, 1991).

70. Jones and Baumgartner, *The Politics of Attention*.

71. Binder, *Stalemate*.

72. Baumgartner and Jones, Agendas and Instability in American Politics, 234.

73. Brady and Volden, *Revolving Gridlock*.

74. The public mood theory is taken from Stephen Skowronek, *The Politics Presidents Make: Leadership from John Adams to Bill Clinton* (Cambridge, MA: Belknap Press of Harvard University Press, 1997). The television-based theory is from Samuel Kernell, *Going Public: New Strategies of Presidential Leadership* (Washington, DC: CQ Press, 2006). The theory of changes in practice is from Jeffrey K. Tulis, *The Rhetorical Presidency* (Princeton: Princeton University Press, 1988).

75. For a cyclical theory, see Skowronek, *The Politics Presidents Make*. For a transition from one era to another, see Kernell, *Going Public*.

76. Pierson, *Politics in Time*.

77. In chapter 6, I track how often policy historians referenced factors related to path dependence in their explanations for policy change, including whether enactments built on previous policies. Reported path dependence reached its peak in the late 1950s but was average during the Long Great Society.

78. Lowi, *The End of Liberalism*; Heclo, "Issue Networks and the Executive Establishment"; Kingdon, *Agendas, Alternatives and Public Policies*.

Chapter 5

1. The presidential announcement is available at: http://www.whitehouse.gov/the-press-office/2011/07/29/president-obama-announces-historic-545-mpg-fuel-efficiency-standard.

2. This chapter is adapted from Matt Grossmann, "The Variable Politics of the Policy Process: Issue Area Differences and Comparative Networks," *Journal of Politics* 75, no. 1 (2013).

3. Jones and Baumgartner, *The Politics of Attention*; Zahariadis, "The Multiple Streams Framework." A content analysis of applications of the ACF found few studies of economic policy, social welfare policy, agriculture, criminal justice, or housing. See Weible, Sabatier, and McQueen, "Themes and Variations." Although there is no equivalent content analysis of the other two frameworks, I noticed few applications of PE to civil rights, science, or transportation and few applications of MS to education or housing.

4 Lowi, "American Business, Public Policy, Case-Studies, and Political Theory."

5. Wilson, "The Politics of Regulation."

6. Kevin B. Smith, "Typologies, Taxonomies, and the Benefits of Policy Classification," *Policy Studies Journal* 30, no. 3 (2002): 379–395.

7. See Jeffrey M. Berry, *The Interest Group Society*, 5th ed. (New York: HarperCollins Publishers, 1989).

8. Heclo, "Issue Networks and the Executive Establishment."

9. Heinz, Laumann, Nelson, and Salisbury, *The Hollow Core*.

10. David Marsh and R. A. W. Rhodes, "Policy Communities and Issue Networks: Beyond Typology," in *Social Networks: Critical Concepts in Sociology*, ed. John Scott (London: Routledge, 2004).

11. Smith, "Typologies, Taxonomies, and the Benefits of Policy Classification," 381.

12. Edward P. Weber, *Pluralism by the Rules: Conflict and Cooperation in Environmental Regulation* (Washington, DC: Georgetown University Press, 1998), 191.

13. Willard W. Cochrane, *American Farm Policy, 1948-1973* (Minneapolis: University of Minnesota Press, 1981), 26.

14. H. Wayne Moyer and Timothy Edward Josling, *Agriculture Policy Reform: Politics & Process in the EU & US in the 1990s* (London: Ashgate Publishing, 2002), 95.

15. Bruce Andre Beaubouef, *The Strategic Petroleum Reserve: U.S. Energy Security and Oil Politics, 1975-2005* (College Station: Texas A&M University Press, 2007).

16. Brownlee, *Funding the Modern American State*, 102.

17. Michael B. Berkman, *The State Roots of National Politics: Congress and the Tax Agenda, 1978-1986* (Pittsburgh: University of Pittsburgh Press, 1993), 40.

18. Michael S. Greve and Fred L. Smith, *Environmental Politics: Public Costs, Private Rewards* (New York: Praeger Publishers, 1992), 67.

19. Charles E. Davis, *The Politics of Hazardous Waste* (New York: Prentice Hall, 1992), 25.

20. Nadine Lehrer, *U.S. Farm Bills and Policy Reforms: Ideological Conflicts over World Trade, Renewable Energy, and Sustainable Agriculture* (Amherst, NY: Cambria Press, 2010), 66–67.

21. Patashnik, *Reforms at Risk*, 61.

22. Since the civil rights issue area is an outlier in this respect, this finding from the case study in chapter 2 does not extend to other domains.

23. Beaubouef, *The Strategic Petroleum Reserve*.

24. Although there are fit statistics proposed for some of these measures (beyond the fitness measure for the core-periphery model), they generally require simulated data and are not usefully compared to familiar statistics. See Stanley Wasserman and Katherine Faust, *Social Network Analysis: Methods and Applications* (Cambridge: Cambridge University Press, 1994).

25. Higher clustering coefficients indicate that, if actors share ties to other actors, they are more likely to be tied. To determine whether actors divide into clustered neighborhoods throughout the network, it is useful to compare the clustering coefficient to the overall density in each network.

26. The indexes are calculated as (number of ties between actors in the two different groups— number of ties between actors in the same group)/(sum of both of these types of ties). They may be measures of the extent of conflict (negative) or cooperation (positive) across groups.

27. Jonathan Bean, *Big Government and Affirmative Action: The Scandalous History of the Small Business Administration* (Lexington: University Press of Kentucky, 2001).

28. Jill M. Hendrickson, *Regulation and Instability in U.S. Commercial Banking: A History of Crises* (New York: Palgrave Macmillan, 2011).

29. Ashley E. Jochim and Bryan D. Jones, "Issue Politics in a Polarized Congress: Roll Call Voting in the House of Representatives," *Political Research Quarterly* (forthcoming).

30. Sheldon Pollack, *The Failure of U.S. Tax Policy: Revenue and Politics* (University Park: Pennsylvania State University Press, 1998), 75.

31. I report an alternative set of results from a different dissimilarity matrix in Grossmann, "The Variable Politics of the Policy Process." That version is based on non-standardized versions of the same variables. It also does not include several measures included here: the liberal proportion of the governing network and of policy enactments in each issue area, the proportion of bipartisan coalitions in each area, and the proportion of enactments associated with factors in each of the three branches of government. All versions of the dissimilarity matrix fail to produce differentiated clusters.

32. Lowi, "American Business, Public Policy, Case-Studies, and Political Theory"; Wilson, "The Politics of Regulation."

33. Kingdon, *Agendas, Alternatives and Public Policies.*

34. Weible, Sabatier, and McQueen, "Themes and Variations."

35. Bryan D. Jones and Frank R. Baumgartner, "From There to Here: Punctuated Equilibrium to the General Punctuation Thesis to a Theory of Government Information Processing," *Policy Studies Journal* 40, no. 1 (2012): 1–19.

36. Wilson, "The Politics of Regulation"; Lowi, "American Business, Public Policy, Case-Studies, and Political Theory."

37. Heclo, "Issue Networks and the Executive Establishment."

Chapter 6

1. Paul Light, *The President's Agenda: Domestic Policy Choice from Kennedy to Clinton*, 3rd ed. (Baltimore: Johns Hopkins University Press, 1998).

2. Jon R. Bond and Richard Fleisher, *The President in the Legislative Arena* (Chicago: University of Chicago Press, 1992).

3. Brandice Canes-Wrone, *Who Leads Whom?: Presidents, Policy, and the Public* (Chicago: University of Chicago Press, 2005).

4. William Howell, *Power Without Persuasion: The Politics of Direct Presidential Action* (Princeton: Princeton University Press, 2003).

5. Binder, *Stalemate.*

6. R. Douglas Arnold, *The Logic of Congressional Action* (New Haven: Yale University Press, 1992).

7. Gilens, *Affluence & Influence.*

8. Ann Campbell Keller, *Science in Environmental Policy* (Cambridge, MA: MIT Press, 2009).

9. Andrew Rich, *Think Tanks, Public Policy, and the Politics of Expertise* (Cambridge: Cambridge University Press, 2004).

10. Christina Boswell, *The Political Uses of Expert Knowledge* (New York: Cambridge University Press, 2009); Saul Halfon, "Depleted Uranium, Public Science, and the Politics of Closure," *The Review of Policy Research* 25, no. 4 (2008): 295–311; Daniel Sarewitz, "How Science Makes Environmental Controversies Worse," *Environmental Science & Policy* 7 (2004): 385–403.

11. David B. Truman, *The Governmental Process: Political Interests and Public Opinion* (New York: Knopf, 1951); Robert A. Dahl, *Who Governs? Democracy and Power in an American City* (New Haven: Yale University Press, 1961); Elmer E. Schattschneider, *The Semisovereign People: A Realist's View of Democracy in America* (New York: Holt, Rinehart and

Winston, 1960); Lee Sigelman, "The American Political Science Review Citation Classics," *American Political Science Review* 100, no. 4 (2006): 668; Lowi, *The End of Liberalism.*

12. Baumgartner, Berry, Hojnacki, Kimball, and Leech, *Lobbying and Policy Change.*
13. Archilochus made this distinction. Isaiah Berlin popularized its application in science.
14. Tetlock, *Expert Political Judgment.*
15. Peter Bachrach and Morton S. Baratz, "Two Faces of Power," *American Political Science Review* 56, no. 4 (1962): 947–952.
16. Jonathan K. Simon, *Governing Through Crime: How the War on Crime Transformed American Democracy and Created a Culture of Fear* (New York: Oxford University Press, 2007), 102–103.
17. Rohde, *Parties and Leaders in the Postreform House.*
18. Gilens, *Affluence & Influence.*

Conclusion

1. The speech is available at: http://www.whitehouse.gov/blog/2013/04/28/watch-president-obama-2013-white-house-correspondents-dinner.
2. See quotations in Jeremy W. Peters, "Hopes, Maybe Misguided, That Food Will Breed Productivity in Capital," *New York Times*, March 8, 2013, A17.
3. Quoted in Andrew Rudalevige, "The Presidential Charm Offensive." *The Monkey Cage*, March 8, 2013. Available at: http://themonkeycage.org/2013/03/08/the-presidential-charm-offensive/.
4. Potentially important Supreme Court cases include *United States v. Windsor*, No. 12-307 and *Hollingsworth v. Perry*, No. 12-144. For agriculture reform, see the Agriculture Reform and Risk Management Act of 2013. For a discussion of education reform via the No Child Left Behind waiver process, see Benjamin Riley, "Waive to the Top: The Dangers of Legislating Education Policy from the Executive Branch," American Enterprise Institute for Public Policy Research. Available at: http://www.aei.org/outlook/education/k-12/system-reform/waive-to-the-top-the-dangers-of-legislating-education-policy-from-the-executive-branch/.
5. This is the definition that *The Macro Polity* authors use for conservative enactments. Policy enactments that are understood as conservative at the time of enactment despite government expansion, such as increased abortion restrictions, are coded as conservative. Their inclusion in the conservative category does not substantially alter the results. My study found 56.6% liberal enactments, 8.9% conservative enactments, and 34.5% neither or both. Erikson, Mackuen, and Stimson found 51.8% liberal, 3.6% conservative, and 44.6% neither or both.
6. See Thomas E. Mann and Norman J. Ornstein, *It's Even Worse than It Looks: How the American Constitutional System Collided with the New Politics of Extremism* (New York: Basic Books, 2012).
7. Matt Grossmann, *The Not-So-Special Interests: Interest Groups, Public Representation, and American Governance* (Stanford, CA: Stanford University Press, 2012).
8. David Espo, "Gang of Eight Tightly Controls Immigration Debate." Associated Press. May 27, 2013. Available at: http://www.realclearpolitics.com/articles/2013/05/27/gang_of_eight_tightly_controls_immigration_debate_118566.html.
9. Baumgartner and Jones, *Agendas and Instability in American Politics.*

Appendix B

1. Each enactment is associated with one of 21 issue areas and 226 subtopics included in the Policy Agendas Project (available at http://policyagendas.org).
2. The variable is coded three for large, two for medium, and one for small. Most enactments are coded as medium.

3. The variable is coded one for liberal enactments, minus one for conservative enactments, and zero for all others.
4. See, for example, Clinton and Lapinski, "Measuring Legislative Accomplishment" and Howell, Adler, Cameron, and Riemann, "Divided Government and the Legislative Productivity of Congress."
5. Mark Smith, *American Business and Political Power: Public Opinion, Elections, and Democracy* (Chicago: University of Chicago Press, 2000).

REFERENCES

Arnold, R. Douglas. *The Logic of Congressional Action*. New Haven: Yale University Press, 1992.

Bachrach, Peter, and Morton S. Baratz. "Two Faces of Power." *American Political Science Review* 56, no. 4 (1962): 947–952.

Bartels, Larry M. *Unequal Democracy: The Political Economy of the New Gilded Age*. Princeton: Princeton University Press, 2010.

Baum, Christopher F. *An Introduction to Modern Econometrics Using Stata*. College Station, TX: Stata Press, 2006.

Baumgartner, Frank R., and Bryan D. Jones. *Agendas and Instability in American Politics*. Chicago: University of Chicago Press, 1993.

Baumgartner, Frank R., Jeffrey M. Berry, Marie Hojnacki, David C. Kimball, and Beth L. Leech. *Lobbying and Policy Change: Who Wins, Who Loses, and Why*. Chicago: University of Chicago Press, 2009.

Bean, Jonathan. *Big Government and Affirmative Action: The Scandalous History of the Small Business Administration*. Lexington: University Press of Kentucky, 2001.

Beaubouef, Bruce Andre. *The Strategic Petroleum Reserve: U.S. Energy Security and Oil Politics, 1975-2005*. College Station: Texas A&M University Press, 2007.

Berkman, Michael B. *The State Roots of National Politics: Congress and the Tax Agenda, 1978–1986*. Pittsburgh: University of Pittsburgh Press, 1993.

Berkowitz, Edward D. *America's Welfare State: From Roosevelt to Reagan*. Baltimore: Johns Hopkins University Press, 1991.

Berry, Frances S., Ralph S. Brower, Sang Ok Choi, Wendy Xinfang Goa, Heesoun Jang, Myungjung Kwon, and Jessica Word. "Three Traditions of Network Research: What the Public Management Research Agenda Can Learn from Other Research Communities." *Public Administration Review* 64, no. 5 (2004): 539–553.

Berry, Jeffrey M. *The Interest Group Society*, 5th ed. New York: HarperCollins Publishers, 1989.

Binder, Sarah A.. *Stalemate: Causes and Consequences of Legislative Gridlock*. Washington, DC: Brookings Institution Press, 2003.

Bond, Jon R., and Richard Fleisher. *The President in the Legislative Arena*. Chicago: University of Chicago Press, 1992.

Boswell, Christina. *The Political Uses of Expert Knowledge*. New York: Cambridge University Press, 2009.

Bosworth, Barry B. "The Evolution of Economic Policy." In *The Great Society and Its Legacy: Twenty Years of U.S. Social Policy*, ed. Marshall Kaplan and Peggy L. Cuciti. Durham, NC: Duke University Press, 1986.

Brademas, John. *The Politics of Education: Conflict and Consensus on Capitol Hill*. Norman: University of Oklahoma Press, 1987.

Brady, David W. *Critical Elections and Congressional Policy Making*. Stanford, CA: Stanford University Press, 1988.

Brady, David W., and Craig Volden. *Revolving Gridlock: Politics and Policy from Jimmy Carter to George W. Bush*. Boulder, CO: Westview Press, 2005.

Brownlee, W. Elliot. *Federal Taxation in America: A Short History*. Cambridge: Cambridge University Press, 2004.

Burns, James MacGregor. *The Deadlock of Democracy: Four-Party Politics in America*. Upper Saddle River, NJ: Prentice Hall, 1963.

Cameron, Charles. *Veto Bargaining: Presidents and the Politics of Negative Power*. Cambridge: Cambridge University Press, 2000.

Campbell, Andrea Louise. *How Policies Make Citizens: Senior Political Activism and the American Welfare State*. Princeton: Princeton University Press, 2005.

Canes-Wrone, Brandice. *Who Leads Whom?: Presidents, Policy, and the Public*. Chicago: University of Chicago Press, 2005.

Capano, Giliberto, and Michael Howlett. "Introduction: The Determinants of Policy Change: Advancing the Debate." *Journal of Comparative Policy Analysis: Research and Practice* 11, no. 1 (2009): 1–5.

Caro, Robert A. *The Passage of Power: The Years of Lyndon Johnson*. New York: Knopf, 2012.

Carpenter, Daniel. *The Forging of Bureaucratic Autonomy: Reputations, Networks, and Policy Innovation in Executive Agencies, 1862-1928*. Princeton: Princeton University Press, 2001.

Christopoulos, Dimitrios C. "Relational Attributes of Political Entrepreneurs: A Network Perspective." *Journal of European Public Policy* 13, no. 5 (2006): 757–778.

Clark, Tom S. "Measuring Ideological Polarization on the United States Supreme Court." *Political Research Quarterly* 62, no. 1 (2009): 146–157.

Clinton, Joshua D., and John S. Lapinski. "Measuring Legislative Accomplishment, 1877–1994." *American Journal of Political Science* 50, no. 1 (2006): 232–249.

Cobb, Roger, and Charles Elder. *Participation in American Politics: The Dynamics of Agenda Building*, 2nd ed. Baltimore: Johns Hopkins University Press, 1983.

Cochrane, Willard W. *American Farm Policy, 1948-1973*. Minneapolis: University of Minnesota Press, 1976.

Converse, Philip. "The Nature of Belief Systems in Mass Publics." In *Ideology and Discontent*, ed. David E. Apter. New York: Free Press, 1964.

Cross, Christopher T. *Political Education: National Policy Comes of Age*. New York: Teachers College Press, 2003.

Dahl, Robert A. *Who Governs? Democracy and Power in an American City*. New Haven: Yale University Press, 1961.

Davies, Gareth. *See Government Grow: Education Politics from Johnson to Reagan*. Lawrence: University Press of Kansas, 2007.

Davis, Charles E. *The Politics of Hazardous Waste*. New York: Prentice Hall, 1992.

DeBray, Elizabeth H. *Politics, Ideology, and Education: Federal Policy during the Clinton and Bush Administrations*. New York: Teacher's College Press, 2006.

Delli Carpini, Michael X., and Scott Keeter. *What Americans Know about Politics and Why It Matters*. New Haven: Yale University Press, 1997.

Edwards, George C. *On Deaf Ears: The Limits of the Bully Pulpit*. New Haven: Yale University Press, 2006.

Epp, Charles R. *The Rights Revolution: Lawyers, Activists, and Supreme Courts in Comparative Perspective*. Chicago: University of Chicago Press, 1998.

Epstein, Lee, and Jeffrey A. Segal. "Measuring Issue Salience." *American Journal of Political Science* 44, no. 1 (2000): 66–83.

Erikson, Robert S., Michael B. Mackuen, and James A. Stimson. *The Macro Polity*. Cambridge: Cambridge University Press, 2002.

Fenno, Richard. *Congressmen in Committees*. Boston: Little Brown and Company, 1973.

Frank, Richard G., and Sherry A. Glied. *Better But Not Well: Mental Health Policy in the United States since 1950*. Baltimore: Johns Hopkins University Press, 2006.

Friedman, Jeffrey, and Wladimir Kraus, eds. *Engineering the Financial Crisis: Systemic Risk and the Failure of Regulation*. Philadelphia: University of Pennsylvania Press, 2011.

Friedman, Sheldon, and David C. Jacobs, eds., *The Future of the Safety Net: Social Insurance and Employee Benefits*. Ithaca, NY: ILR Press, 2001.

Frymer, Paul. "Acting When Elected Officials Won't: Federal Courts and Civil Rights Enforcement in U.S. Labor Unions, 1935–85." *American Political Science Review* 97, no. 3 (2003): 483–499.

Gelfand, Mark I. 1975. *A Nation of Cities: The Federal Government and Urban America, 1933–1965*. Oxford: Oxford University Press.

Gilens, Martin. *Affluence & Influence: Economic Inequality and Political Power in America*. Princeton: Princeton University Press, 2012.

Goldberg, Gertrude Schaffer, and Sheila D. Collins. *Washington's New Poor Law: Welfare Reform and the Roads Not Taken, 1935 to the Present*. New York: Apex Press, 2001.

Graham, Hugh Davis. *The Civil Rights Era: Origins and Development of National Policy, 1960-1972*. Oxford: Oxford University Press, 1990.

Graham, Otis L., Jr., ed. *Environmental Politics and Policy, 1960s-1990s*. University Park: Pennsylvania State University Press, 2000.

Greve, Michael S., and Fred L. Smith. *Environmental Politics: Public Costs, Private Rewards*. Westport, CT: Praeger Publishers, 1992.

Grossback, Lawrence J., David A. M. Peterson, and James A. Stimson. *Mandate Politics*. Cambridge: Cambridge University Press, 2007.

Grossmann, Matt. "Interest Group Influence on US Policy Change: An Assessment Based on Policy History." *Interest Groups & Advocacy* 1, no. 2 (2012): 1–22.

_____. *The Not-So-Special Interests: Interest Groups, Public Representation, and American Governance*. Stanford, CA: Stanford University Press, 2012.

_____. "The Variable Politics of the Policy Process: Issue Area Differences and Comparative Networks." *Journal of Politics* 75, no. 1 (2013).

Grundmann, Reiner. "Climate Change and Knowledge Politics." *Environmental Politics* 16, no. 3 (2007): 414–432.

Guston, David. *Between Politics and Science: Assuring the Integrity and Productivity of Research*. Cambridge: Cambridge University Press, 2007.

Hacker, Jacob S. *The Divided Welfare State: The Battle over Public and Private Social Benefits in the United States*. Cambridge: Cambridge University Press, 2002.

Hacker, Jacob S., and Paul Pierson. *Winner-Take-All Politics: How Washington Made the Rich Richer—and Turned its Back on the Middle Class*. New York: Simon & Schuster, 2010.

Halfon, Saul. "Depleted Uranium, Public Science, and the Politics of Closure." *Review of Policy Research* 25, no. 4 (2008): 295–311.

Hallacher, Paul M. *Why Polity Issue Networks Matter: The Advanced Technology Program and the Manufacturing Extension Partnership*. Lanham, MD: Rowman & Littlefield Publishers, 2005.

Hammond, Thomas H., and Gary J. Miller. "The Core of the Constitution." *American Political Science Review* 81, no. 4 (1987): 1155–1174.

Hart, John. *The Presidential Branch: From Washington to Clinton*. London: Chatham House, 1995.

Hays, R. Allen. *The Federal Government and Urban Housing: Ideology and Change in Public Policy*. Albany: State University of New York Press, 1995.

Heclo, Hugh. "Issue Networks and the Executive Establishment." In *The New American Political System*, ed. Anthony King. Washington, DC: American Enterprise Institute, 1978.

Heinz, John P., Edward O. Laumann, Robert L. Nelson, and Robert H. Salisbury. *The Hollow Core: Private Interests in National Policy Making*. Cambridge, MA: Harvard University Press, 1993.

Hendrickson, Jill M. *Regulation and Instability in U.S. Commercial Banking: A History of Crises*. New York: Palgrave Macmillan, 2011.

Henig, Jeffrey R. *Spin Cycle: How Research is Used in Policy Debates: The Case of Charter Schools*. New York: Russell Sage Foundation, 2008.

Hoff, Joan. *Nixon Reconsidered*. New York: Basic Books, 1995.

Hook, Sidney. *The Hero in History*. New York: Humanities Press, 1950.

Howard, Christopher. *The Welfare State Nobody Knows: Debunking Myths about U.S. Social Policy*. Princeton: Princeton University Press, 2006.

Howell, William. *Power Without Persuasion: The Politics of Direct Presidential Action*. Princeton: Princeton University Press, 2003.

Howell, William, Scott Adler, Charles Cameron, and Charles Riemann. "Divided Government and the Legislative Productivity of Congress, 1945–94." *Legislative Studies Quarterly* 25, no. 2 (2000): 285–312.

Huntington, Samuel P. *American Politics: The Promise of Disharmony*. Cambridge, MA: Harvard University Press, 1981.

Jacobs, Lawrence R., and Robert Y. Shapiro. *Politicians Don't Pander: Political Manipulation and the Loss of Democratic Responsiveness*. Chicago: University of Chicago Press, 2000.

Jochim, Ashley E., and Bryan D. Jones. "Issue Politics in a Polarized Congress: Roll Call Voting in the House of Representatives." *Political Research Quarterly* 66, no. 2 (2013): 352–369.

Jones, Bryan D., and Frank R. Baumgartner. "From There to Here: Punctuated Equilibrium to the General Punctuation Thesis to a Theory of Government Information Processing." *Policy Studies Journal* 40, no. 1 (2012): 1–19.

———. *The Politics of Attention: How Government Prioritizes Problems*. Chicago: University of Chicago Press, 2005.

Jones, Bryan D., Heather Larsen-Price, and John Wilkerson. "Representation and American Governing Institutions." *Journal of Politics* 71, no. 1 (2009): 277–290.

Kaplan, Marshall, and Peggy L. Cuciti, eds. *The Great Society and its Legacy: Twenty Years of U.S. Social Policy*. Durham, NC: Duke University Press, 1986.

Kash, Don E., and Robert Rycroft. *U.S. Energy Policy: Crisis and Complacency*. Norman: University of Oklahoma Press, 1984.

Keith, Nathaniel S. *Politics and the Housing Crisis since 1930*. New York: Universe Books, 1974.

Keller, Ann Campbell. *Science in Environmental Policy*. Cambridge, MA: MIT Press, 2009.

Kelly, Nathan J. "Political Choice, Public Policy, and Distributional Outcomes." *American Journal of Political Science* 49, no. 4 (2005): 865–880.

Kelly, Sean Q. "Divided We Govern? A Reassessment." *Polity* 25, no. 3 (1993): 475–484.

Kernell, Samuel. *Going Public: New Strategies of Presidential Leadership*. Washington: CQ Press, 2006.

Keyes, Ralph. *The Quote Verifier: Who Said What, Where, and When*. New York: St. Martin's Griffin, 2006.

Kingdon, John W. *Agendas, Alternatives and Public Policies*, 2nd ed. New York: Addison-Wesley, 2010.

Klyza, Christopher McGrory, and David J. Sousa. *American Environmental Policy, 1990-2006: Beyond Gridlock*. Cambridge, MA: MIT Press, 2008.

Kotlowski, Dean J. *Nixon's Civil Rights: Politics, Principle, and Policy*. Cambridge, MA: Harvard University Press, 2002.

Krackhardt, David. "Predicting with Networks: Nonparametric Multiple Regression Analysis of Dyadic Data." *Social Networks* 10 (1988): 359–381.

Krehbiel, Keith. *Pivotal Politics: A Theory of U.S. Lawmaking*. Chicago: University of Chicago Press, 1998.

Lapinski, John, and E. Scott Adler. "Defining the Macropolitics of Congress." In *The Macropolitics of Congress*, ed. E. Scott Adler and John Lapinski. Princeton: Princeton University Press, 2006.

Launius, Roger D., and Howard E McCurdy. *Spaceflight and the Myth of Presidential Leadership*. Champaign: University of Illinois Press, 1997.

Lawson, Steven F. *Black Ballots: Voting and Rights in the South 1944-1969*. New York: Columbia University Press, 1976.

Lehrer, Nadine. *U.S. Farm Bills and Policy Reforms: Ideological Conflicts over World Trade, Renewable Energy, and Sustainable Agriculture.* Amherst, NY: Cambria Press, 2010.

Lewis-Beck, Michael S., Helmut Norpoth, William G. Jacoby, and Herbert F. Weisberg. *The American Voter Revisited.* Ann Arbor: University of Michigan Press, 2008.

Light, Paul. *The President's Agenda: Domestic Policy Choice from Kennedy to Clinton,* 3rd ed. Baltimore: Johns Hopkins University Press, 1998.

Lindblom, Charles. *The Intelligence of Democracy: Decision Making through Mutual Adjustment.* New York: Free Press, 1965.

Lowi, Theodore. "American Business, Public Policy, Case-Studies, and Political Theory." *World Politics* 16, no. 4 (1964): 677–715.

———. *The End of Liberalism: The Second Republic of the United States.* New York: W. W. Norton, 1979.

Mann, Thomas E., and Norman J. Ornstein. *It's Even Worse Than It Looks: How the American Constitutional System Collided with the New Politics of Extremism.* New York: Basic Books, 2012.

Manzi, Jim. *Uncontrolled: The Surprising Payoff of Trial-and-Error for Business, Politics, and Society.* New York: Basic Books, 2012.

Marsh, David, and R. A. W. Rhodes. "Policy Communities and Issue Networks: Beyond Typology." In *Social Networks: Critical Concepts in Sociology,* ed. John Scott. London: Routledge, 2004.

Martin, Andrew D., and Kevin M. Quinn. "Dynamic Ideal Point Estimation via Markov Chain Monte Carlo for the U.S. Supreme Court, 1953–1999." *Political Analysis* 10, no. 2 (2002): 134–153.

Mayhew, David R. *America's Congress: Actions in the Public Sphere, James Madison through Newt Gingrich.* New Haven: Yale University Press, 2002.

———. *Divided We Govern: Party Control, Lawmaking, and Investigations, 1946-2002.* New Haven: Yale University Press, 2005.

———. "Lawmaking and History." In *The Macropolitics of Congress,* ed. E. Scott Adler and John S. Lapinski. Princeton: Princeton University Press, 2006.

———. *Parties and Policies: How the American Government Works.* New Haven: Yale University Press, 2008.

McAdam, Doug. *Political Process and the Development of Black Insurgency, 1930-1970.* Chicago: University of Chicago Press, 1982.

McCarty, Nolan. "The Policy Effects of Political Polarization." In *The Transformation of American Politics: Activist Government and the Rise of Conservatism,* ed. Paul Pierson and Theda Skocpol. Princeton: Princeton University Press, 2007.

McCarty, Nolan, Keith T. Poole, and Howard Rosenthal. *Polarized America: The Dance of Ideology and Unequal Riches.* Cambridge, MA: MIT Press, 2006.

Melnick, R. Shep. *Between the Lines: Interpreting Welfare Rights.* Washington, DC: Brookings Institution, 1994.

———. "From Tax and Spend to Mandate and Sue." In *The Great Society and the High Tide of Liberalism,* ed. Sidney M Milkis and Jerome M. Mileur. Amherst: University of Massachusetts Press, 2005.

Mettler, Suzanne. "Reconstituting the Submerged State: The Challenges of Social Policy Reform in the Obama Era." *Perspectives on Politics* 8, no. 3 (2010): 803–824.

———. *Soldiers to Citizens: The G.I. Bill and the Making of the Greatest Generation* (New York: Oxford University Press, 2005).

Milazzo, Paul Charles. *Unlikely Environmentalists: Congress and Clean Water, 1945-1972.* Lawrence: University Press of Kansas, 2006.

Milkis, Sidney. "Lyndon Johnson, the Great Society, and the 'Twilight' of the Modern Presidency." In *The Great Society and the High Tide of Liberalism,* ed. Sidney M. Milkis and Jerome M. Mileur. Amherst: University of Massachusetts Press, 2005.

Mintrom, Michael. *Policy Entrepreneurs and School Choice.* Washington, DC: Georgetown University Press, 2000.

Mintrom, Michael, and Phillipa Norman. "Policy Entrepreneurship and Policy Change." *Policy Studies Journal* 37, no. 4 (2009): 649–667.

Mitchell, Paul. *Federal Housing Policy and Programs: Past and Present*. Piscataway, NJ: Rutgers University Press, 1985.

Morgan, Kimberly. *Working Mothers and the Welfare State: Religion and the Politics of Work-Family Policies in Western Europe and the United States*. Stanford, CA: Stanford University Press, 2006.

Morone, James, and David Blumenthal. *The Heart of Power: Health and Politics in the Oval Office*. Berkeley: University of California Press, 2009.

Moyer, H. Wayne, and Timothy Edward Josling. *Agricultural Policy Reform: Politics and Process in the EU and US in the 1990s*. London: Ashgate Publishing, 2002.

Nadel, Mark V. *The Politics of Consumer Protection*. New York: MacMillan Publishing Company, 1971.

Neustadt, Richard E. *Presidential Power and the Modern Presidents: The Politics of Leadership from Roosevelt to Reagan*, revised edition. New York: Free Press, 1991.

Orren, Karen, and Stephen Skowronek. *The Search for American Political Development*. Cambridge: Cambridge University Press, 2004.

Patashnik, Eric. "After the Public Interest Prevails: The Political Sustainability of Policy Reform." *Governance* 16, no. 2 (2003): 203–234.

Payne, James L. "Show Horses & Work Horses in the United States House of Representatives." *Polity* 12, no. 3 (1980): 428–456.

Perlstein, Rick. *Nixonland: The Rise of a President and the Fracturing of America*. New York: Scribner, 2008.

Pierson, Paul. *Politics in Time: History, Institutions, and Social Analysis*. Princeton: Princeton University Press, 2004.

Piven, Frances Fox, and Richard A. Cloward. *Poor People's Movements: Why They Succeed, How They Fail*. New York: Vintage Books, 1977.

Pollack, Sheldon. *The Failure of U.S. Tax Policy: Revenue and Politics*. University Park: Pennsylvania State University Press, 1998.

Polsby, Nelson W. *Consequences of Party Reform*. Berkeley, CA: Institute of Governmental Studies Press, 1983.

Portney, Paul R., and Robert N. Stavins, eds. *Public Policies for Environmental Protection*. Washington, DC: Resources for the Future, 2000.

Redford, Emmette S. *Democracy in the Administrative State*. New York: Oxford University Press, 1969.

Rich, Andrew. *Think Thanks, Public Policy, and the Politics of Expertise*. Cambridge: Cambridge University Press, 2004.

Rimmerman, Craig A., Kenneth D. Wald, and Clyde Wilcox, eds. *The Politics of Gay Rights*. Chicago: University of Chicago Press, 2000.

Rohde, David W. *Parties and Leaders in the Postreform House*. Chicago: University of Chicago Press, 1991.

Roof, Tracy. *American Labor, Congress, and the Welfare State, 1935-2010*. Baltimore: Johns Hopkins University Press, 2011.

Rose, Mark H., Bruce E. Seely, and Paul F. Barrett. *The Best Transportation System in the World: Railroads, Trucks, Airlines, and American Public Policy in the Twentieth Century*. Columbus: Ohio State University Press, 2006.

Rosenfeld, Sam. "Fed by Reform: Congressional Politics, Partisan Change, and the Food Stamp Program, 1961–1981." *Journal of Policy History* 22, no. 4 (2010): 474–507.

Rudy, Willis. *Building America's Schools and Colleges: The Federal Contribution*. Cranbury, NJ: Cornwall Books, 2003.

Sabatier, Paul A., and Hank C. Jenkins-Smith. *Policy Change and Learning: An Advocacy Coalition Approach*. Boulder, CO: Westview Press, 1993.

Sabatier, Paul, and Christopher Weible. "The Advocacy Coalition Framework: Innovation and Clarification." In *Theories of the Policy Process*, ed. Paul A. Sabatier. Boulder, CO: Westview Press, 2007.

Sarewitz, Daniel. "How Science Makes Environmental Controversies Worse." *Environmental Science & Policy* 7 (2004): 385–403.

Schattschneider, Elmer E. *The Semisovereign People: A Realist's View of Democracy in America.* New York: Holt, Rinehart and Winston, 1960.

Schickler, Eric. *Disjointed Pluralism: Institutional Innovation and the Development of the U.S. Congress.* Princeton: Princeton University Press, 2001.

Schieber, Sylvester J., and John B. Shoven. *The Real Deal: The History and Future of Social Security.* New Haven: Yale University Press, 1999.

Schlager, Edella. "A Comparative Analysis of Policy Theories." In *Theories of the Policy Process,* ed. Paul A. Sabatier. Boulder, CO: Westview Press, 2007.

Schlesinger, Arthur M., Jr. *The Cycles of American History.* Boston: Houghton Mifflin, 1986.

Segal, Jeffrey A. "Separation-of-Powers Games in the Positive Theory of Congress and Courts." *American Political Science Review* 91, no. 1 (1997): 28–44.

Shapiro, Robert Y., Martha Joynt Kumar, and Lawrence R. Jacobs, eds. *Presidential Power: Forging the Presidency for the Twenty-First Century.* New York: Columbia University Press, 2000.

Sheingate, Adam D. "Political Entrepreneurship, Institutional Change, and American Political Development." *Studies in American Political Development* 17, no. 3 (2003): 185–203.

———. "The Terrain of the Political Entrepreneur." In *Formative Acts: American Politics in the Making,* ed. Stephen Skowronek and Matthew Glassman. Philadelphia: University of Pennsylvania Press, 2007.

Shipan, Charles R. "Does Divided Government Increase the Size of the Legislative Agenda?" In *The Macropolitics of Congress,* ed. E. Scott Adler and John S. Lapinski. Princeton: Princeton University Press, 2006.

Shull, Steven A. *American Civil Rights Policy from Truman to Clinton: The Role of Presidential Leadership.* Armonk, NY: M. E. Sharpe, 1999.

Sigelman, Lee. "The American Political Science Review Citation Classics." *American Political Science Review* 100, no. 4 (2006).

Simon, Herbert. "Bounded Rationality and Organizational Learning." *Organization Science* 2, no. 1 (1991): 125–134.

Sinclair, Barbara. *The Transformation of the U.S. Senate.* Baltimore: Johns Hopkins University Press, 1989.

Skocpol, Theda. *Diminished Democracy: From Membership to Management in American Civic Life.* Norman: University of Oklahoma Press, 2003.

Skowronek, Stephen. *Building a New American State: The Expansion of National Administrative Capacities, 1877-1920.* Cambridge: Cambridge University Press, 1982.

———. *The Politics Presidents Make: Leadership from John Adams to Bill Clinton.* Cambridge, MA: Belknap Press of Harvard University Press, 1997.

Skrentny, John D. *The Minority Rights Revolution.* Cambridge, MA: Belknap Press of Harvard University Press, 2002.

Smith, Kevin B. "Typologies, Taxonomies, and the Benefits of Policy Classification." *Policy Studies Journal* 30, no. 3 (2002): 379–395.

Smith, Mark. *American Business and Political Power: Public Opinion, Elections, and Democracy.* Chicago: University of Chicago Press, 2000.

Spring, Joel. *Conflict of Interests: The Politics of American Education.* New York: Longman, 1993.

Staszak, Sarah. "Institutions, Rulemaking, and the Politics of Judicial Retrenchment." *Studies in American Political Development* 24, no. 2 (2010): 168–189.

Steinmo, Sven. "The Evolution of Policy Ideas: Tax Policy in the 20th Century." *British Journal of Politics & International Relations* 5, no. 2 (2003): 206–236.

Stetson, Dorothy McBride. *Women's Rights in the USA.* New York: Garland Publishing, 1997.

Steuerle, C. Eugene. *Contemporary U.S. Tax Policy.* Washington, DC: Urban Institute Press, 2004.

Stolz, Barbara. *Criminal Justice Policy Making: Federal Roles and Processes.* Westport, CT: Praeger Publishers, 2001.

Strickland, Stephen P. *Politics, Science, and Dread Disease: A Short History of United States Medical Research Policy*. Cambridge, MA: Harvard University Press, 1972.

Studlar, Donley T. *Tobacco Control: Comparative Politics in the United States and Canada*. Toronto: University of Toronto Press, 2002.

Switzer, Jacqueline Vaughn. *Disabled Rights: American Disability Policy and the Fight for Equality*. Washington, DC: Georgetown University Press, 2003.

Taylor, Andrew J. "Explaining Government Productivity." *American Politics Research* 26, no. 4 (1998): 439–458.

Tetlock, Philip E. *Expert Political Judgment: How Good Is It? How Can We Know?* Princeton: Princeton University Press, 2006.

Togman, Jeffrey M. *The Ramparts of Nations*. Santa Barbara, CA: Greenwood Press, 2001.

Truman, David B. *The Governmental Process: Political Interests and Public Opinion*. New York: Knopf, 1951.

Tsebelis, George. *Veto Players: How Political Institutions Work*. Princeton: Princeton University Press, 2002.

Tugwell, Franklin. *The Energy Crisis and the American Political Economy: Politics and Markets in the Management of Natural Resources*. Stanford, CA: Stanford University Press, 1988.

Tulis, Jeffrey K. *The Rhetorical Presidency*. Princeton: Princeton University Press, 1988.

Tzankovaa, Zdravka. "The Science and Politics of Ecological Risk: Bioinvasions Policies in the US and Australia." *Environmental Politics* 18, no. 3 (2009): 333–350.

Vietor, Richard H. K. *Energy Policy in America since 1945: A Study of Business-Government Relations*. Cambridge: Cambridge University Press, 2008.

Vinovskis, Maria A. *The Birth of Head Start: Preschool Education Policies in the Kennedy and Johnson Administrations*. Chicago: University of Chicago Press, 2005

Vogel, Steven Kent. *Freer Markets, More Rules: Regulatory Reform in Advanced Industrial Countries*. Ithaca, NY: Cornell University Press, 1996.

Walker, Jack L. *Mobilizing Interest Groups in America: Patrons, Professions, and Social Movements*. Ann Arbor: University of Michigan Press, 1991.

Waltman, Jerold. *The Politics of the Minimum Wage*. Champaign: University of Illinois Press, 2000.

Wasserman, Stanley, and Katherine Faust. *Social Network Analysis: Methods and Applications*. Cambridge: Cambridge University Press, 1994.

Weber, Edward P. *Pluralism by the Rules: Conflict and Cooperation in Environmental Regulation*. Washington, DC: Georgetown University Press, 1998.

Weible, Christopher M., Paul Sabatier, and Kelly McQueen. "Themes and Variations: Taking Stock of the Advocacy Coalition Framework." *Policy Studies Journal* 37, no. 1 (2009): 121–140.

Wilson, Harry L. *Guns, Gun Control, and Elections*. Lanham, MD: Rowman & Littlefield Publishers, 2006.

Wilson, James Q. "The Politics of Regulation." In *The Politics of Regulation*, ed. James Q. Wilson. New York: Basic Books, 1980.

Wisensale, Steven K. *Family Leave Policy: The Political Economy of Work and Family in America*. Armonk, NY: M. E. Sharpe, 2001.

Wlezien, Chris. "The Public as Thermostat: Dynamics of Preferences for Spending." *American Journal of Political Science* 39, no. 4 (1995): 981–1000.

Wood, B. Dan, and Richard W. Waterman. "The Dynamics of Political-Bureaucratic Adaptation." *American Journal of Political Science* 37, no. 2 (1993): 497–528.

Zahariadis, Nikolaos. "The Multiple Streams Framework: Structure, Limitations, Prospects." In *Theories of the Policy Process*, ed. Paul Sabatier. Boulder, CO: Westview Press, 2007.

Zaller, John. *The Nature and Origins of Mass Opinion*. Cambridge: Cambridge University Press, 1992.

INDEX

Page numbers followed by *t* and *f* indicate tables and figures, respectively. Numbers followed by "n" indicate notes.